CW00731542

# Intertextuality

# Intertextuality

## Theories and practices

*Edited by*
Michael Worton *and* Judith Still

Manchester University Press
Manchester and New York

*Distributed exclusively in the USA and Canada by* St. Martin's Press

Copyright © Manchester University Press 1990

Whilst copyright in the volume as a whole is vested in Manchester University Press, copyright in individual chapters belongs to their respective authors, and no chapter may be reproduced wholly or in part without express permission in writing of both author and publisher.

*Published by* Manchester University Press
Oxford Road, Manchester M13 9PL, UK
*and* Room 400, 175 Fifth Avenue,
New York, NY 10010, USA

*Distributed exclusively in the USA and Canada*
*by* St. Martin's Press, Inc.,
175 Fifth Avenue, New York, NY 10010, USA

Reprinted in 1990
Reprinted in paperback 1991

*British Library cataloguing in publication data*
Intertextuality : theories and practices,
   1. Literature. Intertextuality
   I. Worton, Michael   II. Still, Judith
   801'.95

*Library of Congress cataloging in publication data*
Intertextuality: theories and practice/edited by Michael Worton and
   Judith Still.
      p.cm.
   Includes index.
   ISBN 0–7190–2763–2—ISBN 0–7190–2764–0 (*phk.*)
      1. Intertextuality. 2. Literature, Modern—History and criticism.
I. Worton, Michael, 1951–  . II. Still, Judith, 1958–  .
PN98.158158 1990
801'.95—dc20                         89–12603

ISBN 0 7190 2763 2 *hardback*
   0 7190 2764 0 *paperback*

Photoset in Linotron Sabon
by Northern Phototypesetting Company, Bolton

Printed in Great Britain
by Courier International, Tiptree, Essex

# Contents

# Contributors

*Celia Britton* is Lecturer in French at the University of Reading. She is the author of *Claude Simon: Writing the Visible*, 1987, and has just completed 'Structuralist and post-structuralist psychoanalytic and marxist literary theories', a contribution to the *Cambridge History of Literary Criticism*. She has also published articles on the *nouveau roman* and French film.

*Ross Chambers* is Marvin Felheim Distinguished University Professor of French and Comparative Literature at the University of Michigan. Among his recent publications are *Story and Situation*, 1984, and *Mélancolie et opposition*, 1988. His books and articles focus on modern literature, critical theory and cultural politics.

*John Frow* is Professor of English at the University of Queensland and is the author of *Marxism and Literary History*, 1986. He has also published articles on literary theory and on discourse analysis, and in the general area of cultural studies.

*Seán Hand* is Lecturer in French at the University College of Wales, Aberystwyth. He is the editor of the forthcoming *Levinas Reader* and is currently completing a book on Michel Leiris and a critical edition of Leiris's *L'Age d'homme*. He has published articles on Leiris and Edmond Jabès and has translated Kristeva, Deleuze, Lyotard and Levinas.

*Ann Jefferson* is a Fellow of New College, Oxford, and is the author of *The Nouveau Roman and the Poetics of Fiction*, 1980, and *Reading Realism in Stendhal*, 1988, and co-author of *Modern*

*Literary Theory: A Comparative Introduction,* 1982 and 1986. She has also published articles on modern fiction and on aspects of critical theory that relate to fiction.

*Diana Knight* is Lecturer in French at the University of Nottingham. She is the author of *Flaubert's Characters,* 1985 and of articles on feminist theory, French nineteenth-century fiction, and structuralism. She is currently writing a book on Roland Barthes and the concept of utopia.

*Roland François Lack* is currently completing a Ph.D. at University College London on pre-texts to the *Poésies* of Isidore Ducasse. His publications include articles on Lautréamont and translations of Levinas.

*Keith A. Reader* is Senior Lecturer in the School of Languages at Kingston Polytechnic. He has written on French cinema (notably Bresson and Renoir) and on French intellectual life. His most recent book is *Intellectuals and the Left in France since 1968,* 1987. He is currently preparing a book on interpretations of the May 1968 events in France.

*Michael Riffaterre* is University Professor at Columbia University, New York and Director of the School of Criticism and Theory at Dartmouth College, New Hampshire. Among his best-known publications are *Essais de stylistique structurale,* 1971, *Semiotics of poetry,* 1980, *Text Production,* 1983 and *Fictional Truth,* 1989. He has published extensively on various aspects of intertextuality.

*Judith Still* is Lecturer in Critical Theory at the University of Nottingham. She is completing a book on Jean-Jacques Rousseau, and has published the translation of a novel by Djanet Lachmet and articles on Rousseau, George Eliot, aspects of feminism, and critical theory.

*Michael Worton* is Lecturer in French Language and Literature at University College, London. He has published articles on twentieth-century European literature, on the intertextual relations between literature, painting and music, and on critical theory. He is currently writing a book on the politics of Samuel Beckett's theatre and a book on Michel Tournier and quests for origin.

# A note on vocabulary

Different disciplines have different bodies of vocabulary, which have an undeniable use-value in that they can serve as a precise shorthand in which the members of the discipline can communicate with each other about the objects of their study. Value may, moreover, be added through the very business of exchanging ideas in a special language which creates a community of insiders faithful to their *discipline* – impenetrable to the uninitiated. 'Intertextuality' – it should come as no surprise – is a promiscuous inter-discipline, or even a trans-discipline, certainly a transvestite discipline in that it constantly borrows its trappings now from psychoanalysis, now from political philosophy, now from economics and so on. Its practitioners enjoy playing with their own words (newly-coined) and even more so with other people's.

We contemplated providing a *glossary* to explain some of the lexical oddities in this book, but decided that such a lengthy pedagogical gesture would precisely constitute an attempt (albeit blissfully doomed to failure) to restrict the play of intertextual interpretation. If *Symbolic* is used here in a Lacanian context and elsewhere not, then we would hope that for a Lacanian the special sense of the Symbolic sets up an interesting dialogue with the other meanings, and that the inverse is also true – likewise for marxists in the case of *base* or *superstructure*.

We shall take just two instances from literary criticism, seemingly a *home* for intertextuality, to illustrate what we hope will be a fruitful crossing of dialects. Within this volume, *text* is used both in the restricted academic sense to mean 'a work of literature' and in the wider sense to mean anything which can be perceived as 'a signifying structure' from *the spectacle of nature* to *social codes*. The narrower sense can bring with it, perversely, an opening up of meanings thanks to the centuries of subtle and sophisticated readings of the written word from which newer, more sociological studies can profit. *Poet* is used to mean both, in a limited interpretation, 'someone who writes verse', and, in the Classical sense, 'a creative artist' of any kind. What the poet produces (poetry) is variously taken in the Platonic framework to be that which is passionate, pleasure-giving, deceitful and unmanning (hence politically dangerous for the Republic); in the Bakhtinian framework to be that which is unified, centripetal and hierarchical (hence politically conservative and anti-revolutionary); in the Kristevan framework to be that which is plural, centrifugal, intertextual (and hence politically revolutionary); in the Bloomian framework to be that which is Oedipally dialogic and a defence against castration. In such examples each new poet (say, Kristeva following Bakhtin following Socrates) pays homage to her or his precursors and yet the vicissitudes of the vocabulary point to the (creatively) aggressive nature of reading and rewriting.

Judith Still and Michael Worton

# Introduction

'Intertextuality' is a term coined by Julia Kristeva, but which we shall use to cover a somewhat broader range of theories than those which she expounds in her seminal work on intertextuality, 'Word, dialogue and novel' or 'Problèmes de la structuration du texte'.[1] The theory of intertextuality insists that a text (for the moment to be understood in the narrower sense) cannot exist as a hermetic or self-sufficient whole, and so does not function as a closed system.[2] This is for two reasons. Firstly, the writer is a reader of texts (in the broadest sense) before s/he is a creator of texts, and therefore the work of art is inevitably shot through with references, quotations and influences of every kind. Rousseau, for example, does not entitle his autobiography *The Confessions* in ignorance of church practices or of St Augustine's work of the same name. This repetition of past or of contemporary texts can range from the most conscious and sophisticated elaboration of other poets' work, to a scholarly use of sources, or the quotation (with or without the use of quotation marks) of snatches of conversation typical of a certain social milieu at a certain historical moment. The dominant relations of production and the socio-political context – which could be included within a broad definition of *text* – are of course a major force influencing every aspect of a text. Rousseau's work, for example, is marked by the desire to introduce a dynamic (egalitarian) element into static hierarchical relations between men – reproducing, although also problematising, elements of the social context of eighteenth-century France.

Secondly, a text is available only through some process of reading; what is produced at the moment of reading is due to the cross-fertilisation of the packaged textual material (say, a book) by all the texts which the reader brings to it. A delicate allusion to a work unknown to the reader, which therefore goes unnoticed, will have a dormant existence in that reading. On the other hand, the reader's experience of some practice or theory unknown to the author may lead to a fresh interpretation. The modern reader of Rousseau may benefit from the play of comic and inventively salacious connotations which 'Confessions of . . .' now carries, contrasting with the connotations of spiritual seriousness. Some knowledge of the calculated horrors of the Nazi death camps sheds another light of grim verisimilitude on Kafka's fantastic work.

Both axes of intertextuality, texts entering via authors (who are, first, readers) and texts entering via readers (co-producers), are, we would argue, emotionally and politically charged; the object of an act of *influence,* whether by a powerful figure (say, a father) or by a social structure (say, the Church), does not receive or perceive that pressure as neutral. The passionate and the power-relations aspects have, however, been neutralised by certain theoreticians who present the acts of writing or reading as formal structures, without attending to the love-hate which motivates the transfer of texts. Recent work has, however, returned to the erotic and violent aspect of (the bearers of) intertextual relations.[3]

Although the term *intertextuality* dates from the 1960s, the phenomenon, in some form, is at least as old as recorded human society. Unsurprisingly, therefore, we can find theories of intertextuality wherever there has been discourse about texts – both because thinkers were aware of intertextual relations and because our knowledge of the theory makes us, as readers, keen to re-read our source texts in that light. It would be a lengthy task to survey all or even the majority of theories. Consequently we shall focus briefly on a selection of early writers to give a flavour of what theories of intertextuality can be found in the past, and then shift to Bakhtin, Kristeva and other twentieth-century theorists.

Plato is often perceived as the enemy of all poets (a term used to refer to all creative writers) as well as of rhetoric and even of the art of writing in general, and so it may seem strange to start this selection with the Socratic dialogues.[4] There are, however, many reasons for doing so. On the one hand, Plato's opposition to poetry on moral, and hence political, grounds does not exclude him from insights into the way texts function, insights which have much in common with some modern theories of intertextuality. These include: the theory of imitation; the magnetic image of charged interdependence (*Ion*); the passionate poet and reader (likened, for example, to Bacchic maidens), and the notion of texts as subliminal purveyors of ideology (*The Republic*). On the other hand, Plato is himself a poet and the dialogues enact much of what has later been defined as the essence of intertextuality. Longinus points out that Plato is engaged in a fierce rivalry with the arch-poet Homer in terms which remind us of Harold Bloom's *agon*.[5] Bakhtin locates in the Socratic dialogues one of the earliest forms of what he terms variously the novel, hetero-glossia, dialogism – what Kristeva will christen intertextuality.

Neither Platonic nor Aristotelian imitation is to be understood as imitation of nature.[6] In the case of Platonic imitation, the 'poet' always copies an earlier act of creation, which is itself already a copy.[7] Plato terms 'poetry' a realism which is partial and deceptive. Bakhtin follows him, denigrating 'poetry' as monologism, a struc-ture which dupes (the) people, presenting an artefact as the truth to be consumed whole.[8] Plato terms 'philosophy' something like what Bakhtin will celebrate in the dialogic novel: serious truth-seeking via a plurality of voices in a specific narrative context and in an ironic mode. From the perspective of Longinus, or indeed Bloom, Plato is asserting the superiority of his form of creation to that of the (his) beloved Homer.

Plato's typical creation does not have an imposed unity; it is a sometimes meandering and inconclusive discussion, which is charac-terised by digression and which is often playful or even savagely satirical. The starting-point is usually random, apparently accidental – the chance encounter of Socrates with a friend, Socrates coaxed or coaxing others into debate. This leads on to a play of different languages (e.g. those of the authoritarian public figure, the opinionated rhetorician, the naïve and beautiful youth) representing various contemporary belief systems some of which, as in the comic novel, will be unmasked, while others will float, suspended, engaging generations of readers in controversy over their status or meaning. The ambivalence of the dialogues lies not only in the diversity of ideologies evoked, but also in the central image of Socrates, the wise fool, startlingly different from the epic hero. Socrates' lofty purpose is coextensive with both self-deprecation and, sometimes affectionate sometimes biting, irony directed at other points of view.

The form of the Socratic dialogue thus embodies a Bakhtinian intertextuality, as well as the striving of Plato the artist–philosopher

against the influence of Homer. We would argue, in addition, that
Plato's theories of 'poetry' highlight intertextual relations. Certainly
the work of art, for Plato, is not autonomous – it is crossed, for
example, by various references to social knowledge (military tactics,
divination, statecraft, and so on). This glittering and promiscuous
array of citations from various areas of expertise is one reason why
Socrates, as a philosopher, must attempt to rival its seductive
influence. Another reason is given in the very term *seduction*; poetry
moves men, it takes them aside/apart, i.e. *out of* themselves – with
disastrous consequences, according to Socrates.

Aristotle's theory of imitation is rather different from Plato's.[9] For
Aristotle dramatic creation is the reduction, and hence intensifi-
cation, of a mass of texts known to the poet, and probably to the
audience as well. These texts vary from other written works of
literature, to the oral tradition of myths, stock characters or social
codes of conduct. Aristotle's *Poetics,* with its stress on unified and
universal truths, and Aristotelian logic, are both associated by Bakhtin and Kristeva with the monologic pole of discourse. Bakhtin
argues forcefully that the whole discipline of poetics, based upon
Aristotle's source text, is permeated with the sense of organic and
harmonious wholeness, and that Aristotle's concept of poetic
discourse is one of a system of *unitary language* spoken by an
*individual.*[10] Therefore, according to Bakhtin, poetics cannot
account for the novel, a term defined by Michael Holquist in his
Introduction to *The Dialogic Imagination* as the force at work
within a given literary system to reveal the limits of that system.
Bakhtin and Kristeva use the strategy of arguing that, although all
discourse is inherently dialogical/intertextual, there are 'monolo-
gues' which on one level succeed in repressing dialogism. This argument permits a binary opposition which is a useful instrument of
exposition and analysis. Here, however, we are more interested in
undoing that opposition and focusing on the return of the repressed,
the inevitable entry of alien and excluded voices. With the benefit of a
theory of intertextuality, we would argue, with Laurent Jenny, that
the *Poetics* can now be re-read. The Aristotelian account of composition drawing from a variety of sources should make each voice
indeed a polyphony, speaking subjects indeed constructed of alien
languages. Aristotle's 'universal truths' are defined as what a certain
type of person will probably or necessarily say or do in a given
situation (ch. 9), which he opposes to historic truth, to wit, what a

person actually did in a particular situation. Universal, or poetic, truth may therefore be interpreted as a reference to known social language types – the very opposite of the atomic, autonomous self whose behaviour could surely only be described in historic terms and would bring the audience little of the pleasure derived, according to Aristotle, precisely from *recognising* an imitation (ch. 4).

Horace takes up Aristotle's notion of *appropriateness,* referring to a scattered body of theories of style, familiar story-lines and beliefs about the dialects spoken by the young, the powerful, the fashionable and so on, in his advice to the young writer to be consistent.[11] Horace advises following models such as a fierce Medea or a tearful Ino (p. 83), which would not necessarily come from one particular past text, but from a variety of written, oral or pictorial sources combining to create a popular stereotype. It is interesting that he also advises plundering the Socratic writings, Bakhtin's dialogical model, for material. Horace claims that the poet must enter into the emotions he presents if he wishes to move his audience to experience the same emotions, following the pattern of nature (a kind of female artist) who makes us feel passions inwardly before she expresses those passions via our tongues. Again, we should note in passing the feminisation of the ephebe.

Longinus devotes ch. 13 of *On the Sublime* to Plato and the Sublime.[12] He argues that one route to the sublime is imitation and emulation of great historians and poets of the past, representing that relationship variously as catching fire from inspiration, breathing in or impregnation (like the Pythian priestesses). The poet as receiver is thus, as in today's ideology, a feminised figure. Longinus' reader of sublime language is subject to an irresistible force and mastery (ch. 1). The feminising, emotional effect of reading (acting) poetry is a contributory factor in Plato's banning it from the Republic – perhaps his desire to become the lover rather than the receptive beloved contributes to what Longinus describes as follows: '[Plato's] striving heart and soul with Homer for first place, like a young contestant entering the ring with a long-admired champion, perhaps showing too keen a spirit of emulation in his desire to break a lance with him, so to speak, yet getting some profit from the encounter' (ch. 13, p. 120).

The work of Classical Greek theorists has, of course, often been appropriated or interpreted by rhetoricians or intellectual historians who locate therein definitions of discursive tropes which may be refined, restated, amplified, contradicted. Yet on the other hand, few contemporary critics or theoreticians of intertextuality have chosen to examine and exploit Roman theories of *oratory*, which are usually considered merely as programmes for (oral) text production. However, in *De Oratore* Cicero insists that the good orator should attain a good knowledge of all subjects and all arts (I, vi, 20, p. 17), and his mouthpiece Crassus argues that it is the orator who is the founding father and maintainer of social communities (and, therefore, implicitly of socially determined and accepted languages or *sociolects*, see I, viii, 34, p. 27).[13] However, crucially, he asserts that the orator must write as much as possible since writing will always surpass even the best oration and is therefore the best *teacher* of eloquence (I, xxxiii, 150, p. 103). Later, in *Institutio Oratoria*, Quintilian lays stress on the value of reading written texts for a somewhat different reason (I, viii, 34, p. 13): since one can repeatedly re-read and rethink a text, the reader is liberated from the directive determinations of oral delivery (X, i, 19, p. 13).[14]

Aristotle holds that we learn (with great pleasure) through imitating others and that our instinct to enjoy works of imitation is an inborn instinct (*Poetics*, ch. 4); both Cicero and Quintilian emphasise that imitation is not only a means of forging one's own discourse but is a consciously intertextual practice.[15] Of the two major forms of imitation – paraphrase (translation from Latin into Latin) and translation (translation from Greek into Latin) – Cicero, rather like Horace, rejects the former since it is likely to lead either to gratuitous tautology or to a diminution of signifying force.[16] Consequently he prefers the latter form which results in the choice of the best, if familiar, available words or in the 'coining by analogy' of new words (I, xxxiii, 154–5, p. 107).

In his elaboration of Cicero's refusal of word-for-word translation, Quintilian rehabilitates paraphrase which, provided it is not a slavish reproduction, engenders a creative struggle between emulation and agonistic rivalry (X, v, 5–7, pp. 115–17). Imitation is thus not repetition, but the completion of an act of interpretation – and a mode of interpretation which is, as Gadamer says, a highlighting in which the reading and writing translator declares her/himself, while also engaging in a process of self-alienation.[17] Imitation as theory and practice presupposes a virtual simultaneity and identification of reading and writing, but it also implies and depends upon a process of transformation. Quintilian's metaphor for the process is *liquefaction* (X, i, 19, p. 13). By this he means that when we write, we can and indeed should remember only a pulped version of what we have read and thereby make possible an *Aufhebung* of the dialectic between our ov ̄ ̄ present text and its 'originating' model (which need not be a literary text, but could be, for instance, a legend transmitted essentially through an oral tradition). Quintilian's choice of the term liquefaction might seem innocent and undoubtedly had specific resonances in Roman society, but we would suggest that today we cannot but read it through the intertext of contemporary (French) feminisms, recording it as a marker of the apparently inescapable feminisation of readers and reading.

Imitation must therefore be seen as a theory not only of writing but also of reading as a performative act of criticism and interpretation. Joel Weinsheimer has argued that 'an imitation has no independent or autonomous essence ( . . . ) it is neither a copy nor an original' (*Imitation*, p. 2). In his essay in this volume, Ross Chambers refers to Baudrillard's notion of *simulacra* or copies without an original, reminding us of the problematic relationship between physical reality and semiotic reality, but for our Roman theorists imitation presupposes reference to a pre-existent reality which is concrete as well as textual.

Every literary imitation is a *supplement* which seeks to complete and supplant the original and which functions at times for later readers as the pre-text of the 'original'.[18] A testament to the anxiety of influence and an assertive quest for authorial identity, each imitation is also necessarily determined by the literary and socio-linguistic codes in force at the time of its writing (and, analogously, of its reading). Consequently, an imitative text both presents and *is* a tension between two idiolects and two or more sociolects.

For Cicero and Quintilian, the stylistic exercise of imitation is not an end in itself: it serves as an apprenticeship in improvisation, facilitating a liberation from over-investment in admiration for past masters and revealing and actualising the 'inner principle of prolifer-ation' which is the essential feature of language.[19] In this context, sixteenth-century European literature, perceived not only as a parti-cular local and historical moment but as a significant paradigm of global cultural experience, is especially important for an understand-ing of intertextual practice in that, perhaps for the first time in Western culture, writers commit themselves and their readers to discourse as open, unfinished . . . as 'future'. The textual past is explicitly or implicitly present(ed) through quotations or allusions, but in the work of such writers as Bacon, Shakespeare, Erasmus, Montaigne, Ronsard, Du Bellay every reference to a primary (or primal) text is informed by an awareness of the infinity of interpretation which both promises and defers an appropriative return to the/an origin. Modern readings of such works are inevitably problematised by the difference in (legitimate) cultural assumptions: the sixteenth-century author-reader has a historico-literary sophistication which, while often *local,* is different from that of today's readers. Florio's translation of Montaigne, Holland's of Pliny, Chapman's of Homer, for example, would all have been present to cultured spectators of Shakespeare's plays, but modern readers tend to focus on the 'original' pre-text and thus are blind to the workings of contemporary, vernacular intertextuality.[20] This swerve marks one of the main differences between traditional source criticism and intertextual reading, and we would go so far as to suggest that it is desirable to read both the *Urtext* and its translation in order to perceive the mobility of the intertextual relations.

While most Renaissance writers articulate their dependence on imitation of previous texts, we would propose Montaigne as the most interesting for a (pre-) history of intertextuality and so we have chosen to focus on his work as one paradigm of the enactment of intertextuality. His presentation and analyses of a self-regarding subject may seem far removed from twentieth-century post-formalist theories, yet his work *enacts* a theory which is substantially consonant with Riffaterrean notions of intertextual functioning (and even – partially – with the Bloomian concept of the anxiety of influence). Faithful both to the request of his father and to the rhetorical strictures of Cicero, Montaigne commenced his literary career by translating the *Theologia Naturalis* of Raymond Sebond, finding in the exercise of translation the voice that would become his own. In this, he is hardly alone (one thinks of Proust, for instance), but what is important is that in his *Essays,*[21] Montaigne articulates a theory of intertextual reading which is grounded in an almost boastful forgetfulness (*CW,* II, 10, p. 296). Developing the Quintilian metaphor of reading as ingestion (without citing Quintilian), Montaigne asserts that 'It is a sign of rawness and indigestion to disgorge food just as we swallowed it' (*CW,* I, 26, p. 111), since 'To know by heart is not to know; it is to retain what we have given to our memory to keep' (*CW,* I, 26, p. 112).

Like Erasmus for whom writers can assert and maintain their independence only by multiplying and fragmenting their models, thereby avoiding the dominance of one single precursor, Montaigne chooses a diversity of sources, engaging in an active conversation with them rather than in a passive absorption. He often contests the greatness of some of their works: for instance, he judges Cicero's poetry to be bad and, more surprisingly, he states that Plato's dialogues 'drag and stifle his substance too much' (*CW*, II, 10, pp. 301–2). He reads and judges, yet he also feels the need to escape, even physically, from his books and therefore from his precursors. He believes that the 'self' is to be found in a distancing of the reading and writing subject from the anterior 'other'; reading enables an act of interpretation which is also an activity of idiosyncratic creation in that the displacement inherent in imitation engenders a valorisation of the self as writer *because* one reads agonistically. However, this physical alienation from books necessarily leads to the textual amnesia which all writers experience (although they rarely proclaim it quite so defiantly as Montaigne). This amnesia may seem to promise to liberate writers from a (Bloomian) interpersonal struggle with precursor poets, but it also suggests, as Kristeva insists, that their texts function for their readers as intertextual and not intersubjective networks ('Word, dialogue and novel', p. 37). Readers recognise in (or impose on) these texts segments from other writings which may have been forgotten by the writer or even written many centuries later.[22] This may bring about the 'death of the author' more surely than would the tyrannical absorption by a strong precursor.

Imitation and translation may usefully be seen as textual modalities of recognition and transgression of the Law. Analogous to Judeo-Christian laws of obedience to a male-determined God (which also make Eve responsible for the Fall) and to Freudian and Lacanian theories which posit the (symbolic) father as the agent of Law because he prohibits the child's desire for the mother, this cultural Law requires respect for fathers and submission to phallogocentricity. Kristeva has argued that every text is under the jurisdiction of other discourses,[23] and we would further suggest that imitation and translation should also be considered as forms of creative splitting or catastrophe[24] which function both as temporary proofs of the integrity of the writing subject and as transgressive inscriptions of (feminine) fluidity into textuality. Furthermore, they demand that the reader perceive not only the genetic determination of any individual text but also the fact that all Law is textual ideology and consequently not timeless or universal but subject to prevailing cultural codes.

While Montaigne's writing is highly allusive, it is particularly interesting in its use of quotation.[25] As Gadamer says, all tradition in the form of writing is simultaneous with present time (*Truth and Method*, p. 351), yet the writer's (and the reader's) relationship with this tradition is usually, perhaps necessarily, one of contestation, since to believe that one is a latecomer is, as Nietzsche insists, harmful and degrading.[26] Throughout the *Essays*, which are grounded in a tension between the willed presentation of an emerging subject and the active participation in tradition marked by extensive quotation and allusion, Montaigne assails the authority of previous writers whose merit for him lies in their expression, not in any monopoly (or even originality) of thought. His mistrust of mere repetition (*CW*, I, 25, p. 100) leads him to valorise amnesia as a means of escaping the silencing tyranny of predecessors (*CW*, III, 5, p. 666) and deliberately to omit indications of the sources of his quotations – which nonetheless often figure typographically in italics (*CW*, II, 10, p. 296). If Montaigne is suspicious of the value of quotations, it is because they may serve both to diminish and to fragment the latecome text to the detriment of its author. More importantly, perhaps, it is because he is convinced that truth and reason are shared by all and consequently that their articulation must not be attributed to any individual *Witness*, as Hobbes puts it in his later (unacknowleged) rehearsal of the argument.[27]

However, despite Montaigne's suspicion of quotation and his desire to weave a seamless textual fabric (*CW*, I, 26, p. 127), he does quote extensively.[28] While he may believe and assert that his quotations do not 'belong' to him and are therefore marks of his absence from the text, they are not mere ornaments as Compagnon suggests (*La Seconde Main*, p. 296). Rather, they alert the reader to the existence of an already-read, to intertexts which may or may not be locatable. More significantly, they function as textual strategies, as tropological events, as *metaphors*. The use of italics or inverted commas certainly signals a repetition and a ceding of authorial copyright; it also points to an obligatory intertext, to a conscious manipulation of what Barthes calls the circular memory of reading,[29] thereby acting as a blocking mechanism which (temporarily, at least) restricts the reader's free, aleatory intertextual reading of the text. However, we would argue with Kristeva that reading is aggressive participation (*Séméiotiké*, p. 120) and also that the reader inescapably strives to incorporate the quotation into the unified textuality which makes of the text a semiotic unit. The reader thus seeks to read the borrowing not only for its semantic content but also for its tropological or metaphoric function and significance.

Inevitably a fragment and displacement, every quotation distorts and redefines the 'primary' utterance by relocating it within another linguistic and cultural context. Therefore, despite any intentional quest on the part of the quoting author to engage in an inter-subjective activity, the quotation itself generates a tension between belief both in original and originating integrity and in the possibility of (re)integration and an awareness of infinite deferral and dissemination of meaning. Quotation as fragmentation does indeed generate centrifugality in reading,[30] but it also generates centripetality, focusing the reader's attention on textual functioning rather than on hermeneutics. On one level, the quotations in the *Essays* may testify to Montaigne's readings and preoccupations, but they do more: they engage the reader in an activity of tropological analysis and speculation. And it is the reader who thereby founds both Montaigne's subjectivity and the text of the *Essays*. Free to insert or remove the diacritical marks of quotation at will,[31] the reader nonetheless recognises that each quotation is a *breach* and a *trace* – and as such demands a non-linear reading.

A tropological reading of a quotation 'sees it as' something other than it is/was in its original context, sees it as a metaphor. This act of reading is analogous to what Ricoeur describes as the iconic moment in metaphor (*The Rule of Metaphor*, pp. 187–91): the reader passively receives the vehicle and actively tries to understand not only the tenor but also the Gestalt, the figure in which similarity or analogy coheres. The tenor of the quotation-as-metaphor encompasses its first meaning and its interpretation by the quoting author, but the Gestalt, formed or determined by the reader, is ambiguous (like Wittgenstein's duck-rabbit): it is simultaneously the (ultimately locatable) sociolect within which a Montaigne establishes and inscribes his idiolect and that of the reader who reads Montaigne's quotation–translation through the prism of her/his idiolect – and each of these sociolects is susceptible to redefinition. In each encounter with a quotation, the reader perceives that, while there is an obvious conflict between sameness or identity and difference, there is also a covert fusion of differences *within* the single textual utterance. We would therefore suggest that every quotation is a metaphor which speaks of that which is absent and which engages the reader in a speculative activity.[32] This speculation centres not on the/a historical source but on the signifying force of a textual segment which, simultaneously within and without the text, can have its origin only in the moment(s) of reading.

Heidegger affirms that 'every work of art says something other than the mere thing itself is, *allo agoreuei*', positing the work first as an allegory and then as a symbol (*Poetry, Language, Thought*, pp. 19–20). His use of the term 'allegory' may seem surprising if read intertextually in the light of modern theories which characterise allegory by its rigidity and decipherability,[33] but he is surely right in his conviction that the work manifests something other – and the quotation or micro-text does not simply manifest or enact repetition. As an *event* in the text, it depends for its full significance on the activity of a reader who perceives that something is happening rather than simply being said. To quote is not merely to write glosses on previous writers; it is to interrogate the chronicity of literature and philosophy, to challenge history as determining tradition and to question conventional notions of originality and difference. Consequently, to read an explicitly (or even tacitly) quoting text is not to engage in a simple play with and of sources but to recognise and establish criteria of significance.

Both a mode of imitation and an act of apparent appropriation, quotation mobilises the reader's creative performance by alerting her/him to the fact that originality may not be the best way of regarding a work. As Eliot says: 'if we approach a poet without this prejudice [of originality and difference], we shall find that not only the best, but the most individual parts of [an author's] work may be those in which the dead poets, his ancestors, assert their immortality most vigorously' (*Points of View*, p. 24). History as sequence is undone, as is the notion of a single unified, individual voice – so meaning and significance are to be constructed rather than extracted. In other words, hermeneutic activity must give way to semiotic, intertextual analysis.

While all authors rewrite the work of predecessors, many post-Renaissance writers *consciously* imitate, quote and/or plagiarise extensively (as somewhat arbitrary examples we would propose

Hazlitt, Lautréamont, Joyce, the French Surrealists, T. S. Eliot, Borges, D. M. Thomas, Michel Tournier, A. S. Byatt). In various ways these writers are thereby inscribing themselves in *Tradition* and making public a loving gratitude to ancestors – but their works are equally witnesses to an agonistic impulse to demarcate and proclaim their own creative space. Such intertextual practices call into question the difference between poetic voices. Reading Emerson, Coleridge, Wells and Henry James, Borges considers (sympathetically) the pantheistic notion that explains (away) the plurality of authors by erecting the figure of an eternal Spirit-voice which speaks through all poets.[34] We would suggest that for the reader the plurality of authors is both an empirical reality and a poetic illusion. This paradox informs all intertextual reading, but it is the particular ground of the work of Borges – whom we have chosen as our second enactor of intertextuality, largely because of his metapoetical exploitation of imitation. A librarian and so supposedly a guardian of historical taxonomies, Borges chose to write texts that quote in order to deny (slavish) imitation. Like Montaigne, he accords a certain place to the fallacy of intersubjectivity. Equating reading with sex, he writes: 'All men, in the vertiginous moment of coitus, are the same man. All men who repeat a line from Shakespeare *are* William Shakespeare.'[35] Not unlike Gadamer, he denies the existence of a single, sequential time, while admitting the concomitant difficulty of accepting the notion of co-temporality.[36] The products of (meta)critical readings which convince him that tradition is a mere factitious construct, his 'fictional' writings testify to a belief in the creative and modifying power of re-enunciation. Certain that 'each writer *creates* his precursors',[37] he writes constantly from within his (father's!) library which he describes as the chief *event* in his life.[38] Bloom describes Borges's insight as merely 'witty', positing his own theory of Apophrades or the Return of the Dead as 'something more drastic and (presumably) absurd' (*The Anxiety of Influence*, p. 141).[39] However, in his complex writings of and on fictions, Borges challenges the *doxa* of writing as territorialism and demarcation of property, borrowing in order to subvert the concepts of authorial integrity and textual fixity. For him, literature is not mimetic but a form of allegory (interpreted as an intuitive 'seeing as' which mediates between language and reality). Consequently, he engages in a scriptural activity that is grounded in duplication – and in duplicity. Perhaps his most influential intertextual story is 'Pierre Ménard, author of *Don*

*Quixote*' in which Ménard, a figure of Valéry's literary alter ego and *Doppelgänger* Monsieur Teste, has (re)written the 9th and 38th chapters of the first part of *Don Quixote*. Ménard's ambition was not to write just another version but 'the Quixote itself' (*Labyrinths*, p. 39) – and furthermore he wished to do this not through an historical act of intersubjective understanding but by a willed, systematic (re)construction of a text which is 'originally' marked by the workings of chance and spontaneity.[40]

Not insignificantly, Cervantes' *Quixote* itself functions on one level as a conflict between two modes of preformed linguistic discourse – Don Quixote's quotations which are usually inappropriate and Sancho's proverbs which are always apposite. The literary is thus (re)presented as inferior to oral folk-knowledge, if one is judging by criteria of usefulness. This metaliterary irony is magnified and compounded (confounded?) by Ménard's fragmentary rewriting which, absent from the written textuality of Borges's story, is a paradigm of all literature: its duplicitous repetition redefines and locates as posterior the 'original' model, positing itself as a new (if temporary) origin for the infinite speculations of readers.

Gérard Genette has argued that a direct imitation of a text is impossible because it is too easy and therefore insignificant. His view is that one can *parody* an individual text, but *imitate* only a genre, since to imitate is necessarily to generalise (*Palimpsestes*, pp. 91–2). For him Ménard's *Don Quixote* is not a copy but a minimal transformation or a maximal imitation, i.e. a pastiche (*Palimpsestes*, p. 445). Our reading is somewhat different. In Ménard's quotation-as-imitation, we see an articulation not only of irony but of transfiguration: the latecome text tropes (upon) the 'original', metaphorising it and even perhaps making of it a result rather than a cause. Ménard's unfinished (and non-quoted) text might thus be seen as a simulacrum, as a copy without an original which problematises the domimant and domineering European concept of origination. Borges's story has influenced writers perhaps even more than critics: for example, several tales in Tournier's forthcoming *Le Médianoche amoureux* privilege the copy over the original and even D. M. Thomas's controversially plagiaristic *The White Hotel* and *Ararat* may be read in Borgesian terms as 'original'. Much recent fictional writing explicitly contests the intentional self-integrity of texts and explodes the traditional concept of originality, while not falling into the 'trap' of a Shelleyan or an Emersonian belief in a single Spirit-voice. And critical thinking is – happily – increasingly attending to the performative functioning of imitation and quotation which, while superficially signalling an obligatory intertext, mobilise aleatory and metacritical responses from the reader, thereby establishing themselves as powerful operators of intertextuality.

We are now going to turn from our enactors of intertextuality to some twentieth-century theories and theoreticians – though, of course, as the examples of Plato, Montaigne, Borges or Barthes suggest, any distinction between enactors and theorists is a stage in interpretative analysis which is likely swiftly to dissolve as the analysis proceeds. This century has seen a wide variety of positions on what may broadly be termed 'intertextuality', from Riffaterre's poetics to Bloom's anxiety of influence. Again we are not attempting to cover the material exhaustively, but rather to give some brief analysis, starting with Bakhtin, of some of the most important and influential theorists.[41]

Although Bakhtin first published in 1919, for a variety of reasons it is only over the last twenty or so years that he has slowly come to be recognised in circles outside Eastern Europe.[42] What interests us here is the theory of language (everyday dialogism) and of two poles of literature (the monologic and the dialogic). Bakhtin argues that when people speak they use a specific mix of discourses which they have appropriated in an attempt to communicate their intentions. However, they inevitably suffer interference from two sources: words' pre-existing meanings and the alien intentions of a real interlocutor (as opposed to the perfect understanding of a super-addressee). Every concrete utterance is intersected by both centrifugal and centripetal, unifying and disunifying forces (see *The Dialogic Imagination*, p. 272). Unity or plenitude in language can only be an illusion which covers a real excess or lack. Writers of literature can attempt artificially to strip language of others' intentions, a unifying project which Bakhtin calls monologism or poetry.[43] On the other hand, at certain historical moments, writers have artistically elaborated and intensified this heteroglossia, creating what Bakhtin calls the (dialogic) novel. It is important to note that Bakhtin's categories do not correspond to traditional ones, for example, Heine's lyric verse is included by Bakhtin in the category 'novel', whereas Tolstoy's prose is presented as monological. Monologism has, according to Bakhin, been encouraged or imposed by hierarchical and centralising socio-linguistic forces such as Aristotelian or Cartesian poetics, the medieval church's 'one language of truth', or Saussurian linguistics (p. 271).[44] The novel, on the other hand, has been shaped by iconoclastic, even revolutionary, popular traditions; Bakhtin lays particular emphasis on *carnival* and the power of laughter to destroy a hierarchical distance.[45] Novels are enriched by social heteroglossia, by the historicity and social determination of specific languages (p. 285), by the fact that words do not live in dictionaries but in other people's mouths (p. 294).[46]

Bakhtin distinguishes between *double-voiced* discourse (that is to say, speech which serves two speakers' intentions, such as those attributed to novelist and those to character) and poetic or rhetorical tropes. Double-voiced discourse in the novel, for instance irony or parody, is, he argues, a dialogue of two world views. Even though tropes include the figurative use of someone else's imagined speech (say, of accusation), they are merely the formalistic play of particular individuals. Rhetorical *transmission* of another's words (p. 354), unlike double-voiced *representation,* cannot, according to Bakhtin, create that image of a language which reveals the social behind the individual. That image requires two linguistic consciousnesses – the representing and the represented – if it is not to be merely a sample (p. 359).

One of the most important, and earliest, interpretations of Bakhtin's work for a western public was by Kristeva. In 'Word, dialogue and novel' she introduces *Rabelais and His World* and *Problems of Dostoevsky's Poetics.* She adds to Bakhtin's languages ones which she has drawn from fields such as mathematical logic and psychoanalysis. It is also important to note that she refers to literary language as 'poetic language' without the connotations that the term 'poetry' has in Bakhtin. She also privileges the term 'text' in order to remove any apparent bias in Bakhtin towards the spoken word.[47] For Kristeva, the subject is composed of discourses, is a signifying system, a text, understood in a dynamic sense. 'Word, dialogue and novel', written in 1966, illustrates the way in which post-structuralism already inhabits structuralist discourse.[48] Kristeva writes: 'What allows a dynamic dimension to structuralism is Bakhtin's conception of the "literary word" as an *intersection of textual surfaces* rather than a *point* (a fixed meaning), as a dialogue among several writings: that of the writer, the addressee (or the character) and the contemporary or earlier cultural context' ('Word, discourse and novel', p. 36).[49] A structure is generated in relation to *another* structure. In 'Problèmes de la structuration du texte', she argues that a text is in fact a *structuration*, that is, an apparatus which produces and transforms meaning. Kristeva takes up Bakhtin's chain of binary oppositions, but she emphasises that both the monologic and the dialogic poles are to be found in any text. Poetic (dialogic) language is characterised by a logic of non-exclusive opposition (a refusal of the 0–1, true–false opposition of Aristotelian logic) like that of the Unconscious. This suggests that the very opposition between monologism and dialogism cannot be exclusive.

Kristeva also highlights the politically subversive nature of celebrating dialogism/intertextuality. There is, Bakhtin and Kristeva both argue, a deeply serious side to the carnivalesque challenge to official linguistic codes, which is to be contrasted with the kind of parody which upholds what it mocks or attempts to exist without any kind of law. The correlational (non-causal) logic of the dream or the carnival, which persistently refers to sex and death, is a revolutionary refusal of existing hierarchies, and of social and political codes.

Kristeva, along with Riffaterre and other theorists of intertextuality, has sometimes been criticised on the grounds that the literary examples which she cites are too particular or even inappropriate for her argument; Jonathan Culler claims that her work on Lautréamont 'illustrates the way in which the concept of intertextuality leads the critic who wishes to work with it to concentrate on cases that put in question the general theory' (*The Pursuit of Signs*, p. 104). In this volume, Roland Lack takes up that very issue. However, the importance of Kristeva's work is not so much her reading of particular poets, or even of particular poetic genealogies, as her formulation of a theory of the subject and of language. A critique of Plato's reading of Homer by a Homer scholar may be of very considerable interest, but does not necessarily detract from Plato's production of a philosophical position. Kristevan intertextuality suggests, in line with marxist sociology, that meaning is not *given* nor produced by a transcendental ego. Indeed the transcendental ego is itself an effect *produced* in a social context.[50]

Kristeva's recent work has focused more on the peculiar social context which is psychoanalysis, i.e. the meeting of analyst and analysand in the transference, than on that of reading poetry, i.e. the meeting of the reader and the text.[51] But both situations involve the

production of meaning, of moments of structuring, via an exchange
of language (a dialogue). The temporary *meaning* and structure
given to the subject which happens in analysis also occurs outside it –
Keith Reader, in this volume, gives an example of the construction of
the self via the detours of the intertextual, and of the pain–pleasure
attendant upon such moments of recognition. The transference, we
should add, is a love *story*. In *Psychoanalysis and Faith*, Kristeva
concludes that the psychoanalysis cure leads us to consider at once
the word as body (crossed by pre-linguistic forces) and the body as
word (signifying system): 'all plentitude turns out to be inscribed
upon a "void" which is simply what remains when the overabun-
dance of meaning, desire, violence, and anguish is drained by means
of language' (p. 34). This assertion points in the same direction as
Bloom, towards the possibility that intertextual relations are
passionate ones.

Roland Barthes cites Kristeva's work as one of his *intertexts*,
explaining the term as follows: 'The intertext is not necessarily a field
of influences: rather it is a music of figures, metaphors, thought-
words; it is the signifier as *siren*' (*Roland Barthes,* p. 145). Barthes
tells us that he finds certain words as used by certain writers or by
certain schools of thought particularly delicious and seductive. He
acts as an 'echo chamber' (*Roland Barthes,* p. 74), using the
borrowed vocabulary with a certain slippage: he gives as an example
*bourgeois,* which

receives the whole marxist accent, but keeps overflowing toward the aesthetic and the ethical. In this way, no doubt, words are shifted, systems
communicate, modernity is tried (the way one tries all the push buttons on a
radio one doesn't know how to work), but the intertext thereby created is
literally superficial: one adheres *liberally*: the name (philosophic, psychoanalytic, political, scientific) retains with its original system a line which is
not cut but which remains: tenacious and floating. (p. 74)

Other post-structuralist writers have followed the practice of lifting
certain siren signifiers from earlier texts: for instance, Derrida
borrows *supplement* from Rousseau and Kristeva *chora* from
Plato.[52] The words take on a new life in radically new contexts but
retain the character of loans. Kristeva's word *intertextuality* seems to
be one of these sexy (*Roland Barthes,* p. 164) expressions for
Barthes. He uses it for example in *The Pleasure of the Text* as
follows: '[intertextuality is] the impossibility of living outside the
infinite text [. . .]; the book creates meaning, the meaning creates the
life' (p. 36).[53] Here the term means something more than the

pleasure of picking up words (like 'intertextuality' or 'bourgeoisie') which have particularly seductive and/or complicated pasts; rather it explains that we make sense of our lived experience and hence construct our 'lives' in relation to texts, whether these be Proust or television soap operas.

Even before Kristeva's 1965 presentation of Bakhtin in Barthes's seminar, Barthes was evoking something like 'intertextuality' under the name *cryptographie* (which is translated as *cryptogram*).[54] In *Writing Degree Zero*, he uses the term thus:

it is impossible to develop [my selected mode of writing] within duration without gradually becoming a prisoner of someone else's words and even of my own. A stubborn after-image, which comes from all the previous modes of writing and even from the past of my own, drowns the sound of my present words. Any written trace precipitates, as inside a chemical at first transparent, innocent and neutral, mere duration gradually reveals in suspension a whole past of increasing density, like a cryptogram. (p. 23)

This is intertextuality in the sense that a text may appear to be the spontaneous and transparent expression of a writer's intentions, but must necessarily contain elements of other texts. Barthes provides an extraordinary example of this in *S/Z* where he picks out some of the quotations without quotation marks, some of the references to cultural codes, stereotypes, received wisdom and so on in Balzac's *Sarrasine*.

*S/Z* helped to establish Barthes as the most perverse of readers. This expression is high praise in Barthes's terms, but also reminds us of the considerable hostility from the critical establishment to his way of reading.[55] In this volume, Diana Knight analyses Barthes's perverse delight in inversion – both *semantic* inversion (so that 'perversion' is a 'good' rather than a 'bad') and *sexual* inversion – and his delight in precursors such as Socrates, Gide or Proust known for inversion(s).

The 'perverse' reader, in Barthes's vocabulary, is the reader who is a split (and re-split) subject. The reading subject is split like the child who knows that the maternal penis does not exist and yet believes that it does, for s/he knows that the textual events are not real and yet believes in them (*The Pleasure of the Text*, p. 47). S/he is wilfully split again if, like Barthes, s/he enjoys both the hedonistic delight of a culture and the destruction of that culture, both the consistency and the loss of the self (op. cit., p. 14). Even that mastery is a fiction, however, if we define the reading subject according to *S/Z* where the 'I' is an intertextuality, a network of citations, and where each unit of reading functions, not by referring to a fixed content in *Sarrasine,* but by activating certain codes in the reader. The fracturing of the reading subject is inevitably associated with the dissolution of the author, or death of the author as Barthes puts it, evoking Nietzsche as intertext. The author, like the coherent and autonomous subject, is revealed to be a necessary fiction, a reading effect.

Kristeva herself has consistently argued, in accordance with new French psychoanalytic theory, for this redefinition of the subject as always already cleft asunder or even radically dispersed.[56] She later comes to emphasise that the (analytic) subject is speaking the body, is speaking its love. However, it is Barthes, with his reversible figure of body as text/text as body, who is most associated with the eroticisation of intertextuality. Of course the eroticisation of 'philosophy' dates back at least as far as Plato/Socrates; Diana Knight points out how Barthes rewrites Plato (and suggests that Plato has rewritten *history*) in a way which shows eros to conquer death (*thanatos*). Barthes's eroticisation seems to deny the aggression emphasised by Bloom in his Freudian master trope of the Oedipal battle between poets, while enacting it in his rewriting of Plato; he even denies the conflict implicit in Bakhtinian dialogue (*The Pleasure of the Text,* p. 16). Barthes agrees that all narrative is necessarily Oedipal, but defuses that situation of violence.[57] Like Sartre (another intertext), he *denies* that his own personal situation (the only son of a literally dead father) leaves him in the usual Oedipal relationship. He argues indeed that the Freudian reading of 'denial' (as affirmation) is the paranoiac gesture of a would-be totalising discourse (*The Pleasure of the Text,* p. 29).

Barthes's theory is thus of a diffused (or defused) eroticism, which should be detached from meaning and power relations. The expression 'should be' points to a recurring problem in Barthes, Kristeva and Bakhtin, that is to say the slippage between *is* and *ought*. Barthes, like the others, constantly sets up hierarchical antitheses. A fundamental opposition is between the classic work, which is only plural in its meanings, and the modern text, which can be infinitely rewritten by the reader.[58] Does his account of the functioning of the text (like Bakhtin's dialogism) apply only to the small group of 'textes de jouissance' (hence 'ought') or does it apply to all texts ('is')?[59]

Barthes's hailing of the death of the author implies a rejection of authority; does this correspond to the political, indeed revolutionary, thrust which Kristeva emphasises in Bakhtin? The Barthes of *Mythologies* (first published in book form in 1957) refers to 'the revolution', something which would be free of myths; according to *Mythologies,* under capitalism, myths would be the monopoly product of the bourgeoisie. However, Barthes's use of the term 'bourgeoisie' (according to the quotation above) is both a citation from marxist discourse and also, especially later, a link to (desirable) aestheticism. Barthes seems ever ready to politicise seemingly natural matters of taste (a classically marxist task), but also to aestheticise seemingly political issues (*Roland Barthes,* p. 169). The latter strategy works against the tendency of political discourse to become totalising, but where aestheticisation or the theory of intertextuality denies the reality of power relations it can seem dangerously 'neutral'.

Barthes's theory of (inter)textuality is inseparable from his practice as writer. Indeed he constantly blurs generic boundaries: theory or practice, criticism or creation, autobiography or fiction and so on, a blurring which Ann Jefferson explores in this volume. In *A Lover's Discourse: Fragments,* he himself provides the (necessarily incomplete) marginal notations of the erudite reader, who would delight in recognising citations from a variety of sources. The lonely voice of the lover in that text could thus be heard as a polyphony, a chorus of 'friends'. Or perhaps we should theorise Barthes's strategy as providing us with two textile edges which do not quite meet (the lover's discourse and the marginal, plus foot-note, references), the flickering gap between them being the epitome of seduction according to *The Pleasure of the Text* (e.g. pp. 9–10).[60] However, a third possibility might be that the supplementary references are a cloying excess, cutting the reader's appetite, and hence paradoxically impoverishing rather than enriching the reader's feast, filling in the gap (sometimes indicated by an incongruity or 'ungrammaticality' to borrow Riffaterre's language) which invites the reader to undertake an errant search. If I am instructed that a certain thought is inspired by Nietzsche via Deleuze does this inspire play or block it off? Does a reference to a personal friend, indicated by initials, simply invite finite research of the empirical anecdotal kind?[61] This kind of criticism, which appears to delimit the writer's task, may suggest that the author is not just one more fictional character, but rather a special kind of figure. Such criticism would no doubt be ludically and *easily* rejected by Barthes who delighted in commenting on himself to the highest degree possible, for instance by writing a review of Roland Barthes's *Roland Barthes*.

One of the rare theorists of intertextuality to ground his work firmly and extensively in the writings of both Greek and Roman thinkers, Genette proposes in *Introduction à l'architexte* that poetics should be concerned not with the (individual) text, but with the *architext* – which he defines as the set of categories, such as genre, thematics, etc., which determine the nature of any individual text. In many ways an attempt at deconstructing the conventional European tripartite division of literature into lyric, epic and dramatic, his study also offers new definitions of inter-textual relations. Reading Kristeva's notion of intertextuality as referring to the literal and effective presence in a text of another text, he asserts that *intertextuality* is an inadequate term and proposes in its place *transtextuality* (or textual transcendence), by which he means everything, be it explicit or latent, that links one text to others – which is how we in this volume understand and use the term intertextuality. As sub-categories of transtextuality, he posits not only architextuality and 'Kristevan' intertextuality, but also metatextuality or the relationship between a commentary and its object, and paratextuality or the imitative or transformatory relationships that pertain between pastiches or parodies and their models.[62] Genette's book is an introduction in more ways than one – he not only offers new terms in a real attempt to narrow critical focus but also wittily questions the value of his own neologisms and thereby challenges the totalising premises of much critical debate.

Three years after *Introduction,* he published *Palimpsestes* which is both a corrective and sustained elaboration of some of his earlier theories and also, he has told us, his 'last word' on intertextuality. Even more than in *Introduction,* he amusingly alerts his readers to the problems posed by critical 'jargon', but suggests that his own (and others') terms can be genuinely useful as long as they are sufficiently defined by each individual critic–theorist.[63] Insisting again on the globality of his notion of transtextuality (which he recognises as co-extensive with Riffaterre's interpretative use of intertextuality), he now offers five sub-categories: 'Kristevan' intertextuality (now perceived as covering allusion as well as quotation and plagiarism); paratextuality, which he radically re-defines as the relations between the body of a text and its titles, epigraphs, illustrations, notes, first drafts, etc.; metatextuality; architextuality, now defined as a tacit, perhaps even unconscious, gesture to genre-demarcations[64] (and therefore as implying, for the reader, a Jaussian horizon of expectations); hypertextuality. This last domain of enquiry forms the bedrock of the book. Genette defines the latecome text as the *hypertext* and its pre-text as the *hypotext* – although he distinguishes here between metatextual commentaries and literary, transformatory texts, be they imitative or revolutionary (*Palimpsestes,* pp. 7–14). For him, hypertextuality is a practice which includes and informs all literary genres and he goes so far as to assert that the hypertext necessarily gains in some way or another from the reader's awareness of its signifying and determining relationship with its hypotext(s) (*Palimpsestes,* pp. 448–51). Rethinking the Barthesian and Borgesian notions of the functional circularity of memory in reading, Genette ends his study of palimpsestic texts by affirming that hypertextuality has the specific merit of energetically projecting pre-texts into new and different circuits of meaning and meaningfulness. His analyses of individual texts may be less sustained, less close than Riffaterre's, but his work does insistently remind us that memory can be actively 'revolutionary' only so long as it is creative as well as commemorative (*Palimpsestes,* p. 453).

Jacques Derrida, in conversation with Henri Ronse, says 'In what you call my books, what is first of all put in question is the unity of the book and the unity "book" considered as a perfect totality, with all the implications of such a concept' (*Positions,* p. 3). He goes on to point out how this unsettles the notion of authorship. The work signed Jacques Derrida has been highly influential for Kristeva and Barthes as well as for many other writers of the last thirty years. His work assumes intertextuality both in its articulation of theory and in its practice. His writings exemplify intertextual relations both in that other texts (written or otherwise, earlier or later) are read differently after the reader's exposure to the Derridean corpus, and in that he insists that 'above all it is necessary to read and reread those in whose wake I write, the "books" in whose margins and between whose lines I mark out and read a text simultaneously almost identical and entirely other' (*Positions,* p. 4). In this conversation he points out the strange geometrical relationship between three of his own works,[65] each of which is in some way inscribed within the others. Each of these texts, in common with the vast majority of what he has written, takes the form of explicit interpretation or commentary on earlier writers as well as being starred with numerous quotations without quotation marks. In his analysis of other writers he often pays attention to the 'sources' from which they have shied away, pointing out the textual scars or blanks into which the names of missed origins can be inserted. In 'Qual Quelle: Valéry's sources' (*Margins of Philosophy*), he adopts an ex-centric perspective to detect Nietzsche and Freud as the systematically unspoken names in Valéry's writing.

In 'Signature Event Context', Derrida analyses J. L. Austin's *How to Do Things With Words* as representative of a philosophical tradition:

Austin's procedure is rather remarkable and typical of that philosophical tradition with which he would like to have so few ties. It consists in recognising that the possibility of the negative (in this case, of infelicities) is in fact a structural possibility, that failure is an essential risk of the operations under consideration; then in a move which is almost *immediately simultaneous,* in the name of a kind of ideal regulation, it excludes that risk as accidental, exterior, one which teaches us nothing about the linguistic phenomenon being considered.[66]

Quotation is one of these inferior possibilities excluded by philosophical analysis of language. However, a precondition for readability is what Derrida calls 'iterability''. This term means the possibility of being repeated, as well as connoting otherness. No communication is comprehensible unless it could be repeated or cited. This implies that citationality, which entails an utterance being detached from its context, is a characteristic of any sign and not simply an aberrant use of language. In other words, rather than regarding quotation as a parasitic and unusual activity, we could say that any text is inevitably quoting and quotable. Derrida's deconstruction of metaphysical, hierarchical oppositions is thus highly relevant to intertextuality.

While Riffaterre's early work had much in common with Russian and French formalist theories which sought to produce a poetics of literature, he has always insisted on the need to study the modalities of the perception of the literary message,[67] defining the literary phenomenon as '*not only the text, but also its reader and all of the reader's possible reactions to the text*' (*Text Production,* p. 3). Riffaterre has elaborated and refined the notion of intertextuality both through his theoretical pronouncements and through his readings of individual texts: indeed, the main thrust of his thinking is that intertextuality not only grounds textuality but is the main, defining characteristic of (literary) reading. His work must, however, be distinguished from the work of reader-response critics, in that his work is based in and on a concern with textual elements that we are *obliged* to perceive – while also insisting on the need for a theory of literariness rather than of literature.[68] He perceives two stages of reading: the heuristic or initial, linear 'learning' reading, and the subsequent, retroactive hermeneutic readings.[69] In this he might seem merely to be rehearsing a Classical view such as that of Quintilian who insists on the interpretative freedom of the reader as opposed to the restraints imposed on the listener of an oration, yet Riffaterre's theory is much more complex and centres on the determining function of grammatical structures – which determine not only interpretation but even perhaps rhetorical categories. In this regard, his project may be seen as importantly philosophical; for him, as for Paul Zumthor, reading is not only an aesthetic or even hermeneutic activity, but is an epistemological process. The literary phenomenon is, for him, not a dialogue between text and reader, but a *dialectic* (*Semiotics,* p. 1). For this reason, he strives to incorporate into his theory and his practice of reading the hermeneutic activity of the reader who notices in each text 'ungrammaticalities' or instances of *catachresis.* The linguistic and literary competence of readers permits such perceptions of 'breaks' in the fabric of the text, yet readers also know (or at least presuppose) that the text is a unified whole. Consequently the ungrammaticalities are integrated into another system defined as *semiosis,* wherein the reader seeks to discover some originating pre-existent word group (the *hypogram*) of which each segment in the poem is a variant (*Semiotics,* p. 4).

Riffaterre is adamant in declaring that 'textuality is inseparable from and founded upon intertextuality' ('Syllepsis', p. 625). There are objections to his theoretical presuppositions, objections which usually take the form of charges of elitism, of reductionism, of triumphalism, of the monumentalism of literature, or of a belief in a normative or even a 'correct' reading.[70] Such complaints usually emerge from a political response to Riffaterre's theory (and especially to his practice), yet they reveal perhaps a blindness to his conviction that 'the text and the very ideology it embodies are always separable' ('Interview', p. 13). Differing radically from the work of Jauss and other members of the Constance School who are concerned essentially with the horizon of (social) expectations, Riffaterre's insists firmly on the control exerted on the reader by the text. While Riffaterre and Jauss both focus on textual actualisation and on actualisation as reading, Jauss's insistence that reading is a lived experience which modifies the reader's social behaviour and shifts the parameters of that reader's vision of the world is much more committedly grounded in literary history than is Riffaterre's commitment to take 'the real [individual] reader's performance as a litmus test' ('Interview', p. 16).[71] In recent articles Riffaterre has made it clear that we must distinguish between *aleatory* intertextuality (which is not unlike Barthes's notion of 'circular memory' and which allows the reader to read a text through the prism of all and any familiar texts) and *obligatory* intertextuality which demands that the reader take account of a hypogrammatic origin.[72] It is crucial, however, to recognise with Riffaterre that this ultimately locatable intertext need not necessarily be located by the reader who, for reasons of education, time, etc., may never know or find it.[73] What is essential is that in each individual reading, the (various) readers sense, indeed presuppose that there is an intertext through their perceptions of the symptomatic nature of the (un)grammatical articulations of the text itself. The analyst or professional critic/reader must seek and will usually eventually find a matrix text (or texts),[74] but the success or failure of this quest is, in a sense, irrelevant to the experience of intertextual reading: as Riffaterre has himself affirmed, 'the only requisite [for reading] may be a *presupposition* of intertext' ('Interview', p. 16).

Riffaterre has taken pains to distinguish between intertextuality and intertext, since a focusing on the latter would be simply another form of source criticism or literary history – hence his insistence on the performative quality of syllepsis which does not merely speak simultaneously in a literal and a figurative way but which, by means of its own ungrammaticality or textual strangeness, alerts the reader to the presence in the text s/he is reading of an (almost hidden) foreign body, which is the *trace* of an intertext. As Riffaterre says: '*Syllepsis is a word understood in two different ways at once, as meaning and as significance* . . . [and therefore is] the literary sign par excellence' ('Syllepsis', p. 638). Riffaterre's argument here is based on his well-known distinction between mimesis and semiosis, but it reveals more about his project in that it foregrounds undecidability as inescapable in any monotextual reading and implicitly proposes intertextual speculation as the sole (though infinitely elusive) solution to the enigma of reading. Despite what some of his critics have asserted, Riffaterre does accord a place to the consideration of ambiguity, although he usually reads the perception/discovery of ambiguity as the result of inattention to the (un)grammatical functioning of a particular text and indeed has recently suggested that the concept of ambiguity itself is a dubious one ('Interview', p. 16).[75] Increasingly, he insists that the recognition of a particular textual aberration is read as a sign, a pointer to another presupposed (and previously established) grammaticality. If ungrammaticalities can (as they surely do) include such textual strategies as quotation, syllepsis, etc., it is essential to recognise that all 'aberrant' textual utterances 'are but the other face of intertextual grammaticalities' (ibid.). Analogous if not identical with Kristeva's assertion that every text is under the jurisdiction of other discourses which impose upon it a universe, Riffaterre's thesis is that literary reading is possible only if the reader recognises that the text articulates a (generalised) *presupposition* of intertext.

When he defines intertextuality as the *conflict* between the text and the intertext, it is patent that, while not unaware of the socio-historical and psychological factors that may determine an author's *own* (believed, willed) choice of a pre-text, he is concerned essentially with the effect on the reader of a textual presupposition which gives structural and semantic unity rather than fracturing the text under consideration.

The notion of conflict is central also to the theoretical project of Harold Bloom. However, in his elaboration of a theory of influence, Bloom focuses on interpersonal – and imaginary – relationships between strong poets, positing catastrophe as 'the central element in poetic incarnation' (*A Map of Misreading*, p. 10; hereinafter *MM*). In this regard, his thinking is influenced by the work of the pre-Socratic philosopher Empedocles and by Freud's and Ferenczi's readings of Empedoclean catastrophe as a cosmic phantasy: he views catastrophe 'alas' as 'the macrocosmic synecdoche of which masochism and sadism from microcosmic parts' ('Freud's concepts of defense and the poetic will', p. 20). For Bloom, catastrophe-creation by an author is both a defence against and an agonistic struggle with precursors. His theory of influence as an articulation of aggressive–defensive narcissism is often attacked (notably for its phallocentrism). However, his work has made an important contribution to intertextual studies, not only because of his theory of intra-poetic relationships and because he has radically altered our attitudes towards the ways in which we regard and interpret the processes of canon formation,[76] but also because his own discourse is highly idiosyncratic – and intertextual. In all his critical works, we find (Riffaterrean) ungrammaticalities which alert us to the fact that Bloom's texts presuppose intertexts which, ranging from Empedocles and Quintilian to Nietzsche, Freud and Ferenczi, may be unlocatable for individual readers but are an essential, ghostly presence in his own writings – although, as Roland Lack points out in this volume, Bloom chooses to ascribe a particular (and sometimes perverse) meaning to the terms he 'borrows'. In this way, his critical books *enact* intertextuality as they describe it: by liberating the reader (and the potentially writing critic) from the bondage of orthodox critical discourse, they inscribe intertextuality as the major trope, indeed as the essence, of *all* (written) discourse.

Bloom's emphasis on misprision or (mis)interpretation distinguishes him radically from early Kristeva and from Riffaterre in that he insists that poets are engaged in an Oedipal struggle with fathers rather than writing within a discursive space of 'anonymous' networks – although he does crucially, if briefly, admit that these idealised fathers may be composite and that influences are not necessarily poetic (*The Anxiety of Influence*, p. 11; hereinafter *AI*). In all of his work, he articulates a dependence upon Freudian models, interpreting, for example, sublimation as 'the truest of defenses against the anxiety of influence' (*AI*, p. 115) and as a mode of *askesis* or transformative and purgative self-curtailment (*AI*, p. 119). His committed acceptance of the pre-eminent value of sublimation (*AI*, p. 9) may surprise many post-Freudians, as may his translation of the 'nuclear' Oedipus complex into a theory of intra-poetic relationships. In this volume Seán Hand argues that Bloom's relation to Freud is that of the complementarity of desire. We would supplement this notion with the suggestion that Bloom's adoption of the Oedipus complex is just as blind as Freud's reading of the Sophoclean myth, *Oedipus Rex*: both overlook the role of parents in the story, ignoring the motives of Laius who, long before he arrived at the fatal crossroads, was jealous, murderous (and a pederast cursed by his boy victim's father) and equally ignoring the collusion of Jocasta. Bloom's blindness is determined in part by his conviction that literary texts are 'refusals of mortality' which have 'two makers: the precursor, and the ephebe's rejected mortality' (*MM*, p. 19) and which must consequently be read in terms of (particular, uni-directional) love-hate impulses.[77] However, the absence of an exploration both of parental rather than exclusively paternal roles and of the Jungian Electra complex, while faithful to Freud's position, makes Bloom's theory inappropriate for certain feminist readings of women's writing: Emily Dickinson, for example, is read in the same terms as male poets. Such a reading is justifiable on some levels in that she is responding (non-marginally) to a male-ordered theology and literature, but we would suggest that post-Bloomian critics and theorists could include in their thinking some greater sense of difference between writers and attend to notions of class/gender/culture difference.[78]

Bloom's highly allusive and citational texts pose another, different problem to their critic–readers in that, like Montaigne, he rarely gives references. This strategy can result in oppositional, even contradictory readings. One example is the Covering Cherub, 'the power that blocks realization' (*AI*, p. 24), whose shadow lies over Bloom as much as it does over strong poets and their precursors. This figure is taken from Blake who, according to Bloom, took it from Milton, Ezekiel and Genesis, yet Bloom takes virtually no account of its contextual function in Ezekiel, where the Cherub was perfect – until iniquity was found in it. The crucial point is that God's lamentation is to be addressed to the king of Tyre, the maritime arm of Egypt and therefore metonymically a symbol of depravity and corruption, a *false* paradise (Ezekiel 28: 11–19). Furthermore all of Ezekiel's prophetic discourse is preoccupied with punishment and with the *conditions* for ultimate repentance. In Ezekiel, the Covering Cherub's role would seem to be very different from his role in Bloom (or indeed in Blake's 'corrective' readings of Milton), and consequently readers who 'follow up' the genealogy of the figure may discover a Cherub who does not condemn but is condemned, a figure doomed to extinction by the disappointed, angry, punishing male God the Father.

Such an intertextual reading leads to a misreading of Bloom – who *appears* not to have read Ezekiel. Yet this oversight (or forgetting) is precisely what makes Bloom's work so intertextually interesting: in the very moment of their enunciation of a genetic origin for poems, his texts deny a single locatable source by evoking other influencing sources both of the poems and of his own discourse.

Theories of intertextuality have, from the outset, referred at least obliquely to sexual hierarchies. The act of (creative) writing has itself often been regarded as having dangerous 'feminine' or 'effeminate' overtones,[79] while historically writers have been predominantly male and *some* aspects of writing have been celebrated as quintessentially active and hence (in an economy which embraces Aristotle, Freud and many more) virile. The act of creation itself, despite the many metaphorical associations with giving birth, can – warding off that maternal metaphor – be related to the myth of the male god as sole creator: wisdom springs from Zeus's head, and Cicero took pride in his title 'father of the fatherland', arguing that the good orator is indeed the founding father of a community and hence of a sociolect. So what aspects of text production are feared because they are considered to feminise the producer?

We have claimed in this Introduction that all writers are first readers, and that all writers are subject to influence, or that – to generalise the point – all texts are necessarily criss-crossed by other texts. We have also argued that, in any historical period which prizes individual achievement, uniqueness or originality, writers may well experience as a humiliation (the pleasure of) being influenced. Looking back over the arguments which we have cursorily presented, a thread runs through them – a common fantasy. This takes the metaphysical form, unsurprisingly, of a hierarchical opposition.[80] On the one hand, there is phallic monologism or the illusion of unity and self-sufficiency. On the other hand, there is liquefaction, the vehicle of passion – even madness, polyphony, the receptive object penetrated by other voices and so on. The latter pole has been admired, but, more particularly, feared for many centuries. We would argue that it can be read as a figure of 'femininity', of that particular 'other' to *the same*. Celia Britton, in this volume, reminds us of the repressed figure of the passionate/mad woman to be found both in fiction and in 'documents'.

The last thirty years have, however, seen a celebration of plurality and intertextuality. Barthes can happily present himself as an echo chamber, an image which Marguerite Duras has applied to herself[81] and which implies both (feminine) multiplicity and non-originality through 'Echo' and maternity through 'chamber' evoking the womb. However, the intricacies of the sexual figuring of writer–reader relations have only recently begun to be unravelled. Several articles in this volume are examples of this new direction for intertextual studies.

Here, we should like to point out briefly some of the references to femininity or effeminacy in the intertextual theories already mentioned in this Introduction. Plato puts forward the view in *Ion* that good poets compose because they are inspired and possessed like Bacchic maidens under the influence of Dionysus; rhapsodists are therefore the interpreters of interpreters, and spectators are the third in the magnetic chain to be moved by the current of passion. Those who are influenced are not in their right minds: they are not rational nor able to make judgements. Bacchic maidens, known for their sexual excesses, are inspired by the androgynous Dionysus; male poets are similarly taken over by a female muse. We would argue that 'inspiration by the muse' is a figure for the creative process, representing the penetration of the text, via the writer, by *other* past or contemporary texts; this is possible because the poet has first been a spectator or reader – and thus is not only the first to be inspired by the 'muse' but also necessarily the third, a responding and performing spectator.

In Plato's political works, *The Republic* and *The Laws,* poetry and the other arts are presented as potentially dangerous for the virtuous state which must be peopled with rational and virtuous beings. Leo Strauss has argued in *The City and the Man* that the *Republic* abstracts from the body and disregards eros in order to safeguard justice and communality. At the beginning of the *Republic* Cephalus quotes Sophocles, the poet, who praises old age because it brings freedom from sexual desire, from 'bondage to a raving madman'.[82] The society of the Guardians is designed to prevent any servitude to passions, and so poetry, which encourages those who recite it or listen to it to indulge their emotions by imitating those of others, has to be strictly controlled. Plato represents Socrates as speaking out 'in spite of a certain affection and reverence [he has] had from a child for Homer, who seems to have been the original master and guide of all this imposing company of tragic poets' (X, p. 317). He speaks as someone who has overcome the influence of the most influential of predecessors, predecessor in the sense that Homer and the poets were widely (falsely in Plato's view) regarded as guides to right conduct. Plato contrasts the poet/painter who may make many (different sorts of, say) beds – not an indifferent choice of example – with the god who makes one unique Bed, the single ideal Bed. The *philosopher* aspires to know those unique Forms or Ideas rather than being seduced by the multiple appearances and emotions of poetry. Bakhtin has pointed out how Plato's Dialogues are in fact plural, ambiguous and multi-faceted rather than monologic. While Socrates mocks poets because they divide the mind (X, p. 327) and stimulate 'womanish' behaviour (X, p. 330), Bakhtin praises the Dialogues, against univocal poetry, because they represent a multiplicity of voices. Plato/Socrates can be seen as struggling to present himself as manly, the lover who has the strength to reject the meretricious charms of beloved poetry (X, p. 332) rather than as the Bacchic maiden whom he may in fact resemble as much as any other great creative artist.[83]

Plato is not, of course, alone, either in his representation of the muse, the source of inspiration, as female,[84] or in his representation of the inspired as feminine. Longinus compares the new poet, imitating the great poets of the past, to the Pythian priestesses impregnated by Apollo. Quintilian refers to the process of transforming the read into the written as liquefaction, a bodily metaphor which recalls to the modern reader the intertext of, for instance, Luce Irigaray's writing which characterises femininity as fluid as well as plural in its eroticism.[85]

When Montaigne speaks of the desire to create a seamless fabric or text, he is using a traditional metaphor whose etymology links it metonymically to the work of women (weaving). However, his usage actually articulates phallic monologism. Referring to sex changes cited in Pliny, Pontanus and Ovid and to the contemporary case of Marie Germain, he claims that the imagination is so completely fixed on the penis that it would be better if 'once and for all it incorporates this masculine member in girls' (CW, I, 21, p. 69). While elsewhere he states that 'the government of women has a mysterious way of proceeding' (CW, III, 5, p. 651) and, more surprisingly, that 'males and females are cast in the same mould' (CW, III, 5, p. 685), it would seem evident that in the sexual hierarchy which structures his (conscious – or willed) thinking, men are reasonable, less violently passionate than women – and exert a determining, if ambivalent, power, wanting their counterparts to be 'both hot and cold' (CW, III, 5, p. 650). Nonetheless, the image of the codpiece which unjustifiably promises abundance and fertility recurs in the *Essays*, and is often juxtaposed with an assault on prolix and over-citational writing (CW, I, 26, p. 116). The penis, author of children (as of texts which are, though, engendered by a being who is both mother and father, (CW, II, 8, p. 291), is suspect as a 'monumental' reality or image. Indeed, Montaigne concludes his most extensive consideration of sexuality and (inter)textuality with a definition of his commentary of Virgil as an impetuous flux or flow of babble (*CW*, II, 5, p. 684). The feminine is thus inescapable – and reveals itself in the practice of (intertextual) writing as an active, anti-organisational principle of artistic creation.

John Frow points out, in this volume, that there are practical (political) implications which result from the blurring – or erasing – of the ontological distinction between the categories of the textual and the real, not least the problem of determination.[86] But the implications are not only problematic, they are also positive. The analysis of intertextuality, we would like to argue, is inevitably political in its assertion that – at the very least – the 'textual' and the 'extra-textual' inhabit each other, or that – more radically – the 'extra-textual' is another kind of text. However, there is a need to draw out further the relations between social formations (one kind of text) and texts in the conventional sense. Ross Chambers shows how homosociality, making men complicitous and excluding women, is figured in literature's appeal to the reader. Sexual politics is, of course, far from being the only field of repression, nor do any of the forms of repression exist in isolation – the first Mrs Rochester is Creole as well as a woman, Frank Moorehouse's prostitute is an Aborigine, and for Barthes (as for many others) homosexuality evokes transgression of race (North African) and class barriers. The practice of intertexual interpretation is an attempt to struggle against both complicity and exclusion – perhaps something, some shifting of barriers, can thus be achieved even if, in general, none of our thinking can escape constructing identity against differences.

## Notes

All texts are cited only in English in order to economise on space; we refer to published translations of foreign works wherever possible. Page references are given in the text; for full references, see the bibliography.

1   'Word, dialogue, and novel' was first published in 1967; it is translated in *Desire in Language* and reproduced in *The Kristeva Reader* which is the edition to which we shall refer. 'Problèmes de la structuration du texte' is in *Théorie d'ensemble*.

2   While in the narrow sense a *text* means a piece of writing (and so writer and reader are, in the first instance, more or less self-explanatory), *text* is also used in a much more general sense to mean anything perceived as a signifying system – therefore the reader is anyone who (consciously or unconsciously) receives something of the message, and the writer has to be

understood in an abstract sense. This generalisation of the term *text* itself feeds back into our understanding of, say, literary texts and helps us to demystify the notion of *author,* for example. In this volume, John Frow discusses Derrida's use of the idea of a 'general text' and highlights some of the issues raised by a generalisation of textuality to cover all social phenomena.

3    In this volume Ross Chambers makes an analogy between the failure of desire and the failure of interpretation – when both desire and interpretation are predicated upon an 'alter-ego relation', ignoring the crucial role of the third party (the reader). It is when we focus on the creative (writer as) reader that we can acknowledge the power relations at work – rather than clinging to the alter-ego myth of the androgyne as put forward by Aristophanes in Plato's *Symposium* (a key intertext for this volume).

4    Plato was writing in the first half of the fourth century BC. There are a number of different editions of his Dialogues. Page references to *The Republic* are to the edition edited by F. M. Cornford. One of Plato's most famous attacks on writing is to be found in the *Phaedrus.*

5    See Longinus, *On the Sublime,* quoted below, and see Harold Bloom, *Agon.* The term 'agon' comes from the Greek word *agonia* meaning, amongst other things, 'a contest for a prize'. In *A Map of Misreading,* Bloom tropes, 'Poetic strength comes only from a triumphant wrestling with the greatest of the dead' (p. 9); the 'wrestling' takes the form of a *misreading.*

6    See Laurent Jenny, 'Poétique et représentation'.

7    Plato illustrates this by an analogy with the artist who paints a bed, which the carpenter has created by imitating the Form of a bed, which is the product of divine artistry (*The Republic* X, 317–21).

8    Bakhtin discusses the Socratic dialogues in a number of texts, see, for example, *Problems of Dostoevsky's Poetics,* ch. 4: 'The dialogic means of seeking truth is counterposed [in the Socratic dialogues] to *official* monologism, which pretends to *possess a ready-made truth*' (p. 110). Sartre, in *What is Literature?,* and then Barthes, in *Writing Degree Zero,* exclude poetry from literature, classifying it with the plastic arts.

9    Aristotle discusses imitation in *On the Art of Poetry* written in the second half of the fourth century BC.

10    See, for example, 'Epic and novel' and 'Discourse in the novel' in *The Dialogic Imagination,* pp. 5, 8, 269.

11    *On the Art of Poetry,* written 12–8 BC.

12    *On the Sublime,* probably written in the first century AD.

13    Cicero was writing in the first century BC.

14    Quintilian was writing in the first century AD.

15    In '*Imitatio* et intertextualité', 1987, Francis Goyet has sought to distinguish between imitation and intertextuality (which he does not consider to be a valid *theory* but only a description of how *some* texts function). An attack on Riffaterre whom he sees as systematically combatting originality, his essay fails to convince because he bases himself only on *Text Production* (first published in French in 1979), whereas Riffaterre has in fact already met and countered Goyet's objections in his later publications.

16    See Horace, *Classical Literary Criticism,* pp. 80–1.

17    See Hans-Georg Gadamer, *Truth and Method,* pp. 110, 346–8, 352.

18    For a powerful attack on the narrow binary oppositions of Aristotelian mimesis and for a convincing redefinition of minesis, see Richard Kearney, *Poétique du possible.*

19    See Michel Foucault, *The Order of Things,* p. 40.

20    In this respect, see Hélène Naïs, 'Tradition et imitation'.

21    References to Montaigne's *Essays* are made to *The Complete Works of Montaigne* (hereinafter abbreviated as *CW*). We give book and chapter numbers followed by the respective page numbers.

22    Referring to Freud's concept of repression which insists that forgetting is far from being a liberating process, Bloom himself argues that 'Every forgotten precursor becomes a giant of the imagination', *The Anxiety of Influence,* p. 107.

23    See *La Révolution du langage poétique,* p. 339. The English translation of this book does not include the section in which this remark is made.

24    For considerations of Empedoclean catastrophe, see Sigmund Freud, 'Analysis terminable and interminable', *Standard Edition,* vol. XXIII, pp. 245–6; Harold Bloom, 'Freud's concepts of defense and the poetic will', in Joseph H. Smith (ed.), *The Literary Freud,* p. 20; see also Michael Worton, 'The catastrophe of translation: a reading of René Char's "writing" of paintings'.

25    The most sustained analysis of the functionings of quotation is to be found in Antoine Compagnon, *La Seconde Main.* Compagnon makes many illuminating remarks on Montaigne's citational practice. See also his *Nous, Michel de Montaigne.*

26    See *The Use and Abuse of History.* Nietzsche asserts that such a belief 'must appear frightful and devastating when it raises our latecomer to godhead, by a neat turn of the wheel, as the true meaning and object of all creation', p. 51. Nietzsche's position would therefore seem to overlap with both Freud's and Bloom's.

27    *Leviathan,* p. 727. Hobbes refuses to cite Classical sources because quotations are merely 'Words that passe (like gaping) from mouth to mouth' and because 'it is many times with a fraudulent Design that men stick their corrupt Doctrine with the loves of other mens Wit', ibid. It should be pointed out that in this section of the 'Review and Conclusion', Hobbes not only uses the Quintilian and Montaigne metaphors of ingestion/indigestion but also repeats Montaigne's terms of truth and reason: in his attack on quotation he is not only alluding but apparently 'silently' quoting!

28    In 'Of books', Montaigne recognizes that he feels the need to 'hide' his weakness under the great authorities who are his precursors – but this admission is juxtaposed with a request that his readers 'unplume' or 'expose' him and thereby endear themselves to him (*CW,* III, 5, p. 297).

29    *The Pleasure of the Text,* p. 36. Rather like Mallarmé, Jorge Luis Borges goes so far as to equate the library with the universe in 'The library of Babel', *Labyrinths,* p. 51. We would therefore suggest that there is a profound analogy between Barthes's image and Borges's obsessive metaphor of 'circular labyrinths' (cf., for example, 'Theme of the traitor and the hero', ibid., p. 73).

30   See Terence Cave, *The Cornucopian Text,* p. 325.

31   See Compagnon, *La Seconde Main,* p. 387.

32   See Karsteen Harris, 'Metaphor and transcendence', in *On Metaphor,* ed. Sheldon Sacks, p. 82. For a consideration of speculation on sources, see Michael Worton, 'Courbet, Corot, Char'.

33   See for instance Angus Fletcher, *The Theory of a Symbolic Mode,* p. 321, and Henri Morier, *Dictionnaire de poétique et de rhétorique,* pp. 74–5.

34   See 'The flower of Coleridge', *Other Inquisitions: 1937–1952;* cf. also Ralph Waldo Emerson's statement 'I am very much struck in literature by the appearance that one person wrote all the books . . .', this person being for him, not insignificantly, 'an all-seeing, all-hearing *gentleman*' (our emphasis), 'Nominalist and realist', *The Collected Works of Emerson,* Vol. III, p. 137.

35   'Tlön, Uqbar, Orbis Tertius', *Labyrinths,* p. 12; cf. also his (rhetorical?) question in 'A new refutation of time': 'Do not the *fervent* readers who *surrender themselves* to Shakespeare become *literally* Shakespeare?', ibid., p. 224 (the first two emphases are ours; we have chosen to cite this translation since it communicates better than the Simms version Borges's implicit conception of reading as passionate and of the reader as a feminised figure).

36   See 'New refutation of time', *Other Inquisitions,* pp. 176 and 185.

37   'Kafka and his precursors', ibid., p. 108.

38   Though Borges insists on the experiential importance for him of living and working in a library (especially perhaps that of his father?), he, like Montaigne often quotes from memory – and thereby erroneously . . .

39   Michel Tournier, who is one of the most interesting contemporary intertextual novelists, echoes Borges's view (though he claims not to have read him): in his intellectual autobiography, he asserts that a scene in his novel *The Ogre* which has been read as a plagiarism of a scene in Alain-Fournier's *Le Grand Meaulnes* is in fact the 'source' of Alain-Fournier's text – which can be read 'properly' only after his own text has been read (*Le Vent Paraclet,* pp. 53–6). He therefore has 'created' his precursor – but it is interesting that he here avoids the Bloomian terminology of fathers (which he does use elsewhere) and chooses to describe his precursors as 'patrons' or 'bosses'.

40   It is significant that Ménard writes in a letter that his recollection of the *Quixote* is 'simplified by forgetfulness and indifference' (ibid., p. 41): again amnesia is seen as creative and liberating.

41   For reasons of space we could not cover all we would have liked, and decided not to adopt an encyclopedic approach. There are inevitably elements of arbitrariness in the choice and lengths of analyses – omitting, for example, the theories of Hans Robert Jauss (aesthetics of reception), Wolfgang Iser and Stanley Fish (reader response) or the work of Barbara Johnson or J. Hillis Miller.

42   Some of his work is still unavailable in translation. A number of the personal and political reasons for the lack of availability of Bakhtin's work over the years are explained in K. Clark and M. Holquist, *Mikhail Bakhtin.*

43   Bakhtin refers to the *divine* language of poetry, p. 287; the 'novel' is,

by contrast, *human* in its diversity or plurality. While poetry in general has been regarded as a gift from the gods outside the Judeo-Christian tradition, we should like to suggest that it is the monotheistic figure of the Father God which has played a major part in western culture's phallogocentric quest for unity and autonomy. Femininity has often been the figure for rejected humanity.

44   With regard to poetics, it is interesting to juxtapose Michael Riffaterre's particular insistence on the *unity* of the poem. See our discussion later in this Introduction.

45   Bakhtin contrasts authoritative discourse with internally-persuasive discourse, such as that of Socrates, p. 342.

46   The modern invention of 'literary language' is parodied in the novel alongside social discourses.

47   Kristeva returns to the term 'discourse' in her later work, which focuses on psychoanalysis.

48   See Robert Young, 'Post-structuralism: the end of theory', on the relationship between structuralism and post-structuralism.

49   Compare Jacques Derrida, 'Force and signification' first published in *Critique*, 1963, republished in *Writing and Difference*. Derrida writes of structuralism: 'In the future it will be interpreted, perhaps, as a relaxation, if not a lapse, of the attention given to *force*, which is the tension of force itself. *Form* fascinates when one no longer has the force to understand force from within itself. That is, to create. This is why literary criticism is structuralist in every age, in its essence and destiny' (pp. 4–5). Derrida's use of the term 'literary criticism' here could be compared to Bakhtin's use of 'poetics', meaning the concentration on formal unity.

50   See *Revolution in Poetic Language*; Allon White, '*L'éclatement du sujet*: the work of Julia Kristeva', analyses this work's attack on the philosophical tradition which understands the subject as a singular transcendental unity.

51   See, for example, *In the Beginning was Love: Psychoanalysis and Faith*. Seán Hand's essay, in this volume, suggests how the transference relation can be seen as an intertextual relation.

52   See J. Derrida, *Of Grammatology*, for the *supplement*, a term which can be very useful in analysing intertextual relations; and J. Kristeva, *Revolution in Poetic Language*, ch. 1.2, 'The semiotic *chora* ordering the drives', where she explains that she borrows the term from the *Timaeus*, but rescues it from ontology – where Plato confines it(!).

53   We have modified the translation.

54   Stephen Heath points this out in *Vertige du déplacement. Lecture de Barthes*.

55   There are several accounts of particular controversies, see e.g. Philip Thody, *Roland Barthes: A Conservative Estimate*.

56   See Jacques Lacan, for example, *The Four Fundamental Concepts of Psychoanalysis*, on 'the vel of alienation' (pp. 209–13), the division of the subject which, if it appears somewhere as meaning, appears elsewhere as fading (p. 218), or the myth (like Aristophanes' myth in Plato's *Symposium*) of *l'hommelette* which survives any division (p. 197).

57   'Isn't storytelling always a way of searching for one's origin, speaking one's conflicts with the Law, entering into the dialectic of tenderness and hatred? Today we dismiss Oedipus and narrative at one and the same time: we no longer love, we no longer fear, we no longer narrate' (*The Pleasure of the Text,* p. 47). In that text, the Barthesian answer to the rhetorical question seems to be that the textual production turns the two sides of the dialectic into one more antithetical figure rather than creating a logomachia, a battle between irreconcilable positions.

58   *S/Z* proposes the opposition between the readerly (classical) and the writerly (modern) (e.g. p. 4); *The Pleasure of the Text* juxtaposes the text of pleasure (classical) to the text of *jouissance* – translated as 'bliss' (e.g. p. 14).

59   Barthes, Kristeva and Bakhtin each privilege a somewhat different list of writings.

60   This description seems better fitted to the strategy Kristeva uses in 'Héréthique de l'amour', or Derrida in 'Tympan' (*Margins of Philosophy*) where two texts coexist on the printed page without a hierarchy of text and commentary being established.

61   Quintilian and Montaigne both use metaphors of indigestion. We point out earlier how editorial gestures (as in critical editions of Montaigne) can temporarily restrict the reader's aleatory intertextual reading. Barthes does not leave the task to editors. However, the reader always fights back . . .

62   See *Introduction à l'architexte,* 1979, pp. 85–90.

63   See, for example, *Palimpsestes,* pp. 7 and 11.

64   For a consideration of the particular case of the aggressive interaction between the genres of cinema, television and literature, see Keith Reader's essay in this volume.

65   *Of Grammatology, Writing and Difference* and *Speech and Phenomena.*

66   In *Margins of Philosophy*; this is also translated by Samuel Weber and Jeffrey Mehlman in *Glyph* I, 1977, pp. 172–97, which is the translation we use. This question is from Weber and Mehlman, p. 188, *Margins,* p. 323.

67   See, for example, *Essais de stylistique structurale,* p. 268.

68   See 'Interview', p. 13. While working essentially with literary intertexts, Riffaterre also recognises the importance of non-literary texts and of socially determined norms which are often presupposed by quotations; see, for instance, 'Flaubert's presuppositions'.

69   See, for example, *Semiotics of Poetry,* pp. 4–6.

70   See, for instance, Frow, *Marxism and Literary History,* pp. 154–5, and Culler, *The Pursuit of Signs,* pp. 80–99.

71   In Riffaterre's recent work, he has abandoned the much-attacked and unfortunately named concept of the 'super-reader', which was intended merely to designate a *technique* for noticing the elements in a text that called most attention to themselves as ungrammatical.

72   See, for example, 'Production du roman: l'intertexte du *Lys dans la vallée'*, pp. 23–33.

73   See L'intertexte inconnu', pp. 4–7.

74   For a distinction between the reader's competence for discovering the

hypogram and the analyst's inferential positing of a/the matrix, see 'Interview', pp. 14–15, and 'La trace de l'intertexte', p. 18.

75   Objecting to Riffaterre's belief that intertextual reading is essentially sylleptic, Genette prefers to maintain the term and the concept 'ambiguity': for him every hypertext is ambiguous in that it can be read as an autonomous text and also as a relational text which is dependent in one way or another on its hypotext. The difference between these two positions is not simply one of terminology: for Genette hypertextuality is a form of *bricolage*, whereas for Riffaterre an awareness of intertextual functioning confers unity upon the text.

76   See Jauss, 'Goethe's and Valéry's Faust: on the hermeneutics of question and answer', *Toward an Aesthetic of Reception*, pp. 114 and 122.

77   The very term 'ephebe' necessarily inscribes Bloom's theory in the domain of sexual politics, since it signifies a young man who, (re)virilised, could choose as an object of erotic pleasure a 'feminised' boy – though the latter, destined to become in his turn an ephebe, could never identify permanently with his 'passive', feminine role. While virility was privileged in Ancient Greece, the sexual slippages involved in male–male relationships creatively problematise the reading of Bloom's use of the term; see Michel Foucault, *The Use of Pleasure, passim*. For a powerful (if very different) attack on Bloom's intersubjective theory of influence and an affirmation of the need for a 'truly epistemological' theory of poetry, see Paul de Man's review of *The Anxiety of Influence*.

78   See Freud, 'Female sexuality', *On Sexuality*, Pelican Freud Library, VII, p. 375, for his reasons for rejecting Jung's notion. For one analysis of an inter-gender (and agonistic) influence, see Judith Still's articles on George Eliot and Rousseau, 'From Eliot's "raw bone" to Gyges' ring', and 'Rousseau in *Daniel Deronda*'.

79   Some of the arguments about ornamentation as opposed to efficacy are presented by Judith Still in 'Lucretia's silent rhetoric' – this is one of the ways in which the masculine–feminine hierarchy has manifested itself in discussions of literature. Kristeva and Hélène Cixous both include certain male poets, such as Joyce or Lautréamont, within the domain of the feminine.

80   See Derrida, for example, 'Signature Event Context', p. 195, on the recurrence of hierarchical binary oppositions.

81   In 'Structures du silence/du délire: Marguerite Duras/Hélène Cixous', Christine Makward cites Duras's 'Perhaps I am an echo-chamber', relating this statement to what she considers to be the passive and *se-laisser-pénétrer* (letting oneself be penetrated) quality both of Duras's writing and of her heroines (p. 315). The mythical Echo is, as Makward reminds us, a nymph who fades away because of unrequited love and is fated to do no more than reflect the words (desire) of others (other lovers). Duras is sometimes considered to be an example of *écriture féminine*.

82   It is interesting to note the fact that it is a citation, and from a poet, which first hints at one of the guiding themes of the work.

83   See Jacques Derrida, *La Carte postale*, where, within the frame of an exchange of love letters, there is a commentary on an historical reproduction

of the relationship between that most famous couple, Plato and Socrates. This would take the analysis into most interesting realms of speculation.

**84**   Nature is often also female, and often a mother, who acts as source for the artist or, as in Horace, a pattern of creativity for him to follow.

**85**   See, for example, *Ce Sexe qui n'en est pas un*, pp. 105–16.

**86**   Celia Britton, in this volume, analyses one instance where 'fact' is determined by 'fiction' (which is determined by?). See also Barthes's 'Dominici' in *Mythologies*, a real case (which he compares to Camus's fiction (*The Outsider*) of an agricultural labourer condemned to death for murder by bourgeois *language* and a psychology derived from nineteenth-century novels.

### Bibliography to Introduction

All works to which we refer in the Introduction, with one or two additions, are given here as English translations where these are available; in addition we have listed the original versions of texts first published in French which is the foreign language in which most has been produced on intertextuality.

Angenot, Marc. 'L'"intertextualité": enquête sur l'émergence et la diffusion d'un champ notionnel', *Revue des sciences humaines*, CLXXXIX, 1983, pp. 121–35.

Aristotle. *On the Art of Poetry*, in *Classical Literary Criticism*.

Austin, J. L. *How to Do Things With Words*, London, 1962.

Bakhtin, M. M. *Esthétique et théorie du roman*, preface by Michel Aucouturier, trans. Daria Oliver, Paris, 1978. English translation of four of the essays as *The Dialogic Imagination*, ed. Michael Holquist, trans. Caryl Emerson and Michael Holquist, Austin, 1981.

—— *The Formal Method in Literary Scholarship*, trans. Albert J. Wehrle, Baltimore, 1978.

—— *La Poétique de Dostoïevski*, trans. I. Kolitcheff, Paris, 1970. English translation, *Problems of Dostoevsky's Poetics*, ed. and trans. Caryl Emerson, Introduction by Wayne C. Booth, Minnesota and Manchester, 1984. Introduction to French translation 'Une Poétique ruinée' by J. Kristeva, translated in *Russian Formalism*, ed. Stephen Bann and John E. Bowlt, New York, 1973.

—— *Speech Genres and Other Late Essays*, ed. Caryl Emerson and Michael Holquist, trans. Vern W. McGee, Austin, 1986.

Barthes, Roland. *Le Degré zéro de l'écriture*, Paris, 1953, trans. Annette Lavers and Colin Smith as *Writing Degree Zero* with *Elements of Semiology*, London, 1984.

—— *Fragments d'un discours amoureux*, Paris, 1977, trans. Richard Howard as *A Lover's Discourse: Fragments*, New York, 1978.

—— *Mythologies*, Paris, 1957, selection trans. Annette Lavers as *Mythologies*, London, 1972.

—— *Le Plaisir du texte*, Paris, 1973, trans. Richard Miller as *The Pleasure of the Text*, London, 1976.

—— *Roland Barthes par Roland Barthes*, Paris, 1975, trans. Richard

Howard as *Roland Barthes by Roland Barthes,* London and New York, 1977.
—— *S/Z,* Paris, 1970, trans. Richard Miller, London, 1975.
Bloom, Harold. *Agon: Towards a Theory of Revisionism,* Oxford and New York, 1982.
—— *The Anxiety of Influence. A Theory of Poetry,* Oxford and New York, 1973.
—— 'Freud's concepts of defense and the poetic will', in Joseph H. Smith (ed.), *The Literary Freud: Mechanisms of Defense and the Poetic Will,* New Haven, 1980.
—— *A Map of Misreading,* Oxford and New York, 1975.
Borges, Jorge Luis. *Labyrinths: Selected Stories and Other Writings,* ed. Donald A. Yates and James E. Irby, New York, 1964.
—— *Other Inquisitions: 1937–1952,* trans. Ruth L. C. Simms, London, 1973.
Cave, Terence. *The Cornucopian Text,* Oxford, 1979.
Chevrel, Yves. 'Théories de la réception: perspectives comparatistes', *Degrés,* XXIX–XL, 1984, pp. j1–j15.
Cicero. *De oratore,* vol. I, trans. E. W. Sutton, Cambridge, Mass. and London, 1959.
Clark, K. and M. Holquist. *Mikhail Bakhtin,* Cambridge, Mass., 1984.
*Classical Literary Criticism,* trans. T. S. Dorsch, Harmondsworth, 1972.
Compagnon, Antoine. *Nous, Michel de Montaigne,* Paris, 1980.
—— *La Seconde Main ou le travail de la citation,* Paris, 1979.
Cottrell, Robert D. *Sexuality/Textuality: A Study of the Fabric of Montaigne's Essays,* Columbus, 1981.
Culler, Jonathan. *The Pursuit of Signs: Semiotics, Literature, Deconstruction,* London, 1981.
De Man, Paul. Review of *The Anxiety of Influence, Comparative Literature,* XXVI, 1974, pp. 169–75.
—— *The Resistance to Theory,* Manchester, 1986.
Derrida, Jacques. *La Carte postale,* Paris, 1980.
—— *De la grammatologie,* Paris, 1967, trans. Gayatri Spivak as *Of Grammatology,* Baltimore, 1976.
—— *L'Écriture et la différence,* Paris, 1967, trans. Alan Bass as *Writing and Difference,* London and Chicago, 1978.
—— *Marges,* Paris, 1972, trans. Alan Bass as *Margins of Philosophy,* Brighton and Chicago, 1982.
—— *Positions,* Paris, 1972, trans. Alan Bass, London and Chicago, 1981.
—— *La Voix et le phénomène,* Paris, 1967, trans. David B. Allison as *Speech and Phenomena,* Evanston, 1973.
Eliot, T. S. *Points of View,* London, 1941.
Emerson, Ralph Waldo. *The Collected Works, Vol. III (Essays: Second Series),* Cambridge, Mass. and London, 1983.
'La farcissure: intertextualités au XVIe siècle', special number of *Littérature,* LV, 1984.
Fish, Stanley. *Is There a Text in This Class? The Authority of Interpretative Communities,* Cambridge, Mass., 1980.

Fletcher, Angus. *The Theory of a Symbolic Mode,* Ithaca, 1964.

Foucault, Michel. *Les Mots et les choses,* Paris, 1966, trans. unnamed as *The Order of Things,* London, 1970.

—— *L'Usage des plaisirs,* Paris, 1984, trans. Robert Hurley as *The Use of Pleasure,* Harmondsworth, 1986.

Freud, Sigmund. *Standard Edition of the Complete Psychological Works,* general editor James Strachey, London, 1953–74.

—— 'Female sexuality', *On Sexuality,* Harmondsworth, 1986, pp. 367–92.

Freund, Elizabeth. *The Return of the Reader: Reader-response Criticism,* London, 1987.

Frow, John. *Marxism and Literary History,* Oxford, 1986.

Gadamer, Hans Georg. *Truth and Method,* trans. William Glen-Doepel, ed. Garrett Barden and John Cumming, London, 1975.

Genette, Gérard. *Introduction à l'architexte,* Paris, 1979.

—— *Palimpsestes: la littérature au second degré,* Paris, 1982.

Goyet, Francis. '*Imitatio* et intertextualité (Riffaterre revisited)', *Poétique,* LXXI, 1987, pp. 313–20.

Heath, Stephen. *Vertige du déplacement,* Paris, 1974.

Heidegger, Martin. *Poetry, Language, Thought,* trans. Alfred Hofstadter, New York, 1971.

Hirschkop, Ken. 'Bakhtin, discourse and democracy', *New Left Review,* CLX, 1986.

Hobbes, Thomas. *Leviathan,* Harmondsworth, 1968.

Horace. *On the Art of Poetry* in *Classical Literary Criticism.*

Iser, Wolfgang. *The Act of Reading: A Theory of Aesthetic Response,* London, 1978.

—— *The Implied Reader: Patterns of Communication in Prose Fiction from Bunyan to Beckett,* Baltimore, 1974.

Jameson, Frederic. 'Magical narratives: romance as genre', *New Literary History,* VII, 1975, pp. 135–64.

Jauss, Hans Robert. *Toward an Aesthetic of Reception,* trans. Timothy Bahti, Minneapolis, 1982.

Jenny, Laurent. 'La stratégie de la forme', *Poétique,* XXVII, 1976, pp. 257–81, trans. as 'The strategy of form', by R. Carter, in Tzvetan Todorov, *French Literary Theory Today: A Reader,* 1982, pp. 34–63.

—— 'Poétique et représentation'. *Poétique* 58, 1984, pp. 171–95.

Kearney, Richard. *Poétique du possible: phénoménologie herméneutique de la figuration,* Paris, 1984.

Kristeva, *Au commencement était l'amour: psychanalyse et foi,* Paris, 1985, trans. Arthur Goldhammer as *In the Beginning was Love: Psychoanalysis and Faith,* New York, 1987.

—— 'Bakhtin, le mot, le dialogue et le roman', *Critique* 239, 1967, pp. 438–65, trans. Alice Jardine, Thomas Gora and Léon S. Roudiez as 'Word, dialogue and novel' in Moi, 1986 and in Roudiez, 1980.

—— 'Conversation with Rosalind Coward' in *Desire,* ed. Lisa Appignanesi, ICA Documents, London, 1984.

—— *La révolution du langage poétique,* Paris, 1974, the first third is trans. Margaret Waller as *Revolution in Poetic Language,* New York, 1984.

—— *Séméiotiké: recherches pour une sémanalyse*, Paris, 1969.

Lacan, Jacques. *Le Séminaire, livre XI: Les quatre concepts fondamentaux de la psychanalyse*, Paris, 1973, ed. J.-A. Miller, trans. Alan Sheridan as *The Four Fundamental Concepts of Psychoanalysis*, Harmondsworth, 1977.

Lavers, Annette. *Roland Barthes: Structuralism and After*, London, 1982.

Leitch, Vincent B. *Deconstructive Criticism: An Advanced Introduction*, New York, 1983.

Longinus. *On the Sublime* in *Classical Literary Criticism*.

Makward, Christine. 'Structures du silence/du désir. Marguerite Duras/Hélène Cixous', *Poétique*, XXXV, 1976, pp. 314–24

Moi, Toril (ed.). *The Kristeva Reader*, Oxford, 1986.

de Montaigne, Michel. *Œuvres complètes*, ed. Albert Thibaudet and Maurice Rat, Paris, 1962, trans. Donald Frame as *Complete Works*, London, 1958.

Morier, Henri. *Dictionnaire de poétique et de rhétorique*, Paris, 1961.

Morson, G. S. (ed.). *Bahktin: Essays and Dialogues on his Work*, Chicago, 1986.

Naïs, Hélène. 'Tradition et imitation chez quelques poètes du XVIe siècle', *Revue des Sciences Humaines*, CLXXX, 1984, pp. 33–49.

Nietzsche, Friedrich. *The Use and Abuse of History*, trans. Adrian Collins, Indianapolis, 1957.

Plato. *The Republic*, trans. and ed. Francis Macdonald Cornford, Oxford, 1941.

—— *Dialogues*, trans. Benjamin Jowett, Oxford, fourth edition, 1953.

Quintilian. *Institutio Oratoria*, vol. IV, trans. H. E. Butler, Loeb Classical Library, Cambridge, Mass. and London, 1979.

Ricoeur, Paul. *La Métaphore vive*, Paris, 1975, trans. Robert Czerny et al. as *The Rule of Metaphor*, London, 1978.

Riffaterre, Michael. *Essais de stylistique structurale*, Paris, 1971.

—— 'Flaubert's presuppositions', *Diacritics* XI, 4, 1981, pp. 2–11.

—— 'L'intertexte inconnu', *Littérature*, XXXXI, 1981, pp. 4–7.

—— 'Interview', *Diacritics*, XI, 4, 1981, pp. 12–16.

—— 'Production du texte: l'intertexte du *Lys dans la vallée*', *Texte*, II, 1984, pp. 23–33.

—— *Semiotics of Poetry*, London, 1980.

—— 'Syllepsis', *Critical Enquiry*, VI, 1980, pp. 625–38.

—— *La Production du texte*, Paris, 1979, trans. Terese Lyons as *Text Production*, London, 1983.

—— 'La trace de l'intertexte', *La Pensée*, CCXV, 1980, pp. 4–18.

Roudiez, Léon S. (ed.). *Desire in Language: A Semiotic Approach to Literature and Art*, Oxford, 1980.

Sacks, Sheldon (ed.). *On Metaphor*, Chicago and London, 1979.

Sartre, Jean-Paul. *Qu'est-ce que la littérature?*, Paris, 1948, trans. Bernard Frechtman as *What is Literature?*, London, 1950.

Still, Judith. 'From Eliot's "raw bone" to Gyges' ring: two studies in intertextuality', *Paragraph*, I, 1983, pp. 44–59.

—— 'Lucretia's silent rhetoric', *Oxford Literary Review*, VI, 1984, pp.

70–86.

—— 'Rousseau in *Daniel Deronda*', *Revue de littérature comparée*, LVI, 1982, pp. 62–77.

Strauss, Leo. *The City and the Man*, Chicago, 1964.

Tel Quel, *Théorie d'ensemble*, Paris, 1968.

Theis, Raimund and Hans T. Siepe (eds.). *Le Plaisir de l'intertexte: formes et fonctions de l'intertextualité*, Frankfurt am Main, 1986.

Thody, Philip. *Roland Barthes: A Conservative Estimate*, London, 1977.

Todorov, Tzvetan. *Mikhail Bakhtine: Le Principe dialogique*, Paris, 1981, trans. Wlad Godzich, *Mikhail Bakhtin: The Dialogical Principle*, Manchester, 1984.

—— *French Literary Theory Today: A Reader*, trans. R. Carter, Cambridge, 1982.

Tournier, Michel. *Le Vent Paraclet*, Paris, 1977.

—— *Le Vol du vampire*, Paris, 1981.

Vultur, Smaranda. 'La place de l'intertextualité dans les théories de la réception du texte littéraire', *Cahiers roumains d'études littéraires*, III, 1986, pp. 103–9.

Weinsheimer, Joel. *Imitation*, London, 1984.

White, Allon. *'L'Éclatement du sujet': the work of Julia Kristeva*, University of Birmingham Stencilled Occasional Papers, 1977.

Worton, Michael. 'The catastrophe of translation: a reading of René Char's "rewriting" of paintings', *Paragraph*, II, 1983, pp. 1–23.

—— 'Courbet, Corot, Char: du tableau au texte', *Littérature*, LIX, 1985, pp. 15–30.

—— 'Intertextuality: to inter textuality or to resurrect it?', in *Cross-references: Modern French Theory and the Practice of Criticism*, ed. David Kelley and Isabelle Llasera, Leeds, 1986, pp. 14–23.

—— 'Ecrire et ré-écrire: le projet de Tournier', *Sud*, LXI, 1986, pp. 52–69.

Young, Robert. 'Post-structuralism: the end of theory', *Oxford Literary Review*, V, 1982, pp. 3–20.

Zholkovsky, Alexander. 'Intertextuality, its content and discontents', *Slavic Review*, XLVII, 1988, pp. 726–9.

Zumthor, Paul. 'Le carrefour des rhétoriqueurs: intertextualité et rhétorique', *Poétique*, XXVII, 1976, pp. 317–37.

# Intertextuality and ontology

*Intertextuality - Credo*

Let me propose the following theses:

1.   The concept of intertextuality requires that we understand the concept of text not as a self-contained structure but as differential and historical. Texts are shaped not by an immanent time but by the play of divergent temporalities. *(cf. also Jays/ Gadamer)*

2.   Texts are therefore not structures of presence but traces and tracings of otherness. They are shaped by the repetition and the transformation of other textual structures.

3.   These absent textual structures at once constrain the text and are represented by and within it; they are at once preconditions and moments of the text.

4.   The form of representation of intertextual structures ranges from the explicit to the implicit. In addition, these structures may be highly particular or highly general; they may be of the order of the message or of the order of the code. Texts are made out of cultural and ideological norms; out of the conventions of genre; out of styles and idioms embedded in the language; out of connotations and collocative sets; out of clichés, formulae, or proverbs; and out of other texts. *Skinner*

5.   Jenny poses the problem of this disparity of forms of intertextual representation by asking whether one can properly speak of an intertextual relation to a genre. Such a relation is not strictly a relation to an intertext, and it would 'mingle awkwardly structures which belong to the code and structures which belong to its realisation'. But he immediately concedes that it is not possible to make a rigid distinction between the levels of code and text: 'Genre archetypes, however abstract, still constitute textual structures',[1] and conversely reference to a text implicitly evokes reference to the set of

*meaning of reference?*

potential meanings stored in the codes of a genre.

6.  The process of intertextual reference is governed by the rules of the discursive formation within which it occurs. In the case of literary texts (and of readings of literary texts) the relation to the general discursive field is mediated by the structure of the literary system and by the authority of the literary canon.

7.  The effect of this mediation is to effect a metonymic reduction of discursive to literary norms, and so to make possible the reflexive thematisation of the text's relation to the structure of discursive authority. Since intertextuality may function either as trace or as representation, this thematisation need not depend upon conscious authorial intention.

8.  The identification of an intertext is an act of interpretation. The intertext is not a real and causative source but a theoretical construct formed by and serving the purposes of a reading. 'There are no moments of authority and points of origin except those which are retrospectively designated as origins and which, therefore, can be shown to derive from the series for which they are constituted as origin.'[2] The prehistory of the text is not a given but is relative to an interpretive grid.

9.  What is relevant to textual interpretation is not, in itself, the identification of a particular intertextual source but the more general discursive structure (genre, discursive formation, ideology) to which it belongs. This has implications for the kind of knowledge we should expect to be relevant to the reading of texts. It suggests that detailed scholarly information is less important than the ability to reconstruct the cultural codes which are realised (and contested) in texts.

10. Intertextual analysis is distinguished from source criticism both by this stress on interpretation rather than on the establishment of particular facts, and by its rejection of a unilinear causality (the concept of 'influence') in favour of an account of the work performed upon intertextual material and its functional integration in the later text.

I take it that these theses give an account of the sort of range and force the concept of intertextuality carries in its application to literary texts. But the concept has from the beginning also had more radical implications. If, on the one hand, it has transformed the unity and self-presence of the text into a structure marked by otherness

① = Literary implication

and repetition, on the other it has suggested that the exterior of the text is not a monolithic real but a system (or an infinity) of other such textual structures. In its early elaboration by Kristeva, Barthes and ② others it was not restricted to particular textual manifestations of signifying systems but was used, rather, to designate the way in which a culture is structured as a complex network of codes with heterogeneous and dispersed forms of textual realisation. It formulated the codedness or textuality of what had previously been thought in non-semiotic terms (consciousness, experience, wisdom, story, gender, culture, and so on).

The crucial step here is that from thinking intertextuality in relation to a *cultural* text to thinking social structure as a whole through the metaphor of textuality. Insofar as the 'real' signified by literary (or any other) texts is a moment of a signifying process, and indeed is only ever available to knowledge within and by means of a system of representations, it has the form not of a final referent but of a link in an endless chain of semiosis (a chain which may of course be broken for practical purposes and by means of a particular pragmatic delimitation, but in which *in principle* the 'last instance' of representation is always deferred). In this sense the 'reality' both of the 'natural' and the social worlds is text-like in that it can be thought as a grid or a texture of significations, an intrication of heterogeneous materials. Moreover, the metaphor of textuality makes it possible, by overcoming the dichotomisation of the real to the symbolic, or the base to the superstructure, or the social to the cultural, to recognise the semiotic dimension of all moments of the social (to understand the economic in terms of the systemic assignment and circulation of value, and the political in terms of structures of representation; to recognise that the world of things is organised as a system of taxonomically distributed objects, and that the body and its gender are differential cultural constructs). Conversely, the metaphor makes it easier to recognise the material dimension of all signifying structures. Finally, there is a real gain in methodological economy in thinking textual signification in terms of intertextual reference rather than through an ontological distinction between the symbolic and a real which would be external to the symbolic order, a non-signifying terminus to the signifying process.

This is the force of Kristeva's argument that 'the transformational method . . . leads us to situate literary structure within the social whole considered as a textual whole';[3] and it is *at times* the force of

Derrida's important but difficult concept of the 'general text'. Consider this passage from *The Truth in Painting* concerning the relation between the work and the *parergonal* frame: 'With respect to the work which can serve as ground for it, [the frame] merges into the wall, and then, gradually, into the general text. With respect to the background which the general text is, it merges into the work which stands out against the general background.' A few lines previously the *parerga* were said to be separated, successively, not only from the work, the *ergon*, 'but also from the outside, from the wall on which the painting is hung, from the space in which statue or column is erected, then, step by step, from the whole field of historical, economic, political inscription in which the drive to signature is produced'.[4] It is clear from the appositional form of these two passages that the general text is designated as equivalent to the 'field of historical, economic, political inscription', and that it is thus used in the sense of a social text.

At other times, however, the concept of the general text is posited within an immediately problematised *opposition* to some other domain of being. In this passage from *Positions*, for example:

What is perhaps in the process of being reconsidered, is the form of closure that was called 'ideology' (doubtless a concept to be analysed in its function, its history, its origins, its transformations), the form of the relationships between a transformed concept of 'infrastructure', if you will – an 'infrastructure' of which the *general text* would no longer be an effect or a reflection – and the transformed concept of 'ideology'. If what is in question in this work is a new definition of the relationship of a *determined* text or signifying chain to its exterior, to its referential effects, etc. . . . to 'reality' (history, class struggle, relationships of production, etc.), then we can no longer restrict ourselves to prior delimitations, nor even to the prior concept of a regional delimitation. What is produced in the current trembling is a reevalution of the relationship between the general text and what was believed to be, in the form of reality (history, politics, economics, sexuality, etc.), the simple, referable exterior of language or writing, the belief that this exterior could operate from the simple position of cause or accident.[5]

For all its complication of causal relations, this passage continues to rely upon a distinction between the textual and the non-textual; the 'general text' here would be the endless series of relations between signifier and signified which, while never *finally* 'referring' to a sheer non-textuality, is nevertheless other than this *complex* 'exterior'. In this sense the general text is both the structure of textuality itself (that is, a structure of indefinitely postponed presence, the differential, deferred, purely relational structure of signification) and that

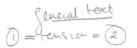
edge or margin of textuality (its frame, its 'context', its institutional space) which problematises its self-containedness, opens it out constantly to an 'outside' which is never properly external to it.

Derrida's most extended meditation on the generalisation of the concept of text is to be found in a long passage in 'Living on'.[6] It begins by arguing that 'if we are to approach a text it must have an edge', but then proceeds to focus on the increasingly problematic nature of 'all those boundaries that form the running border of what used to be called a text, of what we once thought this word could identify, i.e., the supposed end and beginning of a work, the unity of a corpus, the title, the margins, the signatures, the referential realm outside the frame, and so forth'. As a result, the concept of text undergoes a kind of reversal:

> What has happened, if it has happened, is a sort of overrun [*débordement*] that spoils all these boundaries and divisions and forces us to extend the accredited concept, the dominant notion of a 'text', of what I still call a 'text', for strategic reasons, in part – a 'text' that is henceforth no longer a finished corpus of writing, some content enclosed in a book or its margins, but a differential network, a fabric of traces referring endlessly to something other than itself, to other differential traces. Thus the text overruns all the limits assigned to it so far (not submerging or drowning them in an undifferentiated homogeneity, but rather making them more complex, dividing and multiplying strokes and lines) – all the limits, everything that was to be set up in opposition to writing (speech, life, the world, the real, history, and what not, every field of reference – to body or mind, conscious or unconscious, politics, economics, and so forth).

This is the movement of generalisation, of the replacement of the limited notion of text by that of the general text – not a *limitless* text but a principle of textuality that subverts the edges between inside and outside, symbolic and real, signification and reference. But in a final movement Derrida then tries to qualify this generalisation, to set limits to the textualisation of the world, or rather to a perception that the questioning of limits is equivalent to an abolition of all differences and demarcations:

> Whatever the (demonstrated) necessity of such an overrun, such a *débordement*, it still will have come as a shock, producing endless efforts to dam up, resist, rebuild the old partitions, to blame what could no longer be thought without confusion, to blame difference *as* wrongful confusion! All this [this resistance, i.e.] has taken place in non-reading, with no work on what was thus being demonstrated, with no realisation that it was never our wish to extend the reassuring notion of the text to a whole extra-textual realm and to transform the world into a library by doing away with all boundaries, all

framework, all sharp edges (all *arêtes*: this is the word that I am speaking tonight), but that we sought rather to work out the theoretical and practical system of these margins, these borders, once more, from the ground up.

The double movement of this text involves a simultaneous textualisation of the real and recognition of the limits of textuality; and it is the incompatibility or undecidability between these two moments that is governed by the problematic of the edge, the margin, the limit. As Gasché argues, the generalisation of the text (what Derrida elsewhere calls its 'necessary generalisation . . . its extension with no simple exterior limit (which also supposes the passage through metaphysical opposition)', *Positions*, p. 66) does not mean the construction of a new, more diffuse totality; the general text 'has no inside or outside' because 'it is no longer a totality'. Indeed, the general text 'is rather [the] border itself, from which the assignment of insides and outsides takes place, as well as where this distinction ultimately collapses'. The generalisation of textuality 'is not an extension or application of the traditional concept of text to its traditional outside',[7] and it does not imply 'a "theology of the text" '.[8]

It seems, nevertheless, that just because of this problematisation of the border, the question of the extension of the text is finally left open. Moreover, it seems to be the case that the status of the extra- or non-textual in Derrida has essentially to do with the problem of reference rather than with questions of the determination or conditions of existence of textuality. But it is precisely the question of determinacy that comes to the fore in any *politically* interested concern with the extension of the textual metaphor to a generalised intertextuality. The problem is this: while a number of previously intractable theoretical difficulties about the structure of the social and its relation to the symbolic order are solved by the refusal of an ontological difference between moments of the social (between culture and the economic last instance or bottom line, for example), this move nevertheless begs the question of the forms of constraint and determination which operate between a plurality of instances of the social – forms of structural pressure which can no longer be deduced from ontological qualities (such as 'materiality').

The most influential attempt in recent years to develop a non-ontological model of the social, and of a correspondingly complex social causality, has been the cluster of metaphors of the social structure elaborated by Althusser. Like the dispersed and de-centred structure of the text, the non-totalised social whole is made up of disparate temporalities, and its specific form is one 'in which different structural levels of temporality interfere, because of the peculiar relations of correspondence, non-correspondence, articulation, dislocation and torsion which obtain, between the different "levels" of the whole in accordance with its general structure'.[9] The term 'structuration in dominance', borrowed from poetics, is used to describe a causal determination which is entirely constituted by the particular and contingent contradictions for which it is the precondition. In the same way, the concept of overdetermination theorises a relation between the general contradiction between the forces and the relations of production, and the conditions of existence of this contradiction, the so-called superstructures: 'it is radically *affected by them*, determining, but also determined in one and the same movement, and determined by the various *levels* and *instances* of the social formation it animates'.[10] And the concept of structural causality represents an attempt to think a form of determination which is immanent in its effects – that is, which does not depend upon an external and originary principle of determination, nor upon the epiphenomenality of the effects.[11]

In a discussion of Althusser's work, Laclau and Mouffe argue that it represents a radical attempt to think the social in semiotic, and hence in non-essentialist, terms:

The symbolic – i.e., overdetermined – character of social relations . . . implies that they lack an ultimate literality which would reduce them to necessary moments of an immanent law. There are not *two* planes, one of essences and the other of appearances, since there is no possibility of fixing an *ultimate* literal sense for which the symbolic would be a second and derived plane of signification. Society and social agents lack any essence, and their regularities merely consist of the relative and precarious forms of fixation which accompany the establishment of a certain order.[12]

Laclau and Mouffe find, nevertheless, that the concept of overdetermination is limited by Althusser's retention of the concept of 'determination in the last instance' by the economic – even though this last instance 'never comes' (*For Marx*, p. 113). Their own recent work attempts quite explicitly to provide a semiotic and non-reductive account of the social.

The key terms in this project are articulation and discourse. Articulation is defined as 'any practice establishing a relation among elements such that their identity is modified as a result of the articulatory practice. The structured totality resulting from the articulatory practice, we will call *discourse*' (*HSS*, p. 105). Discourse is coextensive with the social, and is not opposed to a non-discursive realm. As in Foucault, it is a complex of linguistic and extra-linguistic acts and entities, but the paradoxical effect of this ontological impurity is not to emphasise but precisely to defuse questions of causal priority. Thus 'the practice of articulation, as fixation/dislocation of a system of differences, cannot consist of purely linguistic phenomena; but must instead pierce the entire material density of the multifarious institutions, rituals and practices through which a discursive formation is structured' (*HSS*, p. 109). Economic practice, for example, is to be thought of as discursive.[13]

When this is spelled out in detail, however, the latent ambiguity (or rather the latent *lack* of ambiguity) of the concept becomes apparent: in explaining the discursive structure of economic practice Laclau and Mouffe argue that 'today we can see that the space which traditional Marxism designated "the economy" is in fact the terrain of a proliferation of discourses' (technical discourses, discourses of authority, of accountancy, of information).[14] The difficulty here is that the term 'discourses' retains its traditional sense of *languages*; and this suggests the difficulty of not reintroducing an opposition between the textual and the non-textual, or the linguistic and the non-linguistic, when the concept of discourse is extended to account for social practices in general.

The counterpart to this problem is the tendency of any such monistically deployed concept to indifferentiation. Let me give a couple of examples. One concerns the status of the 'exterior' of discourse:

> With this 'exterior' we are not reintroducing the category of the extra-discursive. The exterior is constituted by other discourses. It is the discursive nature of this exterior which creates the conditions of vulnerability of every discourse, as nothing finally protects it against the deformation and destabilisation of its system of differences by other discursive articulations which act from outside it. (*HSS*, p. 146, n. 20).

The question this raises is how far this conflictual relation to other discourses is capable of accounting for the 'shape' of any one discourse, for its specificity, and for the *limits* of its construction of reality; it is a question, that is to say, as to whether a model of discursive conflict can account adequately for the manifold *pressures* that act upon discourse. The second example again raises questions of discursive finitude:

> It is not the poverty of signifieds but, on the contrary, polysemy that disarticulates a discursive structure. That is what establishes the overdetermined, symbolic dimension of every social identity. Society never manages to be identical to itself, as every nodal point is constituted within an intertextuality that overflows it. *The practice of articulation, therefore, consists in the construction of nodal points which partially fix meaning; and the partial character of this fixation proceeds from the openness of the social, a result, in its turn, of the constant overflowing of every discourse by the infinitude of the field of discursivity.* (*HSS*, p. 113).

The appropriate counter to this argument would, I think, be Foucault's contention that discourse is characterised by its rarity: that it is an object of social struggle. Here too Laclau and Mouffe's concern with fluidity and with the interpenetration of discourses leads them to disregard the structural and economic (rather than semantic) constraints on this 'infinitude'. My third example, finally, involves their separation of the concept of hegemony from any necessary connection to a hegemonic *class* (see *HSS*, pp. 134–8). To tie hegemony to the shifting and apparently indeterminate play of subject positions (which are themselves the consequence of discursive structures) is to misunderstand the play of stabilisation and destabilisation within the field of force of the social. Geras, in a hostile and often incomprehending review, nevertheless identifies the major weakness in Laclau and Mouffe's discursive metaphor. It is the problem of how to model determinacy within this account of hegemonic articulation (for example, of how to integrate material resources, institutional structures, and so on) – or else, asks Geras, 'must we just assume that openness and indeterminacy of the social mean, here, such a free play of discourses and articulatory practices that *any number* of outcomes is always possible, so that no particular outcome, no specificity, *can* be understood or explained?'[15]

I have discussed Laclau and Mouffe's work at some length because it seems to me one of the most interesting contemporary elaborations of the implications of the concept of intertextuality (although they are not directly indebted to the literary uses of the concept). Their extension of the concepts of text and discourse to the field of the social ultimately begs the question of what it is that conditions the textual – that is, the question of the conditions of existence of textuality. They are in fact quite explicit about the impossibility of this question: 'If the *being* – as distinct from existence – of any object is constituted within a discourse, it is not possible to differentiate the discursive, in terms of being, from any other area of reality', and 'If the discursive is coterminous with the being of objects – the horizon therefore, of the constitution of the being of every object – the question about the conditions of possibility of the being of discourse is meaningless' ('Post-marxism without apologies', p. 86).

This indifferentiation of the concept of a generalised intertextuality can be resolved only by rethinking textuality in terms of its intrication in asymmetrical and unequal relations of force which would not, however, be simply external to the textual. This might mean positing different *modes* of textuality and textual functioning, or postulating an *endless* series of structural constraints, each level of which would in its turn be able to be thought as textual in form and susceptible to further constraint; or it might mean abandoning the concept of textuality for that of discourse, in the Foucauldian sense of an ontologically impure mix of textual structures, practices, institutional sites, and rules of application. But whilst these responses might be more appropriate in theoretical terms, it may be that for strategic and heuristic purposes it is not possible ever finally to move beyond that model of ontological difference which has traditionally been used to think the limits on textuality. In the same way, whilst epistemological questions about the limits of knowledge can be resolved adequately in terms of contradictions between discursive domains and the grids of understanding they carry with them, and whilst scientific *practice* (for example) works largely in terms of the *construction* of objects of knowledge, it may nevertheless be the case that for ordinary purposes we will continue to understand the production of knowledge in terms of the hard resistance to discourse of an ontologically distinct domain of factuality.

The consequence of this for literary study is perhaps a caution about the need to work according to two different sets of rules. On the one hand there is a need to work rigorously with the concept of intertextuality in such a way as to break down the limits between the textual and an apparently external and non-textual ('contextual') domain. On the other there is the need to be constantly suspicious about the extent to which broad domains of social being can thus be incorporated within the single conceptual domain of textuality – and about how this allows us not to attend to the hard resistance of other and disparate domains of discourse.

## Notes

1 Laurent Jenny, 'The Strategy of Form', in *French Literary Theory Today*, ed. T. Todorov, trans. R. Carter, Cambridge, 1982, p. 42.

2 Jonathan Culler, *The Pursuit of Signs: Semiotics, Literature, Deconstruction*, London, 1981, p. 117.

3 Julia Kristeva, 'Problèmes de la structuration du texte', in *Théorie d'ensemble*, Paris, 1968, p. 311 (my translation).

4 Jacques Derrida, *The Truth in Painting*, trans. Geoff Bennington and Ian McLeod, Chicago, 1987, p. 61.

5 Derrida, *Positions*, trans. Alan Bass, Chicago, 1981, p. 90.

6 Derrida, 'Living on/*Border Lines*', trans. James Hulbert, in Harold Bloom et al., *Deconstruction and Criticism*, New York, 1979, pp. 83–4.

7 Rodolphe Gasché, *The Tain of the Mirror: Derrida and the Philosophy of Reflection*, Cambridge, Mass., 1986, pp. 279–80.

8 Derrida, *Dissemination*, trans. Barbara Johnson, Chicago, 1981, p. 258.

9 Louis Althusser and Etienne Balibar, *Reading Capital*, trans. Ben Brewster, London, 1977, p. 108.

10 Althusser, *For Marx*, trans. Ben Brewster, New York, 1977, p. 101.

11 Cf. Althusser and Balibar, *Reading Capital*, pp. 188–9.

12 Ernesto Laclau and Chantal Mouffe, *Hegemony and Socialist Strategy: Towards a Radical Democratic Politics*, trans. Winston Moore and Paul Cammack, London, 1985, pp. 97–8 (hereinafter *HSS*).

13 Ernesto Laclau, 'Populist rupture and discourse', *Screen Education*, XXXIV, 1980, p. 87.

14 'Recasting marxism: hegemony and new political movements', interview with Ernesto Laclau and Chantal Mouffe, *Socialist Review*, 66 (XII, 6) 1982, p. 92.

15 Norman Geras, 'Post-marxism', *New Left Review*, CLXIII, 1987, p. 74; cf. Ernesto Laclau and Chantal Mouffe, 'Post-marxism without apologies', *New Left Review*, CLXVI, 1987, pp. 79–106; and Nicos Mouzelis, 'Marxism or post-marxism', *New Left Review*, CLXVII, 1988, pp. 102–23.

# Compulsory reader response: the intertextual drive

An intertext is one or more texts which the reader must know in order to understand a work of literature in terms of its overall significance (as opposed to the discrete meanings of its successive words, phrases, and sentences).[1] The distinction is paramount because linguistic usage suffices to account for such meanings, even though they may also develop under the further constraint of aesthetic conventions. Readers, however, sense empirically that the overall significance depends less on referentiality (as does standard verbal communication) than on a relation between form and content, or even on a subordination of content to form. The latter, we feel more or less consciously, constitutes the literariness of the verbal work of art.

These perceptions, this reader response to the text, cannot be explained by linguistic structures, since these are observed in non-literary and literary utterances alike. Nor can it be explained by tropology, rhetoric, or any corpus of conventional forms whose objects are already found at sentence level: these may account for discursive phenomena, but could not explain the difference between discursive and textual ones. Literature is indeed made of texts. Literariness, therefore, must be sought at the level where texts combine, or signify by referring to other texts rather than to lesser sign systems.

When we speak of knowing an intertext, however, we must distinguish between the actual knowledge of the form and content of that intertext, and a mere awareness that such an intertext exists and can eventually be found somewhere. This awareness in itself may be enough to make readers experience the text's literariness. They can do so because they perceive that something is missing from the text:

gaps that need to be filled, references to an as yet unknown referent, references whose successive occurrences map out, as it were, the outline of the intertext still to be discovered. In such cases, the reader's sense that a latent intertext exists suffices to indicate the location where this intertext will eventually become manifest.

This type of minimal reader response makes it necessary to distinguish between intertext and intertextuality. The latter is the web of functions that constitutes and regulates the relationships between text and intertext. These functions either are fully activated as they are embodied in perceived relationships, or they are activated in programmatic form, in which case they merely postulate an intertext, reminding readers that their response must be predicated on the hypothesis that the text requires it, showing them how the hypothesis may lead to actualisation, and what kind of intertext is to be expected.

Two modalities of reader response are inseparable. One is the readers' feeling that they need surcease from the demands the text puts on their ingenuity, and from the text's departures from accepted linguistic usage or narrative and descriptive conventions. The other is the constraints or limitations the same text puts on the readers' search for that relief. Indeed, contrary to critics' favourite reaction to difficulty (they too often are content to invoke ambiguity and do not seem to think there may be a way out of deconstruction), facts of reading suggest that, when it activates or mobilises the intertext, the text leaves little leeway to readers and controls closely their response. It is thus that the text maintains its identity despite changing times, despite the evolution of the sociolect, and despite the ascent of readerships unforeseen by the author.

It is obvious that such a process must be an imperative of reading. The urge to understand compels readers to look to the intertext to fill out the text's gaps, spell out its implications and find out what rules of idiolectic grammar account for the text's departures from logic, from accepted usage (that is, from the sociolect), from the cause-and-effect sequence of the narrative, and from verisimilitude in the descriptive. However compelling this reading strategy may be, it cannot account for the actual identification of an intertext, since matching textual ungrammaticalities and intertextual grammaticalities is like trying to find a needle in the haystack of a corpus or of a canon, even if we assume that neither has undergone historical changes that may put them out of the reach of normal readers (that is, readers armed only with their linguistic competence and trying to make do without the philological crutches of footnotes and scholarly gloss). It seems to me that only specific, specialised signs can at once stand for the intertext, point to its locus, and uncover its identity.

I shall try to determine which indices direct readers towards the specific and relevant intertexts, and indeed compel them to look for these intertexts even when cultural changes have made their recovery less likely (obviously, when the culture which the text reflects is still within reach, the readers' task is facilitated by the frequency of references to well-known intertexts, or just by chance encounters with them). These signposts are words and phrases indicating, on the one hand, a difficulty – an obscure or incomplete utterance in the text – that only an intertext can remedy; and, on the other hand, pointing the way to where the solution must be sought. Such features, lexical or phrasal, are distinguished from their context by their dual nature. They are both the problem, when seen from the text, and the solution to that problem when their other, intertextual side is revealed. They therefore belong equally in text and intertext, linking the two, and signalling in each the presence of their mutually complementary traits. Accordingly, I shall call them connectives. And in addition to identifying them, I shall try to show that the connectives combine the sign systems of text and intertext into new semiotic clusters, thereby freeing the text from its dependency on usage and existing conventions, and subordinating its descriptive and narrative devices to a signifying strategy unique to the text.

The text I have chosen as an example is a prose poem by André Breton, an especially arcane and frustrating one because it was written 'under the dictation of the unconscious', the phrase by which French Surrealists defined *écriture automatique*. This mode of writing was to put an end to the traditional literature characterised by laboured style, that which edited out spurts of inspiration, emphasised the approximation of manner to matter, and pursued the *mot juste* – what André Breton called the *littérature de calcul* ('literature of calculation'). In the latter he saw arbitrary conventions, artifice, the tired and tiring repetition of all-too-familiar themes. Whether automatic writing is an immediate product of the unconscious or a concerted attempt at representing it, it privileges associative sequences based on analogy and homophony, and does away with descriptive and narrative logic. And yet our poem eschews arbitrariness and gratuitousness, because intertexts confer authority to apparently random transitions from one set of images to the next. They make up for what automatic writing eliminates: the orderly teleological progress towards a conclusive and unified significance, a systematic development excluded from the text by the mimesis of the unconscious. As a result this development must be achieved from without the text, in its margins so to speak, by a system of exterior references and formal models composed of the intertexts. Automatic writing thus puts the burden of communication on intertextuality and makes its mechanisms easier to observe.

The poem is about sexual desire. Desire, sexual or otherwise, can only be represented in terms of a frustrated present, or of a future, in the anticipation of what is to come. Lasting only as long as it remains unsatisfied, desire must be depicted through suspense or delay, or through an impossibility to satisfy it. Any literary mimesis of desire therefore contains an element of desirability (hope, for example), and an element of interdiction. The latter prevents the former from attaining its goal. These elements generate texts of desire either by saturation or by displacement. Saturation occurs when all nouns in the text receive a positive or negative marker, according to whether anticipation or frustration is being emphasised. Displacement occurs when the nouns in the text are metonyms of the desired object; the object's conflicting features are expressed by metonyms carrying markers of desirability and by metonyms carrying markers of interdiction:

[1] Sur la montagne Sainte-Geneviève il existe un large abreuvoir où viennent se rafraîchir à la nuit tombée tout ce que Paris compte encore de bêtes troublantes, de plantes à surprises. [2] Vous le croiriez desséché si, en examinant les choses de plus près, vous ne voyiez glisser capricieusement sur la pierre un petit filet rouge que rien ne peut tarir. [3] Quel sang précieux continue donc à couler en cet endroit que les plumes, les duvets, les poils blancs, les feuilles déchlorophylées qu'il longe détournent de son but apparent? [4] Quelle princesse de sang royal se consacre ainsi après sa disparition à l'entretien de ce qu'il y a de plus souverainement tendre dans la faune et la flore de ce pays? [5] Quelle sainte au tablier de roses a fait couler cet extrait divin dans les veines de la pierre? [6] Chaque soir le merveilleux moulage plus beau qu'un sein s'ouvre à des lèvres nouvelles et la vertu désaltérante du sang de rose se communique à tout le ciel environnant, pendant que sur une borne grelotte un jeune enfant qui compte les étoiles; [7] tout-à-l'heure il reconduira son troupeau aux crins millénaires, depuis le sagittaire ou flèche d'eau qui a trois mains, l'une pour extraire, l'autre pour caresser, l'autre pour ombrager ou pour diriger, depuis le sagittaire de mes jours jusqu'au chien d'Alsace qui a un oeil bleu et un oeil jaune, le chien des

anaglyphes de mes rêves, le fidèle compagnon des marées.[2]

(On Saint Geneviève Hill there is a broad watering-trough where, at night-fall, what Paris still has of disturbing beasts, of surprise-springing plants, come to refresh themselves. You would think it had run dry if, on closer inspection, you did not see sliding capriciously over the stone a thin red trickle that nothing can dry up. What precious blood, then, keeps on flowing in this place, that the feathers, the down, the white hairs, the leaves without chlorophyll which it passes divert from its apparent course? What princess of royal blood devotes herself after her disappearance to the upkeep of all that is most sovereignly tender in the flora and fauna of this country? What saint with her apron of roses has made this divine extract flow through the veins of the stone? Each evening the wonderful hollow cast, more beautiful than a breast, opens itself to new lips, and the thirst-quenching power of the rose-blood spreads to all the surrounding sky, while against a mounting stone a young child sits shivering and counts the stars; soon he will drive home his herd with their millenia-old hides, from the sagittarius or arrow-head that has three hands, one for extracting an essence, the other for caressing, and another yet for casting a shade or pointing directions, from the sagittarius of my days to the Alsatian dog with one blue eye and one yellow eye, dog of the anaglyphs of my dreams, faithful companion of the tides.)

The poem sketches a nocturnal scene, a landscape paradoxically uniting city and country. In the very centre of Paris, in the heart of the Latin Quarter, on the *montagne Sainte-Geneviève*, there exists the magic kind of spring that folklore normally locates in the wilderness, a watering-hole frequented by fantastic animals and plants miraculously endowed with motion. Nearby, a young shepherd watches over a herd that is just as strange, since instead of sheep, the creatures of the Zodiac graze under his care.

The reader will easily recognise in this the well-known legend of the miraculous spring whose pure water flows at the scene of a crime, gushing from the spot where a virgin has been raped and murdered; the crystal clarity of the flowing water either effaces the traces of wrongdoing, or else symbolises the victim's purity. A modern version of this legend can be found in Ingmar Bergman's film *Virgin Spring*, in which the victim is a princess. Sentence 4 in the poem indeed alludes to a princess ministrating to the needs of the thirsty after her own death. Blood, rather than water, flows from the trough, a different and more supernatural variant also well attested to in folklore. But the poem conflates the two alternating liquids by transferring to blood the property of quenching thirst which belongs to water. Since this property is miraculous in blood, blood therefore becomes a desirable drink.

Readers readily accept the fountain of blood miracle because it conforms to accepted rules of the fantastic. Within the descriptive system of the word *fountain*, blood instead of water and a flow that never dries indicate the miraculous. The description is grammatical, self-sufficient, in no need of bolstering by comparison with the legends in which gory springs gush forth to commemorate the sacrifice of a saint.[3] True, if readers chance upon such stories, they verify the poem as a variant of a theme, and this theme exemplifies the fantastic. This verification, however, remains aleatory. While it does enhance plausibility within the fantastic by connecting this story in a tradition, the story itself only actualises a given of the fairy tale genre that would be interpretable and enjoyable for a reader quite innocent of folktales. Rather than recognising an intertext here, it is better to speak of a theme: the text is understood by reference to usage and to standard tales.

Intertextuality would add to this elementary reading mechanism only if we had to know other variants of the theme in order to understand that this blood is good. This is not the case. The medliorative process merely consists in a paradigm of variants in praise of blood repeating the word *blood* positively each time by its figurative acceptations, but also in its literal sense by embellishing associations. The whole series first makes blood an object of wonder. The expression *royal blood*, for example, can literally designate the blood of a monarch, or it can simply be a metonym for 'royal family' (cf. *princesse du sang*). 'Essence' (*extrait*) is a word borrowed from the vocabulary of chemistry, and specifically that of perfume-making; it designates the precious liquid distilled from rose petals that is used in the rarest perfumes. The literary synonym for this essence is in French conventional poetic language *sang des roses* ('blood of roses', or 'rose-blood'). 'Precious blood' (*sang précieux*) commonly signifies exactly that, but it is also, in religious discourse, the term for the blood of Christ and more to the point, it is that blood when it becomes drinkable: the phrase designates the transubstantiated wine of the Eucharist. This meaning still needs no more than normal linguistic competence to be understood, but its unexpected aptness for the poem's symbolism does not become evident until the next rung on the paradigm's ladder, the vision of the blood spreading through the sky. This image signals a major shift from blood as an object of admiration to blood as an object of desire – that is, a blood one thirsts for.

This shift is specific to the poem and indeed constitutes its idiosyncratic, topical significance. But it is also with this shift that the poem departs from grammaticality most visibly. Readers could be satisfied with the truth and beauty of the rose-blood as a metaphor for the sky coloured by the setting sun. They are denied this natural and obvious reading, however, for it is precluded by the fact that the subject of the sentence is not the rose-blood itself, but its *vertu désaltérante*, a quality equally nonsensical for speaking of celestial hues and of a rose distillate.

This is the point at which an intertext intervenes, making a second reading possible and indeed compulsory, an intertext that authorises the seemingly gratuitous and absurd sentence where thirst-quenching power can serve as a subject for the predicate 'spread through the sky'. This intertext is a literary one, but it is also the subject of paintings by Tintoretto and Rubens, a fact that must have increased its currency: the myth of Juno forced to suckle Hercules at her breast, despite the child's being Jupiter's bastard. The errant king of gods pushes the famished babe against the bosom of Juno asleep. Awakened by the voracious lips of Hercules, she turns and pushes his mouth away from the breast that he has already grasped. But the divine infant's suction is so powerful that the stream of milk still flowing from the nipple spreads across the heavenly canopy: thus was the Milky Way created.

Better still, now that this ungrammaticality is further emphasised by the intertext that redeems it, readers' attention reverts to the beginning of the poem and to a first ungrammaticality that may have escaped them in the initial jumble of contradictory images. Instead of just depicting a miraculous fountain in accordance with folktale practice, the second sentence is at variance with the fantastic of the motif because of the double anomaly of a trough. A farmyard implement is ungrammatical in a big-city context, and it is ungrammatical in a virgin-spring context. The verisimilitude of the supernatural tale (a literary genre) is compatible with the locus amoenus of a bucolic setting, in which a rivulet trickles over pebbles through a verdant mead, or a silent pond reflects the leafy shade, etc. By contrast, it would seem to exclude the prosaic utilitarian décor of the farm.

The mythological intertext does provide a transition back to the fantastic. Even though the Juno myth has cultural connotations which somewhat defuse the direct impact that the fantastic has in a Celtic tale of fountains, both the breast and the spring are clearly supernatural. But replacing the breast with its own cast, and making it still function as a spring, ceases to be absurd when we grasp the similarity between the cast's hollow and that of the trough, a similarity confirmed by the fact that both produce a beneficent blood. The whole transformation still remains painfully far-fetched, however, until we relate it to the intertext that lurks behind *moulage*. This word functions as the connective here because it is even more of a technical term than *abreuvoir*. It is borrowed straight from the sculptor's studio, designating the plaster templet moulded on a model's breast, or on a sculpture created in her likeness: molten bronze poured into the cast takes the shape of that breast and immortalises its beauty. The cast is thus halfway between the trough and the breast, partaking of the artificiality of the former and the eroticism of the latter. The intertext illustrates this with a well-known motif of pathos about the irony of Fate, where Nature herself is the sculptor, and the cast is accidental, the negative impression left by a woman's breast in the hardened lava of Pompeii.

Théophile Gautier's short story, *Arria Marcella*, offers a fully developed version of this intertext:

> . . . he was looking at a piece of coagulated black ash with a hollow imprint. It looked like a fragment from a statue's mould, broken during the casting procedure. An artist's knowledgeable eye would have easily recognized the outline of a wonderful breast and of a waist whose stylistic purity was worthy of Greek statuary. Any traveller's guidebook will tell you that as this lava grew cold around the body of a woman, it kept her charming contour. The caprice of an eruption which destroyed four cities has preserved until our day a noble shape that had fallen to dust two thousand years ago. The rounded outline of a bosom has endured through centuries while so many empires have vanished without a trace.[4]

There are quite a few other versions of the cast-moulding-a-breast story, to which I shall refer later. The Pompeii variant is the one most frequently invoked, and the one most likely to be remembered, for two reasons. The first is its complexity; its effect is heightened by two other themes. One is that the love or desire inspired by the bosom triumphs over death. The other is that art or beauty survives the fall of empires, with the added twist that the more apparently perishable the media, the more it endures (a motif made famous by Horace celebrating the power of poetry, that outlasts bronze statues, *monumentum exegi aere pereenius*). Gautier's story gives narrative proof of desire made eternal when the dead beauty appears to the young tourist in his dreams and seduces him. We are left uncertain as to whether all this is but a figment of the aroused sleeper's erotic dreams, or whether it is an actual visitation by the undead risen from the grave. Despite whichever version happens to be correct, both spell out the maximal form of the axiom of desire: if frustration is eternal, then the libido must accordingly be undying.

But the other reason for the Pompeii version's fame is that its melodramatic tension makes more visible the function of a structure which is nothing less than the basic mechanism of intertextual exchange. If praise of a woman in love poetry can be done by depicting her as statuesque, an equally effective praise does the reverse by imagining her as the mould from which a statue will be cast (e.g., the motif of the bereft lover drinking to his dead mistress's memory from a cup moulded on her breast). A further reversion of the intertextual shuttle then describes a female shape through the detour of a figurative, or literal, hollow mould. This mechanism is central to the entire poem because the comparison of the body and of the artefact is being misused or diverted, as it were, in the statement about the *cast more beautiful than the breast*. This would appear paradoxical or nonsensical if the poem were about the real thing. The intertextual manipulation here builds on the fact that the word *abreuvoir* designates a hollowed-out stone, and that images derived from it may be easier to recognize as synonyms of it if the stone component is preserved, which is the case for *cast*. The cast therefore imagistically designates a wet mould of flesh which, we will soon discover, is literally a more beautiful sex object than the breast itself.

The two intertexts (*moulage* and the galaxy) conjured up together by the same sentence and knotting together two images of desire (sex and thirst), posit an idiolectic rule, applicable only within the poem and germane to its significance, whereby blood's newly established equivalency with milk makes it a synecdoche for the whole woman.

But the question remains: why is blood made into an object of desire? And if it flows as a memorial to the victim of a tale of rape and murder, who is she? The answer, of course, is a shepherdess. She who gave her name to the Paris hill, the city's patron saint and therefore a metonym for it, was a shepherdess, but most readers would not think of it. The name itself may however become a connective, or one of the connectives, when readers become aware that the whole tale narrated or hinted at in the poem is but the long periphrasis for a repressed word, *bergère*. The very nature of a periphrasis is that it beats around the bush hiding the word that is that periphrasis's lexical equivalent. The periphrastic meandering itself, and the multiple question marks lead readers towards identifying the victim with *bergère*, and eventually to guessing which aspects of the sememe 'shepherdess' enable it to function as an exemplary object of desire, and consequently to give the poem its textual identity.

As always in literary texts, a number of secondary signals ensure that even the most absent-minded readers will find the thread leading to the solution. These signals consist in repeating words from the descriptive systems[5] of 'shepherd(ess)' or aimplifying these words into periphrases each of which constitutes a mini-description to make the point explicit. The very size of the space occupied by the developing representation emphasizes it. The child of sentence 6 is a shepherd himself, as we are told twice through two periphrases. The first amounts to a definition and suscitates a rich intertext of poetic allusions to the mythical birth of astronomy. It is a well-known theme, in France and elsewhere, that the first people who were able to discern and name asterisms were those men whose occupation kept them awake at night, watching over their herds and contemplating the starry skies – the pastors of ancient Mesopotamia. Then a new periphrastic approach to the key is made via metonyms of the shepherd. First, the herd itself, which being the Zodiac, confirms the supernatural, or perhaps just figurative or symbolic, nature of the whole tale. Then, the shepherd dog, twice described as such through its species and through its characteristically varicoloured eyes.[6] And now that we have shepherd, herd, and shepherd dog, only the shepherdess is missing. Not for long, however, because a dog is a symbol of fidelity, and the text leaves blank only the space where the name of that fidelity's beneficiary should be. That this space should be filled out with the renewed nonsense of *tides* makes it even more necessary for readers to correct this with the only appropriate word so far left unuttered. Of course, any feminine character could be an object of desire. But it so happens that *bergère*, which was so difficult to uncover, is a word ideally suited for this role since, as a conventional character of the pastoral, she embodies sexuality in the bucolic genre. This proceeds from the idylls of ancient literature through seventeenth- and eighteenth-century *bergerades* in poetry and in painting down to vulgar usage. To this day, *bergère* is a colloquialism for lover or even for a 'loose' girl. Add to this phrases like *l'heure du berger*, a humorous euphemism designating the moment of surrender of a willing female, and *étoile du berger*, another name for the planet Venus. This name, by the way, is also a synonym for the first sign of the Zodiac, and an occasional synecdoche for the word *zodiac* as well, bringing us back sylleptically to the other facet of the poem, the mimesis of the fantastic, and thus realising once more the interface of vision and of sexuality.

The intertext summarised and represented by *bergère* selects therefore from the descriptive system based on that word those descriptive details and narrative situations that may actualise sexuality literally or figuratively, especially in the hyperbolic form of male desire: rape. A shepherdess, alone and defenceless in the solitude of woods and meadows, is a natural symbol of feminine vulnerability, so much so that the development of a poetic genre, the medieval *pastourelle*, is but a narrative expansion on *rape*. The modality of experience that defines the shepherdess would seem to be feminine availability. So powerful is this stereotyped derivation from the very name of the character, that it involves or contaminates even those components of the descriptive system that have nothing to do with the strategy of the act itself. First, the dog. He was supposed to protect his mistress. Instead, he becomes an accomplice in her demise. Second, the spring of water. Third, the tree shading the scene. These two were but props in the setting of the bucolic *locus amoenus*. They now symbolically re-enact the unutterable scene that transforms the pastoral bower of bliss into a dramatic stage of violent lust.

An early instance of the intertext gives us an example of the dog's new function. Marmontel wrote a short story, *La Bergère des Alpes,* first published in his *Contes moraux* that so aroused his readers' fantasies, that the musical stage version of it was produced in 1766, plagiarised as a comedy by abbé Desfontaines in 1795, and developed into a full-fledged five-act drama in 1852 by Desnoyers and Dennery. It tells the seduction of the heroine by a hunter who loses his way in the mountains and is saved by the dog. The dog brings him to her hut. She becomes pregnant, but all is well that ends well: they get married. The dog turning from protector into procuror is an instance of role reversal, and of resulting suspense, common in melodrama. But that structural shift permanently endows the animal with literariness and makes him a fixture of the seduction tale, with the effect that his presence alone indicates what is going on.

A later version of the intertext provides us with a more complete example of the transference, transforming the dog and the surroundings into a symbolic account of the event. In that version, from Jean Giraudoux's 1926 novel *Bella*, a Parisian dandy takes a walk in the countryside. He is sexy (*Pan en veston*, 'Pan in morning coat') and Spring is beckoning. A shepherd dog befriends him (rather than the more usual way around) and brings him to his mistress. The dog's literary function (as opposed to its role of guardian in reality) as a metonym for his mistress in her role as sex object, is clearly expressed: the dog does the wooing (*le chien de la bergère l'avait séduit*) and the shepherdess has the same varicoloured eyes as the animal. The metonymic transference is repeated through the name: the dog is called, unaccountably, Red Stockings, a riddle solved by the indirection in the narrative derived from the name. Instead of a straight account of the scene's climax, the text alludes to it circuitously by having the wench display to the passer-by the top of her own red stockings. Finally, a variation on the vernal theme repeats the story as if it were a commentary on Breton: '. . . the setting *seduced him* rather than the shepherdess herself. How splendid, how *potent* the mountain-ash looked, beneath which she was sitting. The tree was *raping* the earth that was *fighting back*. A spring was flowing: it would soon be good to *touch its water*.'[7]

I have italicised images that may seem merely ornate and fairly artificial stylistic devices. The instant we perceive their common implication, these images assume a new function as members of a paradigm of synonymous representations of desire. We therefore read them as figurative paraphrase of the implicit rape story.

The recovery of *bergère* from under *tides* is unmistakable and cannot fail, as we have seen, because the phrase *faithful companion of* for a shepherd dog cannot be completed except with *berger* or *bergère,* and of the two only the latter is still available. But even if the descriptive system I have described were not actualised, thus facilitating the proper interpretation of the riddle, or rather making it foolproof, the substitute chosen for the predicate of *faithful companion* would have pointed to *shepherdess,* for *tides* makes sense only with the feminine. Given the blood paradigm, *tides,* suppressing the designation of a woman, must be read as a metaphor for menstruation. All mythologies have concurred in linking women's menses as well as tides to the phases of the moon. The plural of *tides* makes the substitution even more imperative since French *règles* ('period') is used only in the plural.

As soon as the reader makes this discovery, nonsense disappears. While the whole paradigm of synonyms describes the blood as desirable, this intertext reveals it as prohibited, since menstrual blood is impure blood in all western religious traditions. The connective, therefore, actualises the frustration component in the mimesis of the libido. After all, Leviticus prohibits intercourse with a woman during her period. In consequence, both miraculously thirst-quenching spring and taboo liquid, menstrual blood is a perfect metaphor for desire.

Nevertheless, the prose poem still presents images that appear arbitrary. The fusion of two incompatible settings, urban and rustic, remains entirely gratuitous, and its relation to the blood-symbolism remains far-fetched. Miraculous fountains are usually hidden in forests and dales like the nymphs that once frequented them. But so long as a man-made trough was substituted for the natural spring, the latter could have transferred its magic to the former, while remaining in the background as an intertextual footnote. The substitution itself is the real problem: not even the usefulness of a trough to shepherds could explain it, since ponds and springs would do the job just as well, especially in the bucolic genre.

Actually, the key to the riddle is not the thing itself, but the word for it. *Abreuvoir* sticks out in context because it is a technicism of sorts, a term found only in the special vocabulary of animal husbandry, that would seem appropriate only in a realistic description of a farmyard. So conspicuous a presence, and one so estranged from its context, impels readers to search for its reason. Since contextual justification is lacking, readers turn to outside associations for an answer. They find it in a lexical look-alike of *abreuvoir* whose near identity at the phonetic level is bound to attract attention, the more so because it combines so disparately at the stylistic level. The two words so close in shape, so far apart in style, thus constitute a near syllepsis. The farmyard word happens to be related to only one other term in the whole lexicon, a term that paradoxically is used only in conventional literary contexts, the verb *abreuver* or *s'abreuver*, 'to slake thirst'. Moreover, the thirst in question is metaphorical (its seldom-used literal sense is always melodramatic), the thirst for blood, as in *s'abreuver du sang de l'ennemi*, 'to slake one's thirst for enemy blood', certainly a desirable activity.

This bloodthirsty hyperbole would have been long forgotten, buried in the rhetoric of political polemics of the Revolutionary period, Classical tragedy, or outdated epics, were it not kept alive in France's national anthem. No French reader can go from *abreuvoir* to *s'abreuver* without recognising this intertext, of which he is reminded at every public event, when most people to this day join in the refrain:

> Aux armes, citoyens! Formez vos bataillons!
> Marchons! Marchons!
> *Qu'un sang impur abreuve nos sillons!*
>
> [Take up arms, citizens! Form your batallions!
> Let us march! Let us march!
> May our furrows be slaked with impure blood!]

Impure blood; the thirst for this blood; and the word *sillons*, 'furrows', rather than *champs*, 'fields', or *labours* 'tilled fields', a synedoche for *campagnes*, 'countryside'; and finally the fact that in the first stanza, *campagnes*, 'our fields' invaded by foreign violators, rhymes with their intended victims, *nos compagnes*, 'our women': all these components are now in place to form a series of double meanings that trace the silhouette of women and of bloodthirsty aggressors. *Sang impur* refers to the blood of France's enemies, but it is also a pompous euphemism for menstrual blood, while *sillon* is a salacious euphemism for the female genitals. The optative form of the verb for thirst-slaking expresses a programme of desire. Thus *sillon* in this explicit intertext caps a paradigm of erotically charged images of hollowness: the watering-trough, and the cast of a breast. Obscene equivocations on the refrain are found in off-colour jokes about intercourse, and about defloration in particular. *Sang impur* paves the way for a retrieval of the intertext. Despite its archaism, the phrase exists in present everyday usage, and always with a comical, parodic tinge, because in spoken French there is this one phonetic liaison, that seems to contradict spelling, in which the final *g* in *sang* is pronounced as a *k*, and the example that schoolchildren memorise when they learn this strange rule is the same *sang impur* line about thirst and furrows.

The intertextual role of the patriotic refrain is special. Contrary to the intertexts that transform one sentence at a time, the impact of the *Marseillaise* affects the whole poem at once. It causes readers to recognise, however unconsciously, that the trough and the *moulage*

are synonymous, as are the princess, the female saint, and the shepherdess. All three are identical in the single respect that they are
overflowing with desirable blood. This intertext therefore, by providing the model that sets the rule of transformation to be applied to
the other intertexts, has the same function as the interpretant in C. S.
Peirce's definition of the sign: a sign stands to somebody for something in some respect, creating in the mind of that person an
equivalent sign, the interpretant.[8] Translated at the level of textuality, this would read: a text stands to the reader for an intertext,
creating in her or his mind an equivalent sign system. The interpretant intertext embodies that system and keeps it in store for all
future readers as a written guarantee that they will all end up with the
same interpretation.

The power of the interpretant results from its repression: once
readers identify this intertext, they still have to cope with the *double
entendre* of *sillon,* to perceive that that word is relevant only in a
prurient intertext repressed and therefore directed to our attention
by the patriotic bombast of the song in its official use.

It must be emphasised that it is not the actual context of the French
anthem which constitutes the interpretant. If the refrain itself were a
key to interpretation, it would be a quotation or an allusion, not an
intertext. For the intertext to play its role as a supplement to the text,
it need not be more than a structural referent, a model authorising
certain verbal connections which are unacceptable in usage. These
may be predications, syntagms, or fragments thereof. Or they may be
mere juxtapositions; words otherwise unrelated in language, and
belonging to different syntagms in the intertext, are still close enough
to one another to be remembered together. Their nearness is
valorised because we observe it within the compass of a familiar
intertext. The refrain is not, therefore, involved in its entirety. It only
provides an abstract frame endowed with the power to give
authority to whatever fits into it; a hallowed textual space in which
*s'abreuver* presupposes a craving for blood; a space in which that
particular libido demands that the blood be impure; a space where
the locus of fulfilment is a furrow. Only because of that abstract
frame, only because of its ability to consecrate a specific verbal
combination, does a second step become possible: the activation, the
accession to relevancy of the already present but dormant sexual
*double entendre* of 'furrow' (as if to make sure that readers will not
miss the cue, another sylleptic intertext urges them to the second

step: *moulage* is an abstract connective, corresponding to a literal mould in the intertext, to a metaphorical one in the text where it stands for vulva).

This activaticn doubles back, as it were, onto the text. As soon as the water-trough is revealed for what it is, thanks to the discovery of the *furrow* interpretant, details of the hollowed stone's description that were as yet unexplained become in turn the interpretants of *sillon,* which latter now functions as the primary sign.[9] Consequently, these details too acquire a sexual significance. The feathers, hairs, down, and leaves through which blood trickles therefore appear as a periphrasis for two stereotyped images, *toison,* 'head of hair' or 'fur', and *forêt,* 'forest', the alternately literary or colloquial metaphors for pubic hair, in lofty poetic style as well as in lowbrow or vulgar discourse.

So wide an impact, so totalising a transformation, presupposes that the multiple meanings of the text should be modified together and given a common significance simultaneously, irrespective of their discrete referents. It could not therefore depend on a connective whose own meaning might differ from and obscure the aim of the overall transformation. This is why the connective for an interpretant intertext must be a syllepsis – that is, a word that has two mutually incompatible meanings, one acceptable in the context in which the word appears, the other valid only in the intertext to which the word also belongs and that it represents at the surface of the text, as the tip of an iceberg. As a word, the syllepsis has two meanings, each of which generates its own derivation in its separate text; yet as a connective, it has no meaning of its own. The connective is therefore empty, since it is a mere phonetic shape which can be filled in turn by two otherwise alien universes of representation. As such it is vastly more powerful than a metaphor, which needs some semes common to both its tenor and its vehicle for the tropological substitution to work. The syllepsis, on the contrary, resting as it does on homophony, is a connective in the abstract, a mere sign of equivalency.

The syllepsis's power over the reader lies in the paradoxical combination of two factors. One is the unmistakable obviousness of the connective, the other is the distance between the connected texts. Obviousness: one word is at once the question and the answer, having both textual and intertextual relevances (sometimes two words almost identical as is the case here but with the same radical, which makes them look like a declension or conjugation on one radical). Distance: the irresistible lure for readers is an enormous return for a modest investment, and also an effect of transgression, of pleasurable release from a repression, such as the titillation we experience when a wording safe from any embarrassing connotation yields to minimal changes (e.g., letter or syllable permutations in spoonerisms) and produces an outrageous or even taboo derivation.

The other cases of intertextuality I have discussed are equally compelling, but they differ from syllepsis on two major points. Far from being empty, the connective carries a double semantic load. And instead of being a lexical Janus, one word with two faces, the connective is a puzzling substitute for the term that should have been lifted from the intertext in order for the text to produce significance. The instances found in Breton belong to two different types, but in both of them the key word or phrase common to text and intertext is missing, and is replaced with another in such a way that readers cannot fail to sense a substitution. This makes the recovery of the intertext both urgent and unavoidable.

Our poem presents no other type, not, I think, because of its limitations, but rather because the examples at hand cover all possible alternatives. Substitution is the clue, because the semantic or lexical incompatibilities it creates between the substitute and the sentences surrounding it are blatant forms of ungrammaticality. For the incompatibilities to be experienced, the verbal sequences they modify must have some stability, some permanence, barring which we could not recognise them and compare their original form to the altered version before us. These sequences may be found either in a text signed by an author, or in the potential, inchoate or fragmentary narrative and descriptive sequences floating in the limbo of the corpus of myths, stories, exempla, etc. of which a sociolect is comprised. But their permanence, their stability can only take two forms. It can manifest itself, first, in one-sentence cliché predications, phrases that go unchanged in any context, or even in stereotyped full-length stories, admitting of few variations from one version to the next, such as themes, motifs, and myths. Any repressed component of the above category is sure to be recovered because it is presupposed by its context. The second kind of permanence is that of descriptive systems, within which a repressed component is readily identified as a metonym or synecdoche of the system's kernel word. The two instances I have discussed correspond to the possibilities:

stereotypes (Milky Way), and textual models (*bergère* descriptive system).

Within these categories, the recovery of an intertext proceeds in two stages both so overdetermined that they are unlikely to elude for long any reader equipped with basic linguistic competence. Over-determination is the more inescapable because it is an in-built self-contained model accessible in its entirety through the semanalysis of the matrix word from which the stereotyped text or descriptive system is derived. At the heuristic stage, readers instantly notice the substitution of a connective because it disturbs an expected verbal sequence. At the interpretive stage, they easily recover the substi-tuted component because anything missing can be deduced from the extant components.

The question arises as to whether intertextuality ceases to work if the reader is unfamiliar with the intertexts involved. One might think the Breton poem would become a dead letter if the sculptor's mould were to go unrecognised (and its implications ignored), if Gautier's short stories were no longer accessible to French readers, or if British readers were to tire of Bulwer-Lytton's *Last Days of Pompeii,* in which the same negative of a bosom is depicted. Experience suggests otherwise. The cast emptied of its statue has many other variants. One would be a sultry scene in Rousseau's *Nouvelle Héloïse*: when a lover, waiting for his mistress in her boudoir, loses himself in fervid contemplation of the girdle and bra strewn about him, he muses, 'every item of your underwear offers to my burning imagination the parts of your body they conceal . . . Delicious imprints, I kiss you a thousand times.'[10]

The passage could serve as an emblem of the mechanism of desire: the object of desire, reduced to an outline, is both represented and missing; it is literally visible in its very absence. A prurient immediacy is added through vicarious sensory perception; the sight and touch of undergarments is so strongly associated with the body that they are already stereotyped metonyms for it. Indeed, they are as forbidden as those parts of the body they cover (it is not so long ago that they were still called *unmentionables*). Just to name them is as potent as a striptease.

Nor is there any need to know printed versions of this generalised variant (Rousseau's novel is also losing popularity), since linguistic competence (that is, familiarity with the clichés of the sociolect) should suffice for readers to recognise the reversed form of an erotic stereotype (fantasising about the suggestive swelling curves at once hidden and displayed by feminine attire). The only difference is that published variants enjoy the momentary authority of the canon. If we further hypothesise the loss of the stereotypes, there is little chance that any full shape can ever be perceived or conceived of without its counterpart, the hollow outline that complements it, especially when the strategies of clothing, fashion and sexual symbolism valorise them together as mutually alternative. Furthermore, we should not assume that the survival of intertextuality depends on whether or not the reader's libido is aroused. Although the examples discussed are heated up by libidinal drives, they are but especially valorised variants of a universal structure of intertextuality: the semiotic shuttle between polar opposites, trading them back and forth, and treating them as if they were mutually equivalent, one pole being the negative of the other. The widespread literary practice of depicting nature in terms of artefacts and vice versa is an example of this.

Finally, words correspond to sememes, and sememes contain, in a potential state of suspense, the semes that can, at any time, develop into a narrative. A sememe is an inchoate text. Conversely, a text from which a crucial component is missing can be rebuilt by reversing the generating process; that is, by performing a semanalysis. This is why the gradual vanishing of mythology from readers' memories is unlikely to hamper the recovery of *milk,* although it is displaced by the *sang* substitute. In any language in which a major galaxy is called the Milky Way, one easily surmises that the convention of describing a symbolic liquid spreading over the sky has for its authority the metaphorical phraseology of popular astronomy that represents stardust as milk. We do not have to know the details or the names, let alone read obscure mythographers like Hyginus, who spins the tale in his *Astronomica.* The Juno story itself is but an early rationalisation of the original semanalysis of the popular name for the galaxy: that semanalysis merely deduced the breast from the milk, and supernatural nurse and nursling from the cosmic proportions of the spectacle.

The stability of intertexts, and the reader's ability to compensate for their losses, should not lead us to assume that intertexts are just themes and motifs. In terms of content and even of form, intertext and theme may indeed coincide, but they differ radically from each other in terms of their impact on the reader, let alone in terms of the

reader's awareness. In fact, a theme's impact can be quite independent of the reader's recognition of the theme: narrative and stylistic
devices, the actualisation of diegetic structures – in short, the very
features that explain its success and its becoming a theme as a result –
these same features will arouse even a reader who does not suspect
the existence of other versions. In fact, it is not unusual for a theme to
be known as such only by specialised readers, by comparatists.

By contrast, intertextuality exists only when two texts interact,
whether or not they are themes as well. There cannot be an intertext
without our awareness of it. This awareness, as I have tried to
demonstrate, rests either on the transparency of the syllepsis or on
the momentary opaqueness of a substitution.

In other words, even if the intertext can also be described as a
theme, it will differ in one major respect: it will either be a theme
missing a key word, relevant only if rephrased as a riddle (the
substitute type), or a theme made inseparable from another story
with which it shares a key word (the sylleptic type) to the exclusion of
anything else. This implies the erasure of any identifying structure
previously built with traits definable as thematic. Any significance
attached to the similarity between versions, from which we deduce
the existence of a theme, is superseded by the illogical relationship
(unjustifiable in referential terms) produced by the mere pun that the
syllepsis ultimately is.

Before concluding, I should like to point out one final (but
essential) difference between intertext and theme, a trait common to
both types of connectives. Because it is specific to intertextuality, this
trait excludes the synonymous or antonymous kind of relationship
that exists between versions of a theme. Instead, this trait is the
combinatory nature of the connectives. Each connective has, as we
have seen, two components: the substitute in the text, and its corollary or correspondent, the item substituted for, that remains *praesens
in absentia* in the intertext, displaced or repressed, but in no way
suppressed, inactive, or dormant. Intertextuality of the sylleptic type
provides, in an intertext unconnected with the text except for the
purely formal pun that indicates their relationship, the rule or programme for the interpretation of the text; the paradigm associating
the cattle's watering-trough and the artist's mould would remain
cryptic without the explicitness of the one word (*sillon*) that has
remained behind in the intertext, while *abreuvoir* and *sang* are
transferred to the text. Intertextuality of the substitutive type fuses

together the mimesis of the repressed element and the mimesis of the repressing one. Consequently, the solution to the riddle posed by the substitution can never be just a reductive strategy that would not, for instance, go beyond recovering *bergère* from under *marées*. Far from being a momentary conundrum to be erased the minute it is solved, the substitution triggers a semiosis which isolates and privileges, within the sememe 'shepherdess' as a sex symbol, a seme 'menstruation'. Without the connective, that seme would remain untapped. Hence a lexical hybrid, a ghost portmanteau-word holding together a peasant girl and the vast sea's ebb and flow. As a mimesis, this defies visualisation, but its role is to try an equation (not unlike the oxymoronic structure of an adynaton) on the reader's imagination. Hence, in a fleeting but illuminating reconciliation, a compound sign, in which a character from conventional bucolic poetry, indicating the legitimacy of sex, and the menstrual component of femaleness, indicating the illegitimacy of sex, stand together, one and indivisible, for *desire*.

The combinatory nature of the connectives accounts, it seems to me, at one fell swoop for three aspects of intertextuality. It explains the fact that intertextuality enables the text to represent, at one and the same time, the following pairs of opposites (within each of which the first item corresponds to the intertext): convention and departures from it, tradition and novelty, sociolect and idiolect, the already said and its negation or transformation. It explains also that intertextuality should be the one trope that modifies a whole text rather than a sentence or phrase, as a metaphor, say, or a synecdoche would. Indeed, it takes a whole text to compensate for the disappearance of the repressed intertext, and at the same time to transfer to that text (i.e., to the periphrastic derivations of the repressed item) a significance issuing from the intertext.

It explains above all that the most important component of the literary work of art, and indeed the key to the interpretation of its significance, should be found outside that work, beyond its margins, in the intertext.

In conclusion, the concept of combinatory connectives explains why the recovery of the intertext is an imperative and inevitable process. We should not be misled by the fact that in the Breton poem this process is bolstered by its coincidence with a structure of desire. It is true that the reader's compulsion to lift the veil on the lust for menstrual blood can be explained in psychoanalytic terms.[11] And, generally speaking, we are justified in drawing a parallel between intertextuality and the unconscious, since the text plays the role of a screen. Thus the intertext is to the text what the unconscious is to consciousness. Reading, therefore, is not unlike analysis.[12] Nonetheless, we must recognise that what impels the reader to pursue the search for the intertext, to experience the intertextual drive, as it were, is above all not just the material fact of the binary structure of the connective, but its being consistent with, or a variant of, the ubiquitous mechanism of tropes. In a response rendered compulsive, and facilitated by this familiar model, as soon as the reader notices a possible substitutability, s/he automatically yields to the temptation to actualise it. The intertextual drive, therefore, is tropological rather than psychoanalytical, a reader response dictated by the tantalising combination within each connective of the enigma and the answer, of the text as Sphinx and the intertext as Oedipus.

## Notes

1   For a sensible introduction to these problems, see the Intertextuality issue of *Texte: revue de critique et de théorie littéraire*, II, 1983. It includes an exhaustive bibliography by Don Bruce, pp. 217–58.

2   This piece is the eighth of thirty-two prose poems entitled *Poisson soluble* published in 1924 (Breton, *Œuvres complètes,* ed. Marguerite Bonnet, Paris, 1988, Vol. I, pp. 347–99). There is no visible intertextuality between this and the other pieces. I tried my hand at a reading of this poem, from a different viewpoint, in 'Désir, représentation, textualité', *Degrés,* XLIX–L, Spring–Summer 1987, esp. pp. 6–11.

3   A majority of these legends attribute the origin of the fountains of blood to the violent death of women, whether victims of rape or martyrs of the faith. The second case would seem free of sexual overtones. Far from it: the woman is decapitated or cut to pieces, and blood or water gushes forth from the spot where her head or breasts fall.

4   First published in *Un Trio de romans* (1852), reprinted in Théophile Gautier, *La Morte amoureuse, Avatar et autres récits fantastiques,* ed. Jean Gaudon, Paris, 1981, pp. 167–8.

5   A descriptive system is a network of words associated with one another around a kernel word, in accordance with syntactic relationships between the semes of that nucleus' sememe. Each lexical component of the system functions as a metonym of that nucleus.

6   Actually, the dog's membership in the *shepherd* descriptive system is symbolised three times, the last time, revealingly, through the obscure image of *anaglyphs.* The word should refer to a kind of *bas relief,* but instead refers to a gadget or toy of the twenties, a kind of stereoscope whose yellow and blue lens created an effect of relief, like the goggles American spectators had to put on thirty years later to watch 3-D movies. Three times then

*shepherd(ess)* is referred to, translated or disguised, in *dog* code.

7   *Bella,* Paris, 1926, p. 194.

8   I summarise one of C. S. Peirce's definitions of the sign (*Collected Papers,* Harvard, 1931, 2:228); cf. my discussion of it in 'The interpretant in literary semiotics', *American Journal of Semiotics,* III, 1985, pp. 44 ff.

9   This is a conspicuous effect of continuous semiosis. Cf. Peirce, *Collected Papers,* 2.300: a sign 'is anything which determines something else (its interpretant) to refer to an object to which itself refers (its object) in the same way, the interpretant becoming in turn a sign, and so on ad infinitum'.

10   Rousseau, *Julie ou la nouvelle Héloïse,* 1761, Part I, letter 54.

11   Cf. D. H. Lawrence's near glossolalia about it in his 1929 essay on *Chatterley*: 'The phallus is a column of blood that fills the valley of blood of a woman. The great river of male blood touches to its depths the great river of female blood – yet neither break its bounds. It is the deepest of all communions, as all the religions, in practice, know ...' (*Sex, Literature, and Censorship,* ed. Harry T. Moore, New York, 1959, p. 101). It goes without saying that in Breton this lust for blood is but a metaphor of the lust for desire *per se.* To think otherwise would be a reductive reading here. But a literal lust is not excluded for other texts: Michelet, for instance, offers striking examples of obsession with feminine blood, an obsession coupled with creative writing (see Thérèse Moreau, 'Sang sur: Michelet et le sang féminin' *Romantisme,* XXXI, 1981, pp. 151–65.

12   I have developed these views apropos Proust in 'The intertextual unconscious' in Françoise Meltzer (ed.), *The Trial(s) of Psychoanalysis,* Chicago, 1988, pp. 211–26.

# Missing you: intertextuality, transference and the language of love

Psychoanalysis is a listening process in which a narrative is composed from an interaction between at least two persons, who in fact always turn out to be more than two. In this sense psychoanalytic representation is predetermined by the possibility of reception. The act of transference which this involves creates an intertextual space in which the story changes as it is listened to and worked on. As this process continues we come to recognise that this sense of development has existed from the beginning. A search for the narrative's forgotten origin is replaced by a recognition of the active process of constructing the narrative. The heart of the matter is increasingly viewed as essentially, even necessarily missing, as transference highlights not just the missing past event but the language of love dramatised by the analyst and analysand, a desire which revolves around the object *existing as missing*.

It is clear already from such a characterisation of psychoanalysis that an examination of its concrete workings in the analytic session, that is, the central fact of transference, is a useful way in which to think through the various characterisations of intertextuality, all of which make similar claims about the nature of narrative and the supposed origins of a text. In Freud's writings the concept of transference assumes an increasing importance. It is initially viewed as a displacement of unconscious ideas onto the analyst by the patient. In the 'Psychotheraphy of hysteria',[1] this transference onto the physician takes place through a 'false connection', and as a specific object is viewed only as an obstacle to treatment, erected precisely as a resistance. This obstacle has an actual source which may be rediscovered by taking 'the patient back to the moment at which it had originated' (pp. 303–4). Transference is a negative phenomenon, an illusion that melts away with the conclusion of the analysis (p. 304). The dissolution of this object leads to the restoration of a therapeutic relationship in which the analyst's role is that of Virgil to the patient's Dante.

The 1905 'A case of hysteria' (henceforth called *Dora*) sustains this conception of transferential objects as 'merely new impressions' of 'a disease [which] must be combated like all the earlier ones' during the progress of the analysis.[2] Only after this localised phenomenon has been resolved can a patient arrive at 'a sense of conviction of the validity of the connections which have been constructed during the analysis'. But a subtle transformation has already taken place here. On the one hand, these phenomena are still viewed as isolated and individual. But on the other, they are described as 'new editions or facsimiles' (p. 157) of pre-existing factors brought to light as unconscious phantasy in the course of treatment. This gives transference an increasingly symbolical status, which can be used in the therapeutic process. As a result Freud can say that 'transference, which seems ordained to be the greatest enemy to psychoanalysis, becomes its most powerful ally' (p. 159).

With the incorporation of the Oedipus complex, transference now begins to represent the entire analytic situation and define the cure through its eventual dissolution. The conquering of transference resistance obliges the analyst to sustain the demand represented by a symptom. 'Transference-love' (1915) consequently takes up where *Dora* leaves off in stating 'as a fundamental principle that the patient's need and longing should be allowed to persist in her in order that they may serve as forces impelling her to do work and make changes'.[3] Already, then, the analyst is seeking to persevere in a course that moves away from real-life models towards the installation of psychical structuration. This can be seen in Freud's rewriting of a section of *The Interpretation of Dreams* in 1907, 1914 and 1919 in order to stress that '*physical* reality is a particular form of existence not to be confused with *material* reality'.[4]

Beyond the pinpointing of the phenomenon's source, then, lies the recognition of the permanence and indestructability of phantasies. A simplistic notion of calquing or reproduction of old symptoms becomes more subtly textual as the transferential relation is increasingly viewed as semiotic. These editions, facsimiles, impressions and reprints are permanently revised actualisations of symbolic reality. This dynamic construction is described explicitly in the 1914 essay on 'Remembering, repeating and working-through': the patient's compulsion is admitted into the transference 'as a playground' which may be used as an intermediate region in which to create an artificial illness accessible to intervention.[5] Real experience is now treated as a constructed transference-neurosis, a form of discourse in which transitional stages may be enacted. The desire to achieve cathexis henceforth replaces the search for the source of resistance with the idea of a 'phototype' or 'plate': as 'The dynamics of transference' showed in 1912, the drama now unfolds within 'the physical "series" which the patient has already formed'.[6] The ambivalent situation in which transference may be simultaneously negative and positive defers judgement and obliges the entire analytic situation to be 'played out almost exclusively in the phenomena of transference' (p. 108). This *relation* now structures the whole treatment, replaces a pedagogical or curative function with a more complex involvement in a psychical network, and introduces a specular identification into a general economy that will be encountered in every serious analysis. What we now have, to borrow a term from Derrida and Kristeva, is a *hinge* that joins and separates resistance and revelation in an opening and closing movement.

This movement becomes ever more insistent as we come closer to the supposed origins of a 'pathogenic complex', as if to reveal that the source of the symptom is precisely the phantasy of an object, an object that exists as the cause of desire. And indeed, we can trace a genealogy of the object in Freud that seems to confirm both a continual deferment of its source and the recognition of its transferential nature. This runs from the 1905 *Three Essays on the Theory of Sexuality*, where the prototype of source, the mother's breast, provokes a search for the lost object in the form of the compulsive repetition of mistakes; through the 1915 'Instincts and their vicissitudes', where the object becomes an instinctual (sexual) object only when lost and consequently undetermined; through the 1925 'Negation' with its recognition of the link between desire, negation and truth, and the subsequent *hallucinatory* nature of the desired object; to the very rock of castration in the 1937 'Analysis terminable and interminable'.

This move from transference as localised phenomena to transference as a general economy revolving around a lost object or source of desire provides a useful comparison with the notion of

intertextuality. Such a comparison would, of course, be self-contra-
dictory were psychoanalysis envisaged here as a cathartic method for
the unscrambling of intertextual effects.[7] Instead, my description of
transference has stressed how analysts must acknowledge the dissolution of their own knowledge in order to resist and reveal the
discourse's intention. The notion of text as transference can therefore be used in a truly intertextual way in order to think through both
the relationship between book and reader (where reader may include
author) and the work's situation within an intertext.

It is clear that such a comparison can be illuminating. Freud
himself equated transference and textual phenomena in *Dora*. The
transferential phenomena we have noted (the notions of prototype
and psychical series, the deferment caused by simultaneous resistance
and revelation, the increasing postponement of the very source of the
external object from which everything springs) could easily be
described in terms of Barthes's view of intertextuality. In both transference and intertextuality, 'there is no first reading, even if the text is
concerned to give us that illusion by several operations of suspense'[8]
since any text is composed from a topos of codes, each of which 'is a
perspective of quotations, a mirage of structures' and consequently a
fragment of something already read (p. 20). The playful nature of
this rereading process which has displaced a simple consumption of
the text as unambivalent source of information, and the move to a
stress on the reader's performance, rather than acquired knowledge,
which this entails, uncannily echo both Freud's description of transference as the playground of repetition and his assertion that it is 'the
one thing the presence of which has to be detected without assis-
tance' (*Dora*, p. 58).

In both transference and intertextuality, then, hermeneutic codes
are built on lost origins, involving language as a general network
(*langue*) and any particular instance of it (*parole*) in a relation of
infinite regression. This regression is 'controlled' or 'handled' only
by the recognition of how the narrator is forced to conceptualise
from the point of the other. The dynamics of transference therefore
resemble intertextual theories which locate meaning not in the
author or reader but in the intermediate region of reading. To take
one example, Peter Brooks has productively used the concept of
transference to examine 'the dialogic struggle and collaboration' of
reader and text 'in the activation of textual possibilities in the process
of reading', a process that properly makes the reader analysand as

well as analyst.[9] The objection subsequently made by Terence Cave that this evocation of the dynamics of transference is merely metaphorical moreover leads Brooks to Freud's late 'Constructions in analysis' of 1937 in order to show how the 'delusional system' of the analysand is *formally* equivalent to the analyst's constructions. Both are part of a larger narrative intertext where the analyst's position is constructed by his or her recognition of the erotics of form and the psychic investments of rhetoric. From this perspective, such a recognition is similar to Cave's description of *anagnorisis*, or the poetical concept of recognition, as 'the perception of an ineradicable – but also seductive – asymmetry between the recogniser and the recognised'.[10] A model of intertextual transference therefore appears to satisfy both Brooks's view of narrative transmission and Cave's reading of 'circuits of recognition'.

Rather than press the question here of the scientificity of psychoanalysis, the point of dissension between Brooks and Cave, what appears more urgent is to recognise the contradiction that has now become apparent at the heart of many theories of intertextuality which are content to regard the vicissitudes of textuality as the object of their analysis. The way in which certain critics do not succeed in 'mastering the transference in good time' (*Dora*, p. 160) leads to their retention of a metalanguage or of an unproblematically personal sense of the performative in order to determine the text's degree of explicitness in its intertextual germination. There is thus no conception of the other in their use of a focal text that keeps control over the meaning. Once the semantic possibilities of the text are gauged against a second-degree immobile architext in this way, intertextuality is reduced to a montage whose implications are realised by a self-confirming critical recuperation. Such theories refuse to recognise their own involvement in the transference: instead they locate and annotate an intertextual conjuncture which condenses disparate material into an accomplished re-presentation.[11] This transumption of metonymy by metaphor is something to which I shall return at the end of this essay.

The use of psychoanalysis as a critical tool in such an operation can merely intensify the contradiction through a misconception of transference. Wolfgang Iser, for example, is right to criticise both Norman Holland's *The Dynamics of Literary Response* and Simon Lesser's *Fiction and the Unconscious* for the way in which they view literature as a psychomachia and consequently exalt certain

psychoanalytic concepts. But an ignorance of the dynamics of transference means Iser repeats the gesture by having recourse to a specular intersubjectivity in order to assert a consensus on the level of plot,
and to a narcissistic aggressivity in order to dictate the closing of a
gestalt:

> On the level of plot, then, there is a high degree of intersubjective consensus,
> but on the level of significance selective decisions have to be taken which are
> subjective not because they are arbitrary, but because a gestalt can only be
> closed if one possibility is selected and the rest is excluded. The selection will
> depend on the reader's individual disposition and experience, but the inter-
> dependence of the two types of gestalten (plot-level and significance)
> remains an intersubjectively valid structure.[12]

The resolution of tensions between signs, here seen as necessary to
the successful closing of a gestalt, is dependent on a principle of
coherence in which the reader closes a circuit of illusion by meeting
and eliminating obstacles to a coherent meaning. 'Intersubjective
accessibility' here translates into psychoanalytic terms as wishing to
talk Dora out of her belief and orchestrate 'a triumph of the girl's
affection . . . over all her internal difficulties' (*Dora*, pp. 150–1). The
illusion of an intersubjectively valid structure resolves tensions
between signs in a unilateral act of aggression that repudiates one's
involvement in intertextuality. This can be seen in Freud's postscript
to *Dora*. Freud wishes to conclude: 'In the meantime the girl has
married, and indeed – unless all the signs mislead me – she has
married the young man who came into her associations at the
beginning of the analysis of the second dream'. The significance of
this second dream should be that Dora has been 'reclaimed once
more by the realities of life'. But later Freud is forced to add: 'This, as
I afterwards learnt, was a mistaken notion' (p. 164).

The resolution of intertextual tension by individual disposition is
apparent in two major theorists: Harold Bloom and Michael Riffaterre. This has been explicated clearly by Jonathan Culler in *The
Pursuit of Signs*[13] but can be restated here in terms of our particular
preoccupation. In Bloom, a narrow view of transference as Oedipus
complex reduces poetic crisis to a personal and familial romance.
Thus, in *The Anxiety of Influence* individual authors struggle to
attain maturity by swerving away from their precursors (*clinamen*),
completing them (*tessera*), breaking with them (*kenosis*), mythifying
them (*daemonization*), purging all links (*askesis*) or assuming their
place (*apophrades*).[14] By shifting back from text to author in this

way, Bloom views intertextuality as the vigorous development of an ego seeking to recover a primary narcissism from which it is withheld by its immediate precursor. He concentrates not on the structuration of this development but precisely on the imaginary identifications of the drama. Resolution is here brought about by the ego's victory, a move which reduces the transferential relation to 'a psychic battlefield',[15] the increasingly general economy of the pathogenic complex to the struggle with a single precursor, the metonymies which produce an endless narrative network of analysis to the Kabbalistic troping of an object of satisfaction. Bloom's genetic chain, in which the tensions of intertextual production are resolved by strong personal 'misreadings' of particular precursors and origins inevitably reduces the 'dialogue struggle' to the armwrestling of strong poets. So when Bloom describes how Freud made 'the solitary crossing from a realm where effect is always traced to a cause, to a mode of discourse which asked instead the economic and agonistic questions of comparison',[16] this agon is in fact seen as the conscious scepticism of an old man who has triumphed in his strong misreadings of anterior texts and broken through into a peculiar form of sublime self-revision. Bloom's relation to Freud here appears to be precisely that of the complementarity of desire.

The same identification of origins turns Riffaterre's theories of intertextuality into a practice that relies on 'the reader's praxis of the transformation' undergone by a particular work.[17] This creates a peculiar contradiction. On the one hand, Riffaterre propounds the theory that 'intertextuality is not a felicitous surplus, the privilege of a good memory or a classical education [but is] the perception that our reading of the text cannot be complete or satisfactory without going through the intertext'.[18] On the other hand, the personalising note at the end of this quotation indicates a homologising practice: 'the text *does not signify* unless as a function of a complementarity or contradictory intertextual homologue' (pp. 143–4, my emphasis). The critic's role is dominated by the rationalising force of interpretation such that the examination of a particular signifying structure becomes the triumphalist decipherment of a previously baffling puzzle. The belief that 'intertextuality cannot avoid being hermeneutic' (p. 160) translates in practice into a reading that is more or less held to be self-evidently superior ('The real agent of the poem's efficacy, it seems to me, and one that no accident of the reading process can alter, is the word "glazed" ' (p. 145)) or into a systematisation of stereotypes, polarities, connectors in order to resolve tensions by asserting the complementarity of sonnet and sociolect: 'The sonnet is powerful not because it substitutes an unexpected code for the one expected in the description of a city but because it substitutes a powerful structure for its negative homologue. Everything is so simple, so beautifully mechanical, so close to automatic writing that narrative motivation would actually weaken the effect' (p. 154). Transference here takes place not between text and reader but between the origins of the poem and Riffaterre – and the origins of the poem's construction are used to discover coherence and resolve contradiction. Riffaterre's theories are more subtle than Bloom's, for rather than having recourse to a mysterious affectivity they concentrate on the reconstruction of meaning through an examination of the dialectical movement in which the particular work occurs. But where transference would recognise how such a movement normally translates an *error* on the part of the analyst, Riffaterre, rather than take his bearings from the meaningfulness of this error, imposes the limits of coherence on the intertext by falling back into a genetical interpretation of the text's workings and worth. Thus the resolution of what Riffaterre terms the *écoute flottante* still boils down to 'the reader's individual reactions', a goal pursued through restricting oneself to a text-dictated segmentation, where one spots anomalies and eradicates ungrammaticalities.[19] Intertextuality is here a psychoanalytic 'mimesis of repression' where we may recognise two different units as being variants of the same structure by retaining in our minds the self-confirming principle of relevancy or pertinence. My unease at the circular form of this interpretation is confirmed by the all too relevant examples which Riffaterre takes from Proust: fantasies of fellatio.

The work of Julia Kristeva, on the other hand, stands in opposition to the attenuation of crisis by a timeless hypogram. Her theory of signification 'refuses to identify with the recumbent body subjected to transference onto the analyser' – as I would argue the work of Bloom and Riffaterre ultimately agrees to do.[20] Instead her early semiotic work unequivocally centres on the truth revealed in the transference relation, namely an impossibility of coincidence that is the very condition of a signifying process. Kristeva's definition of intertextuality, or transposition, in *Revolution in Poetic Language* corresponds perfectly to a transference that is effected not between persons but between subject positions within the intertext of the unconscious, or 'instinctual intermediary common to the two systems' (p. 60). Her description of the signifying field is therefore a perfect comment on a true transference between analyst and analysand: 'Its "place" of enunciation and its denoted "object" are never single, complete, and identical to themselves, but always plural, shattered, capable of being tabulated' (p. 60). Only this approach permits the symbolic field within which transference is situated to come into play through language. (Concentrating as we are on the formal relation of transference rather than the 'ideational content' of the subject of the unconscious, the contradiction which Kristeva sees between the subject of psychoanalysis and the poetic subject does not here obtain.)

This linguistic equation of transference and transposition in Kristeva now impels us to take a closer look at certain specifically non-linguistic theories of transference, particularly in light of the way in which Riffaterre can be said to close his gestalt in 'The intertextual unconscious' by 'the closing of the circle of orality'. This corresponds to the psychoanalytic concept of identification. In this notion the subject orally incorporates the lost object by regressing to an oral stage object-relationship. The narcissism which this entails elucidates the constructions of both Bloom and Riffaterre since, in 'On narcissism: an introduction', 'Freud introduces the dialectic which links the narcissistic object-choice (where the object is chosen on the model of the subject's own self) with identification (where the subject, or one or other of his psychical agencies, is constituted on the model of earlier objects, such as the parents or people around him)'.[21] The bodily ingestion contained in the intertextuality of Riffaterre and Bloom points to an intersubjective introjection that forms the basis for several psychoanalytic theories of transference, particularly in the case of Sandor Ferenczi and Michael Balint. The term 'introjection', first used by Ferenczi in 'Introjection and transference' (1909) designates a 'passion for the transference' that results in the transposition of objects and their inherent qualities into the ego. Language is viewed in the context only of 'stimulus-words'.[22] Instead, since Ferenczi views introjection as synonymous with transference to the physician (p. 53), his approach to the transferential cure is based on 'sympathy' (p. 57). Balint's *Primary Love and Psycho-Analytic Technique* views transference as the transference of emotions onto the well-polished lifeless mirror of the analyst. As an inanimate object, the latter marks the limits of a dialectical relation which takes place in what Balint calls a two body psychology. This primary love, whose prototype is the mother-child relation, is a closed circuit of satisfaction, as Balint unwittingly demonstrates in 'On transference and counter-transference', when he discusses 'the problem of the cushion':

(a) the cushion remains the same for every patient, but a piece of tissue paper is spread over it, which is thrown away at the end of the hour; (b) the cushion remains, but every patient is given a special cover, distinguishable from the others by its shade or design, and for each hour the cushion is put into the appropriate cover; (c) each patient has his own cushion and must use only his; (d) there is only one cushion or only two or three of them for all the patients and it is left to them to use them as they like, etc.[23]

Our examination of intertextuality shows how 'the problem of the cushion' is another example of the 'beautifully mechanical' systematisation of a mere personal past designed to lead to integration and synthesis through a strengthening of the ego. The intersubjective relation becomes an inter-objectal one, grounded in the 'naturalist propaedeutics'[24] of two bodies coming together. Balint's cushion has parallels with Riffaterre's misreading of Proust, for in Marcel's jealous imagination we can see how the ideal of an inanimate object precisely lends support to a 'perverse desire sustained by the annihilation either of the desire of the other, or of the desire of the subject'.[25]

The passion for the transference is in fact an imaginary love, one that cannot lead to true symbolisation. This is borne out by Freud's reference to love in 'On narcissism: an introduction'.[26] The closed world of need satisfaction which Freud outlines precisely involves a bodily rather than linguistic relation. In narcissistic love (*Verliebtheit*) one loves what one is, was, would like to be, or once contained. But anaclitic love (*Anlehnung*) is no less imaginary, since it is based on a reversal of identification in which one loves the woman who feeds and the man who protects. The love of parents is therefore merely 'a revival and reproduction of their own narcissism' which has been transformed into object-love by the necessity of sublimating the self-directed aims of the ideal ego outwards onto an ego ideal that takes account of society. To be content with this leads to 'a subduction of the symbolic'[27] which we in turn naturally find seductive (as in Culler's subtly ambiguous descriptions of Riffaterre as 'engaging' and Bloom as 'daring' and 'powerful' (*The Pursuit of Signs*, pp. 98, 108, 109); or Lacan's view of Balint as 'very interesting

. . . extremely pleasurable . . . often bold' (*The Seminar of Jacques Lacan*, p. 204)). Unless we operate within a form of transference, or intertext, that is beyond the imaginary and can lead to the full recognition of the other, the analysis sees only the mirage of *Verliebtheit*, the object of a narcissistic investment. Recognition must take place on the plane of speech, therefore, for it is here that love participates in the symbolic register. True intersubjectivity is given in the manipulation of the symbol in analysis such that imaginary crystallisations may play a role in the transference.

We may therefore agree with Kristeva that 'analytic speech is a discourse of love'.[28] But we must analyse this transference–love at the level at which the representation of affects takes place – in the founding medium of speech. That is to say, in order to avoid reducing intertextuality or transference to identification, we must continue to concentrate on the structure that articulates the narcissistic relation. Through a positive passivity, we refrain from forcing identifications with the intertext, and so allow the signifiers of the subject's drama to emerge continually. By sustaining demand in this way, true otherness is recognised in the transferential movement of the object of fantasy, what Lacan terms the *objet a*. We can then move beyond an intersubjective relationship by viewing the intertextual unconscious as 'the sum of the effects of speech on a subject'[29] and by recognising that the cause of this unconscious, in both senses, is a lost object. This lack is the conflictual motor for a real intertextual or transferential process. Unless we are induced into the false termination of love, then, the very centre of intertextual and transferential repetition is that which is continually *missed*.

Kristeva perhaps falls into a mystical joy when she characterises this position as 'a simple listening, lovingly absent-minded',[30] for the wish to be loved makes nothing less simple. But she is right to finish *Tales of Love* with the words: 'A permanent crisis' (p. 383). In the permanent crisis of continuous utterance, the model or source (*Vorbild*) in transference or intertextuality becomes the prototype (*Vorbild*) or first event of an endless chain. In other words, the generalised intertextuality which I am suggesting here is already moving us from the metaphorical notion of transference as the eventual dissolution of a fantasmagoria into a consideration of its metonymic dimension, where its effectiveness lies 'in the *continuity* of its rhythm with a *vaster form of discourse*, that which we never stop having with ourselves and which is held with us'.[31] Freud continued to view the ego as both metaphor and metonymy, seeing it as both a surface and the projection of a surface.[32] And we cannot in turn transcend *this* metaphor, for we would fall into the dream of a pure scientific language.[33] Instead, metaphor and metonymy are the double axes of repetition and derivation that mark the origin and prototype of being: 'Beyond any derivations of vocabulary, beyond even a derivation of new concepts, it is the derivation of certain psychical "beings", the formation of psychical "entities" which we deal with in psychoanalytic practice that can be illuminated through reference to these two fundamental axes' (p. 138). It is therefore by concentrating on the structuring phenomenon of language, where both the semiotic and symbolic are revealed, that we can observe a passion for the transference which enables us to think of intertextuality not as the result of an intersubjective introjection, but as revolving around the *objet a* as cause of desire.

In this way psychoanalysis and intertextuality would finally read themselves not simply as hermeneutic enterprises, but as the time of a larger intertextual narrative which from the beginning is a revised edition, carried over and derived from the pure book of origins.

## Notes

Works by Freud are referred to throughout by their English title in *The Standard Edition of the Complete Psychological Works of Sigmund Freud* (24 Vols), London, 1953–73, hereinafter abbreviated *SE*.

1   'The psychotherapy of hysteria' in *Studies on Hysteria, SE*, II, p. 302.

2   'Fragment of an analysis of a case of hysteria', *SE*, VII, p. 116.

3   'Transference-love', *SE*, XII, p. 165.

4   *The Interpretation of Dreams, SE*, IV–V, p. 620.

5   'Remembering, repeating and working-through (further recommendations on the technique of psycho-analysis, II)', *SE*, XII, pp. 145–56.

6   'The dynamics of transference', *SE*, XII, p. 100.

7   I have echoed many of my criticisms of non-reflective theories of intertextuality in this essay in 'Double indemnity: the ends of citation in Edmond Jabès', *Romance Studies*, XII, 1988, pp. 76–85.

8   Barthes, *S/Z*, New York, 1974, p. 16.

9   'The idea of a psychoanalytic literary criticism', in *Discourse in Psychoanalysis and Literature*, ed. Shlomith Rimmon-Kenen, London and New York, 1987, p. 14.

10   *Recognition*, Oxford, 1988, p. 270.

11   See Laurent Jenny: 'La stratégie de la forme', *Poétique*, XXVII, 1976, pp. 256–81, translated in *French Literary Theory Today*, ed. Tzvetan Todorov, Cambridge, 1982, pp. 34–63; 'Poétique et représentation', *Poétique*, 1984, pp. 171–95.

12   Iser, *The Act of Reading: A Theory of Aesthetic Response*, London and Henley, 1978, pp. 123–4.

13   *The Pursuit of Signs*, London and Henley, 1981, chs. IV and V.

14   *The Anxiety of Influence: A Theory of Poetry*, Oxford, 1973, p. 68.

15   Bloom, *Poetry and Repression*, New Haven, 1976, p. 3.

16   *Agon: Towards a Theory of Revisionism*, Oxford, 1982, p. 117.

17   Riffaterre, *Semiotics of Poetry*, Bloomington, 1978, p. 12.

18   'Intertextual representation: on mimesis as interpretive discourse', *Critical Inquiry*, XI, 1984, p. 143.

19   Riffaterre, 'The intertextual unconscious', *Critical Inquiry*, XIII, 1987, pp. 371–2.

20   Kristeva, *Revolution in Poetic Language*, New York, 1984, p. 15.

21   Jean Laplanche and Jean-Baptiste Pontalis, *The Language of Psychoanalysis*, London, 1982, p. 206.

22   Ferenczi, 'Introjection and transference' in *First Contributions to Psycho-Analysis*, London, 1952, p. 51.

23   Balint, 'Transference and counter-transference' in *Primary Love and Psycho-Analytic Technique*, London, 1952, p. 214.

24   Jacques Lacan, 'Intervention on transference' in *Feminine Sexuality*, ed. Juliet Mitchell and Jacqueline Rose, London, 1982, p. 64.

25   *The Seminar of Jacques Lacan: Book I, Freud's Papers on Technique, 1953–1954*, ed. Jacques-Alain Miller, Cambridge, 1988, p. 222.

26   'On narcissism: an introduction', *SE*, XIV, pp. 67–102. See also chs. VII and VIII of *Group Psychology and the Analysis of the Ego*, *SE*, XVIII, pp. 65–143.

27   *The Seminar of Jacques Lacan*, p. 142.

28   *In the Beginning Was Love: Psychoanalysis and Faith*, New York, 1987, p. 4.

29   Lacan, *The Four Fundamental Concepts of Psycho-Analysis*, Harmondsworth, 1979, p. 126.

30   Kristeva, *Tales of Love*, New York, 1987, p. 382.

31   Jean Laplanche, *Life and Death in Psychoanalysis,* Baltimore and London, 1976, p. 138.

32   *The Ego and the Id*, *SE*, XIX.

33   Laplanche, *Life and Death in Psychoanalysis*, p. 136.

# Roland Barthes: an intertextual figure

In 1974 Barthes published his 'first text', a schoolboy pastiche of the Socratic dialogue in which Crito visits Socrates on his last day in prison, and fails to persuade him to save his life by allowing his friends to help him escape. In Barthes's version ('A footnote to the *Crito*') Socrates' reason and virtue collapse in the face of the sensual temptations represented by a plate of juicy figs. Socrates gives in to his friends, leaving Plato to arrange matters with history. Barthes accompanies his text with a preface, in which he explains that it was modelled on a book of pastiches (*Footnotes to . . .*) in which Jules Lemaître had rewritten the endings of famous classical works. Thus Barthes saw himself as producing a second degree pastiche: his own pastiche of a Lemaître pastiche of the *Crito,* a text he had just studied all year at school. With familiar interpretative skill Barthes reads his own juvenile creation intertextually, recognising that he had staged all the languages present in his head at the time: some Gide and Flaubert, but above all 'the babble of school lessons', imbued with the style of 'Greek translation' and 'French composition', yet totally silent on one whole area of Greek culture – 'you had to get out of the Greek class to realise that Greece might also have something to do with sexuality'.[1] With everything accounted for, and all passing discourses historically placed, only one detail remains to be explained.

That leaves the figs. There were figs in the family garden at Bayonne; they were small and purple, and always underripe or overripe; my distaste was aroused in turn by either their milk or their rottenness and it was not a fruit that I liked (though I was later to discover another side to it in Morocco, and recently, again, at the Voltaire restaurant where figs are served up in large dishes of cream). (p. 4)

*Is this a joke?*

Whatever, asks Barthes with wilful naïvety, made him make of the *fig* (which he didn't even like) a beguiling, an immoral, a philosophical fruit? The first answer, is simple and disappointing: the figs too are an intertextual, *literary* product ('a literary, biblical, Arcadian fruit'). But this is a mere rhetorical feint, designed to set off the final throwaway line: 'Unless, perhaps, lurking behind the fig, lies *le Sexe* ['Sex/the Sexual Organs'], *Fica?*'. By unmasking the figs as a symbol of sexuality Barthes's 1974 preface does two things: it invites a particular reading of the 1933 text, but it also sets up intertextual ripples in the rest of his writing. From figs to sex – it is a short step from intertextuality to intersexuality.

Barthes claims to have first discovered figs in the family garden at Bayonne, the very garden later identified in *Roland Barthes by Roland Barthes* as the locus of childhood sexuality.[2] He was apparently converted to their merits in Morocco, a locus of homosexuality in his work.[3] Not only are the figs twice described in Barthes's pastiche in a way that indeed connotes the male sexual organs, but Barthes departs from historical fact to include 'the handsome Alcibiades' (p. 5) in the band of friends, using him as the chief vehicle of figgish temptation: 'Above all, Alcibiades' speech had tempted him cruelly' (p. 6). If this part of Barthes's pastiche is read against the famous Alcibiades episode in the *Symposium,* it becomes likely that submission to Alcibiades – the plate of figs or the seaside idyll (with fig tree) conjured up in his speech – might have something to do with an option for homosexuality. In the *Symposium* Alcibiades arrives drunk at the dinner party, and recounts his former rejection by Socrates, whereby the latter had resisted a sustained campaign of amorous advances (culminating in a night in each other's arms), despite appearing to reciprocate Alcibiades' desire.[4] Now the *Symposium* is an important intertext in Barthes's *A Lover's Discourse,* little commented upon by critics despite many explicit textual and marginal allusions. It is obviously interesting as a homosexual intertext, even if in general Barthes resists distinguishing between heterosexual and homosexual love in this work. Barthes refers specifically to the Platonic theme of sublimation of a homosexual desire which is nevertheless necessary as its starting point: 'Two powerful myths have persuaded us that love could, *should* be sublimated in aesthetic creation: the Socratic myth (loving serves to "engender a host of magnificent discourses") and the romantic myth (I could produce an immortal work by writing of my passion)'.[5] If the relationship between desire and 'aesthetic creation' in Barthes's writing is hardly one of expression, it is certainly not one of sublimation. To begin to sort out what it might be, I should like to look at another reference to Alcibiades, written into the ending of Barthes's own paper at the 1977 Cerisy colloquium on his work.

Here Barthes brilliantly links the rejection of Alcibiades to the aggression of language. Discussing the problem of his own image and of the imposition of images on others (the site of a typical Barthesian power struggle), he introduces the Greek term *Mache* to designate both combat in general and more specifically the linguistic trapping of the other through an enforced logical contradiction. He then introduces *Acolouthia* as an opposite term meaning 'the transcendence of contradiction (which I interpret as the opening of the trap)'.[6] In a typical homage to the 'friends' he often celebrates as necessary to his way of working and thinking, Barthes calls up a second meaning of *Acolouthia* as:

> the retinue of friends who accompany me, guide me, in whose hands I place myself. [. . .] In that *colour* of intellectual work (or of writing), there is something Socratic: Socrates employed the discourse of the Idea, but the step-by-step *method* of his discourse was erotic; in order to speak, he required the guarantee of inspired love, the assent of a beloved whose replies marked the progression of reasoning. Socrates knew *Acolouthia*; but (and this I resist) he maintained in it the trap of contradictions, the arrogance of truth (so it is no surprise that he ultimately 'sublimated' – rejected Alcibiades). (pp. 357–8)

Socrates' dialectical method is an amorous one but it scores points. Barthes wants to accept in the method 'the guarantee of inspired love', but he doesn't want to gain or maintain the upper hand – a lack of aggression which he equates with *not* rejecting Alcibiades. And when one of the audience at Cerisy asks Barthes: 'what might Socrates produce, if we imagine a Socrates who lived after Freud, who knew a bit about psychoanalysis, and who kept Alcibiades?', Barthes replies in his own name and about his own work.[7]

Pointers to the Socratic intertext are therefore launched at least three times by Barthes in the mid 1970s, and twice rather specifically in the context of a Barthes surrounded by his much younger disciples-cum-friends.[8] If there are obvious links between Barthes and Socrates as famous teachers and supposed corrupters of the young (and ironic parallels such as the trauma of their deaths for an academic    generation    both    intellectually    and    emotionally dependent), I wish to extract the rewriting of the rejection of Alcibiades as the most interesting feature of the 1933 pastiche, and to suggest that it is this, rather than some vague option for hedonism, that Barthes himself intended to underline in 1974.

This is precisely the period when Barthes is openly signalling his homosexuality to the public, and in 1975 he does it through the more obvious method of a sudden declaration of allegiance to Gide, both in *Roland Barthes,* and through the relaunching of another early text, his 1942 essay on Gide. In the well-known passage of the autobiography where Barthes (tottering quite deliberately on the brink of stupidity) identifies Gide as his *Abgrund* and *Ursuppe,* it is clear that the identification is less with a slippery value system than with the figure of Gide himself as meeting point of writing and homosexuality:

Can one – or at least could one formerly – take up writing without taking oneself for someone else? The history of figures should be substituted for the history of sources [. . .] I begin to produce by reproducing the person I should like to be. This first wish [*voeu*] (I desire and I pledge myself [*me voue*]) establishes a secret system of fantasies which persist from age to age, often independently of the writings of the desired author. [. . .] a diagonal cross-breed of Alsace and Gascony, as Gide was of Normandy and Languedoc, Protestant, having a taste for 'letters' and fond of playing the piano, not to mention the rest – how could he have failed to recognize himself, to desire himself in this writer? (p. 99)

One might assume that 'not to mention the rest' can only refer to Gide's homosexuality and is the real point of this list of otherwise mundane biographical coincidences. It seems a more likely catalyst of desire in the adolescent Barthes than the location of Alsace and Gascony relative to Normandy and the Languedoc. It is clearly the homosexual '(Gide)' who is lined up opposite '(desire to write)' in Barthes's table of 'Phrases' (p. 145). The point is spelled out less obliquely in the 1942 essay: 'Many entries in the *Journal* will doubtless irritate those who have some prejudice, secret or other-wise, against Gide. These same entries will delight those who have some reason, secret or otherwise, to believe themselves like Gide. This is true of any personality who *compromises themself.*'[9] As the young Barthes most appropriately says of Gide: 'it is never without a reason that Gide writes a critical work. His preface to selections from Montaigne, indeed his very choice of texts, tells us as much about Gide as about Montaigne' (p. 5).

When Barthes declared in *The Pleasure of the Text* that Proust's work represented for him the ultimate intertext ('*the* reference work, the general *mathesis,* the *mandala* of the entire literary cosmogony'), it might have seemed that Proust's homosexuality was an incidental feature.[10] Barthes claims in an interview that Proust is 'a complete world-reading system', and that 'there is no incident in our daily lives, no encounter, no trait, no situation which doesn't have its reference in Proust'. Nevertheless, Proust represents a fairly arbitrary personal system for engaging with the world: 'dependent on very specific givens (social, psychological, philosophical, neurotic) [. . .] which I certainly don't keep constantly in mind: I'm not "a Proust specialist" '.[11] This could be read as an invitation to explore the personal motivation for Barthes's investment in Proust, but on the surface that investment seems to have more to do with the Proustian narrator's exemplary status as a *future writer* than with the nature of the author's sexuality. Proust first played an important intertextual role in Barthes's work in the 1963 preface to *Critical Essays,* where Barthes somewhat tortuously struggles to establish the literary critic as someone who will one day become a writer (though insists also on introducing affect and desire into what the critic-cum-writer will write).[12] By 1975 he ventures to label a photo of himself as a toddler with the legend: 'Contemporaries? I was beginning to walk. Proust was still alive, and was finishing *A la recherche du temps perdu*' (*RB,* p. 23). The invasive presence of Proust culminates in a near-total identification with both author and work in the 1978 lecture '*Longtemps je me suis couché de bonne heure . . .*', in the 1979 text 'La lumière du sud-ouest', and in the 1980 essay on photography, *Camera lucida.*[13] To explore in detail the place of Proust in Barthes's work, and above all to situate him relative to an emerging ethic of homosexuality, is too large a task for this essay. However, I should like to focus briefly on a short 1971 essay: 'A research idea'.

The 'idea' behind this dense and suggestive essay is what Barthes identifies as a very frequent narrative structure in *A la recherche* – the reversal of a state of affairs into its complete opposite: 'these notations are so frequent, they are applied so consistently to such different objects, situations, and languages, that we may identify in them a form of discourse whose very obsessiveness is enigmatic' (*RL,* p. 272). Barthes decides that, provisionally at least, he will call this obsessive form *inversion*; as the essay unfolds it is interchangably labelled *inversion* and *renversement* ('reversal/turning upside-down'). Now for the first half of the text this formal figure doesn't appear to have anything to do with sexual inversion as a theme, though the example through which Barthes gets the essay going is the morally dubious princesse Sherbatoff, whom the narrator takes for a brothel keeper, but who turns out to be a woman of the highest rank and pearl of the Verdurin salon. The 'surprise' engendered by inversion also turns out to be positively orgasmic, the high point of a Proustian erotics of discourse: 'veritable jubilation, so complete, so pure, so triumphant (as is proved by the success of its expression), that this mode of inversion can only derive from an erotics (of discourse), as if the inscription of *renversement* was the very moment of orgasm of Proust's writing' (p. 273). Two-thirds of the way through Barthes's essay he suddenly introduces sexual inversion as exemplary, 'but not necessarily primary'. Yet the famous hornet scene, in which the narrator discovers the 'Woman' in the Baron de Charlus, 'is theoretically equivalent to any reading of the play of opposites', and from this point on 'in the whole work, homosexuality develops what we might call its enantiology (or discourse of *renversement*)'. The entire movement of the plot represents the gradual overturning of a heterosexual world into a homosexual one: 'there is a pandemia of inversion, of *renversement*' (p. 274). Barthes claims that the figure of *renversement* is not a movement from illusion to truth, but a metaphorical process which is infinitely circular. As with the surprise convergence of Proust's 'two ways': 'to speak of these opposites is finally to join them in the very unity of the text, of the journey of writing' (p. 275). Can homosexuality then be inverted back into heterosexuality? The question seems to me a crucial one. On the one hand the surprise revelation of homosexuality is exemplary and subsumes all the other examples; on the other it is superfluous because what is described is already an erotic structure. Is the erotic structure either way a homoerotic one? Is Barthes's own erotics of writing always a homosexual one?

In the case of Barthes's reading of this Proustian figure of *inversion*, I would suggest that his very choice of vocabulary blocks the movement back to heterosexuality. A passage from Renaud Camus's *Notes achriennes* offers possible support. Camus, who has just rejected the notion of a specific homosexual writing (*écriture homosexuelle*), is referring to his very Barthesian set of fragments, *Buena Vista Park*:

That, by a *formal* extension, homosexuality might inspire writing processes such as *inversion* – the anagram or, more perfectly, the palindrome. As for its *semantic* extension, a small book of short fragments published by myself [. . .] could well have been called *Le retournement*; a figure to which a centuries-old joke (in dubious taste) gives, as we know, a homosexual connotation.[14]

The figure of *retournement* is central to Barthes's preface to Pierre Loti's *Aziyadé* (published in 1971, the same year as 'A research idea'). Barthes typically begins by interrogating the wonderful title for its intertextual resonances, manages to find a list of seven of them, but basically detects a Proustian *disappointment* in the gap between a splendid signifier and a derisory signified: 'the preconception of dealing with a quaint, insipid and conventionally sentimental novel'.[15] One may question Barthes's good faith in fostering the sad image of an outdated novel in the first place, since Barthes later draws from this very outdatedness the *déshérence* ('escheat') which is prized (both in *Aziyadé* and elsewhere), for its *phantasmatic* qualities.[16] However, the feigned disappointment is necessary to his strategic *retournement*:

> However, from another region of literature, someone gets to their feet to tell us that we should always turn [*retourner*] the disappointment of the proper name back against itself, and that we should make of this turning back the itinerary of an apprenticeship: the Proustian narrator, starting out from the phonetic glory of the Guermantes, finds the world of the duchess to be quite other than what the orange slendour of the Name had led him to expect, and it's by retracing the disappointment of his narrator that Proust is able to write his work. Perhaps we too might learn to make the name of Aziyadé disappointing in the right way and, having slipped from the precious name to the sad image of an outdated novel, we might make our way back towards the idea of a *text*: a fragment of infinite language which doesn't recount anything but which is crossed by 'something unprecedented and murky'. (pp. 170–1)

The phrase 'something unprecedented and murky', presented here as an integral feature of *text*, is taken from the scene in *Aziyadé* which first introduces homosexuality into the plot. Barthes's preface inverts an initial sense of disappointment into an opposite pleasure, but does so precisely by 'discovering' sexual inversion as the novel's transgressive theme. Between Barthes, Proust, Loti and the strategy of *retournement*, homosexuality emerges yet again as an overdetermined signified.

As the preface unfolds Barthes settles into a reading of *Aziyadé* which is perfectly convincing and which could well have been introduced from the outset. At the level of plot, transgression is superficially displaced to an unhappy passion for a forbidden woman. However, this 'odyssey of an expatriate soul' is equally 'the muted and allusive tale of an oriental-style debauchery' (pp. 186–7) – a decentred tale of homosexual desire drifting free through a night-time city. It is best characterised by Barthes's highlighting of the phrase 'pale debauchery': 'that of daybreak, as a whole night of erotic meandering draws to a close [. . .] Istanbul and Salonica (their poetic descriptions) take the place of encounters which are hypocritically declared irksome, of the stubborn pursuit [*la drague*] of young Asian boys; the harem stands in for the prohibition on homosexuality (p. 178). Thus it is not so much the woman Aziyadé, but Istanbul and its pale debauchery, that Loti will finally choose against his country, his family, and his career. If the fictional hero of the novel dies as a result of the death of Aziyadé, Loti the author takes over from him: 'having disposed of the lieutenant in a suitably noble manner, the author will go on describing cities of Japan, Persia and Morocco, that's to say he will indicate and stake out (by emblematic discourses) the space of his desire' (p. 179).

It is tempting to substitute Barthes for Loti in these elaborations of desire adrift in the city. Such substitution may be dubiously voyeuristic in the Morocco or Paris of the posthumously published *Incidents* and *Soirées de Paris* (Paris Evenings),[17] but is in accordance with Barthes's own deliberate pointers to the Tokyo of *Empire of Signs*: 'A happy sexuality found its naturally corresponding discourse in the continuous, effusive, jubilant happiness of the writing: *in what they write, everyone champions their sexuality*' (*RB*, p. 156). In an interview he speaks of his unusual behaviour and energies, of his happiness in distant *quartiers* at four in the morning: 'nocturnal wanderings, in a huge city, the largest in the world, a city completely unfamiliar to me, and I don't speak a word of Japanese' (*GV*, p. 230). It is true that Barthes displaces his desire on to the city itself – its 'incidents', its life-style, and the general texture of what he calls the *romanesque* ('novelistic'): 'these infinitesimal adventures (of which the accumulation, in the course of a day, provokes a kind of erotic intoxication'.[18] Where *la drague* ('cruising') becomes a quasi-theoretical concept central to Barthes's aesthetic of reading, writing, and of everyday life, it is arguably being used metaphorically:

La *drague* is the voyage of desire. The body is in a state of alert, on the lookout for its own desire. [. . .] La *drague* is an act which repeats itself, but the content of the act is absolutely new each time. [. . .] That's why *la drague* is a notion I can easily transfer from the order of the erotic quest, where it originates, to the quest for texts, for example, or for novelistic features. What comes with the surprise of the 'first time'. (*GV*, p. 231)

Nevertheless, I do not think that *la drague* would work as a route into geographical or textual spaces if it were *merely* metaphorical. It might be more accurate to speak of *metonymy,* for the subsumed sexual dimension gives the world its erotic edge. Reading *Empire of Signs* through the 1975 commentaries, and more especially through *Incidents,* it is impossible to ignore its more literal subtext of an erotic quest or *histoire de drague.*

This is built in at an early stage through Barthes's little lists of Japanese vocabulary for the *rendez-vous.* The theme of the *rendez-vous* first appears in a hand-written caption illustrating the 'Without words' chapter. Barthes discounts the idea that understanding the language is necessary to communication; indeed communication is likely to be all the richer and more subtle if words are opaque. For in Japan (*là-bas*) it is not the voice but 'eyes, smile, hair, gestures, clothing' which communicate, 'according to a pure – though subtly discontinuous – erotic project':

Fixing up a meeting (by gestures, drawings on paper, proper names) may take an hour, but during that hour, for a message which would be over with in an instant if it were to be spoken (simultaneously essential and insignificant), it's the other's entire body which has been known, savoured, received, and which has displayed (to no real purpose) its own narrative, its own text. (p. 10)

Turning the other's body into a *text* depends on the physical presence of that body. The *rendez-vous* itself, which might seem less important than the pleasurable mechanics of its lengthy organisation, turns out to be the reason for travelling at all: 'Open a travel guide: usually you will find a brief lexicon which strangely enough concerns only boring and useless things: customs, post offices, hotels, barbers, doctors, prices. Yet what is travelling? Meeting people. The only lexicon that counts is that of the *rendez-vous.*' (p. 13) Barthes provides (in his own handwriting) a series of specially designed lexicons of the *rendez-vous.* The first two are dispersed in his chapters on Japanese food (*where?'*, *when?*, *both,* and so on, pp. 17 and 23); the third, and most equivocal (*maybe, tired, impossible, I want to sleep,* p. 37) is to be found in the chapter 'No address', which again stresses the delicate *bodily* communication involved in the drawing of makeshift street plans.

(Homo)sexuality circulates in the text of *Empire of Signs* through the metaphorical transpositions that link writing and the body with cooking, bowing, Pachinko, violence, bunraku, etc. One crucial link between writing and sexuality seems to be the *hand,* both as metonym for the body and as the instrument of writing. In one at least of Barthes's examples, it is actually connoted as the instrument of masturbation. The paintbrush of ideographic writing 'has its gestures, as if it were the finger [. . .] it has the carnal, lubrified flexibility of the hand' (p. 86). I suspect, too, that Barthes's gloss on the game of Pachinko is intended as a sustained anal or masturbatory metaphor. Despite his claim that the Pachinko halls are full of a varied public of both sexes, the players in his colour photo are all men, lined up by their individual machines with the dubious legend: 'Mangers and latrines'.[19] Barthes omits the latrines in his verbal description, but it is impossible to put aside the allusion to male public lavatories that accompanies the illustration:

What is the point of this art? to regulate a nutritive circuit. [. . .] The machines are mangers, lined up in rows; the player, with an abrupt gesture, renewed so rapidly that it seems uninterrupted, feeds the machine with marbles; he stuffs them in, the way you would stuff a goose; from time to time the machine, gratified beyond measure, releases its diarrhea of marbles; for a few yen, the player is symbolically spattered with silver. We can understand then the seriousness of a game which counters the constriction of capitalist wealth, the constipated parsimony of salaries, with the voluptuous flood of silver marbles, which, all of a sudden, fill the player's hand. (pp. 28–9)

Once the text has become saturated in this way with its own sexual connotations, it is tempting to read its closing lines on the Shikidai gallery at Kyoto (a microcosm of Japan as an Empire of Empty Signs), as a sort of *mise en abyme* of its homosexual subtext. Around the middle of *Empire of Signs* Barthes accompanies a picture of the Shikidai gallery with the recommendation: 'Turn the image upside down: nothing more, nothing else, nothing' (pp. 50–1). The point is expanded on the last page:

Centreless, space is also reversible: you can turn the Shikidai gallery upside down and nothing will happen, except an inconsequential inversion of top and bottom, of right and left: the content is irretrievably dismissed: whether you walk through, cross over, or sit down on the flour (or the ceiling, if you invert the image), there is nothing to *grasp*. (p. 110)

*Inversion* and *retournement* are here associated with Barthes's favourite value of the *non-vouloir-saisir* ('no-will-to-grasp'), as he reaffirms in *Roland Barthes*: 'the golden rule of any *habitation*, discerned in the Shikidai gallery: *no will-to-grasp and yet no oblation*' (p. 59). It is actually linked to the idea of *la drague* in a 1977 interview, where he explains that the *non-vouloir-saisir* is a notion borrowed from oriental philosophy: ' "*Ne pas saisir*" the object of love, and to let desire circulate freely. At the same time, not to "sublimate": to master desire in order not to master the other' (*GV*, p. 297). If *retournement* is in itself a homosexual figure, it is associated here with an affirmation of non-aggression and a rejection of sublimation. I would want to link both back to Barthes's identification of linguistic aggression with Socrates' rejection of Alcibiades.

The association of homosexuality and gentleness is made on Barthes's own behalf by Renaud Camus, in a suitably Proustian response to Philippe Sollers's homophobic caricature of Barthes (through the character of Werth in *Femmes*):[20] 'In my opinion the very relative (and too long postponed) liberation of the man relative to social constraints is the chief cause, in the writer's relationship with meaning, meanings, writing and the world, of that quality of 'gentleness' which the elderly Bergotte, in the case of style, valued more than anything.'[21] Camus declares himself 'on the side of those who desire' precisely because 'nothing is more benevolent [*bien-veillant*] than desire, nothing is more gentle or less aggressive' (p. 241). By a circular process it seems to be these qualities that arouse his desire in the first place: 'I find *bienveillance* erotically exciting, or at least essential to excitement' (*Notes achriennes*, p. 158). The overlaps between the two writers' evaluation of homosexuality are even more apparent in Barthes's 1979 preface to Camus's exceedingly funny *Tricks*. Despite the graphic detail in which forty-five brief encounters between the narrator and previously unknown partners are recounted, the text has a paradoxical quality of innocence which Barthes convincingly locates in its *tone* and its 'ethics of dialogue':

This ethic is that of *Bienveillance,* which is surely the virtue most contrary to the amorous pursuit, and hence the most rare. Whereas ordinarily the erotic contract is presided over by harpy-like figures, who leave each party in a state of chilly solitude, here it is the goddess Eunoia, the Eumenid, the *Bienveillante,* who accompanies the two partners [. . .] Moreover, this goddess has her retinue: Politeness, Kindness, Humour, Generous Impulse.[22]

The goddess of homosexuality has already figured in Barthes's writing, and what is more as a product of another reversal. A page of *Roland Barthes* reproduces drafts of Barthes's text in the form of three hand-written filing cards, individually labelled 'in bed . . .', '. . . out of doors . . .', '. . . or at a work table' (p. 75). The page bears the general legend '*Renversement*: of scholarly origin, the filing card follows the twists and turns of unconscious desire [*la pulsion*]'. This upturning of a scholarly aid into an agent of drifting desire serves as a commentary on a draft of Barthes's fragment *The goddess H*. In the final version (pp. 63–4) there are two H's: homosexuality and hashish. In the reproduced, handwritten draft 'the goddess Homo' stands alone: 'Homosexuality: all that it allows us to say, do, understand, know, etc. Hence a crystalliser, a mediator, an intercessory figure: → The Goddess Homosexuality'. Clearly, homosexuality is figured by Barthes as an *intertextual* goddess. As such, she recalls the mediating qualities of Charles Fourier's highly valued character type, *la Papillonne* ('Butterfly'), whom Barthes twice links to the figure of the *dragueur,* and with whom he himself identifies in *Roland Barthes*. A list of all the ways he creates minor distractions for himself (instead of working) is headed *La Papillonne* and ends: '*je drague*: (*la drague* relates to that passion which Fourier called the Variating, the Alternating, the Butterfly)' (p. 72). In his essay on Fourier this is glossed as: 'the disposition of the subject who doesn't invest in a stable manner in the "good object": a passion whose mythical prototype is Don Juan: individuals who endlessly change their jobs, crazes, affections, desires – incorrigible *dragueurs* (unfaithful, renegade, subject to "moods", etc.): a passion disdained in Civilization, but one Fourier places very high.'[23]

If for me Don Juan somewhat spoils the image of the gentle, non-aggressive *dragueur,* there is no doubt that Barthes gives *la drague* and *le trick* a very positive and non-sordid connotation, which spills over into the spheres in which it operates metaphorically:

*Trick* – the encounter which takes place only once: more than a *drague,* less than a love affair: an intensity, which passes without regret. Consequently, for me, *Trick* becomes the metaphor for many a non-sexual *aventure*; the encounter of a glance, an idea, an image, an intense but ephemeral association, which accepts its own easy dissolution, an unfaithful kindliness: a way of not getting bogged down in desire, though without evading it; all in all, a kind of wisdom. (*RL*, p. 295)

In the concluding lines of Barthes's inaugural lecture at the Collège de France, where he recommends to himself the experience of *unlearning,* kindly infidelity is similarly juxtaposed with wisdom. He proposes

yielding to the unforeseeable revision which forgetting imposes on the sedimentation of the knowledges, cultures, and beliefs we have traversed. This experience has, I believe, an illustrious and outdated name, which I shall venture to appropriate here, without inhibition, at the very crossroads of its etymology: *Sapientia*: no power, a little knowledge, a little wisdom, and as much flavour as possible.[24]

As usual, an intertextual reading will sexualise the context. For a start the lecture is full of Barthes's familiar, metaphorically erotic vocabulary – clichés, for example, 'loiter' in language, and Barthes can only speak at all by 'picking them up' (p. 461). More specifically, the contiguity of 'crossroads' and 'etymology' echoes Barthes's earlier image for the writer (and hence certainly himself) as a *prostitute* at the crossroads of discourses:

A writer [. . .] must have the persistence of the watcher who stands at the crossroads of all other discourses, in a position that is *trivial* in relation to the purity of doctrines (*trivialis* is the etymological attribute of the prostitute who waits at the intersection of three roads). In short, to persist means to maintain, over and against everything, the force of a drift and an expectation. (p. 467)

The idea of conducting a series of *promiscuous* relationships with the discourses of his day often appears where Barthes is discussing the question of 'influence'. In *Roland Barthes* the theoretical intertext appears as a vast terrain through which he wanders as a *dragueur,* in search of someone to love. For example he has *crushes* on concepts: 'hence the work proceeds by conceptual infatuations, successive flushes, short-lived crazes. Discourse advances by minor twists of fate, by amorous crises' (p. 110). Of the woolliness (*mollesse*) of important words, he declares, wonderfully: 'other words, finally, are *dragueurs,* they follow whoever they meet' (p. 126). Ideas, basically, are something with which one *cohabits*: 'a sort of cohabitation which is both risky and intensely pleasurable [*jouissive*], yet responsible at the same time. It's a sort of love affair.'[25] And, as if worried by having to admit the fidelity of his desire for *language,* even here Barthes decides to lower the tone:

My work seems to be made up of a succession of 'disinvestments': there is only one subject from which I have never withdrawn the investment of my desire [. . .] it's language which I have chosen to love – and of course to hate at the same time: entirely trusting yet entirely suspicious of it; but as for the methods of approach, dependent on ideas developed around me and which drew me to them in distinctive ways, they may well have changed, that is to say: been tried out, given pleasure, transformed themselves, or been left behind: it's as if you always loved the same person but you tried out new erotic practices with them.[26]

On the one hand, Barthes's constant recourse to metaphors of prostitution, *la drague*, and the drift of a literal desire are his way of eroticising the world and of sexualising all theoretical issues. At the same time, the discovery (with the publication of *Incidents*) that the learned professor of literary semiology was living out his metaphors in real life, might truly seem to turn him into a Proustian 'surprise' – worthy of the princesse Sherbatoff. Since many readers have found *Soirées de Paris* a depressing text to say the least, I propose that the strategy of *retournement* be invoked one final time. For Barthes's infamous assassination of the author was simply the necessary first stage of the inversion of the biographical author into an intertextual 'novelistic figure':

a text can make contact with any other system: the inter-text is subject to no law but its infinite reworking. The Author himself – that somewhat decrepit deity of the old criticism – can or could some day become a text like any other [. . .] the critical undertaking [. . .] will then consist in *overturning* [*retourner*] the documentary figure of the author into a novelistic, irretrievable, irresponsible figure, caught up in the plural of his own text: a task whose adventure has already been recounted, not by critics, but by authors themselves, by a Proust or a Jean Genet.[27]

by a radical reversal [*renversement*], instead of putting his life into his novel, as is so often said, [Proust] made his life itself a work of which his own book was the model, so that it is quite clear to us that it's not Charlus who imitates Montesquiou, but Montesquiou, in his anecdotal, historical reality, who is only a secondary, derived fragment of Charlus. (*RL*, p. 51)

Proust, Genet, Roland Barthes . . . Not for nothing does a street name remind Barthes of Charlus in the opening scene of *Soirées de Paris*. Turn his real-life behaviour on its head (turn it back on him) and we make of Roland Barthes a secondary fragment, a mythical *dragueur*, an intertextual metaphor dispersed in his own text.

### Notes

1   Roland Barthes, 'Premier texte', *L'Arc*, LVI, 1974, p. 3. All references in this essay are to published translations where they exist, although I have

introduced modifications in some cases. Other translations are my own. After the first reference, all page numbers follow quotations in the body of the text.

2  *Roland Barthes by Roland Barthes,* New York, 1977, trans. Richard Howard, p. 10 (hereinafter *RB*).

3  See especially *Incidents,* Paris, 1987, pp. 21–61.

4  Plato, *The Symposium,* Harmondsworth, 1951, trans. W. Hamilton, pp. 96–113.

5  *A Lover's Discourse: Fragments,* New York, 1978, trans. Richard Howard, p. 97.

6  'The image', in *The Rustle of Language,* Oxford, 1986, trans. Richard Howard, p. 357 (hereinafter *RL*).

7  See *Prétexte: Roland Barthes,* Paris, 1978, ed. Antoine Compagnon, pp. 320–1.

8  The volume of *L'Arc* in which 'Premier texte' appears is a special issue on Barthes containing essays by members of his teaching seminar. It includes Barthes's utopian 'To the seminar' (see *The Rustle of Language,* pp. 332–42).

9  'On Gide and his journal', in *Barthes: Selected Writings,* Glasgow, 1983, ed. Susan Sontag, p. 4.

10  *The Pleasure of the Text,* New York, 1975, trans. Richard Miller, p. 36.

11  *The Grain of the Voice: Interviews 1962–1980,* London, 1985, trans. Linda Coverdale, p. 194 (hereinafter *GV*).

12  See Barthes, *Critical Essays,* Evanston, 1972, trans. Richard Howard, pp. xi–xxi.

13  See *The Rustle of Language,* pp. 277–90; *Incidents,* pp. 13–20; *Camera Lucida,* London, 1984, trans. Richard Howard.

14  *Notes achriennes,* Paris, 1982, p. 138. *Achrien* is Camus's neologism for homosexual. Camus foregrounds his own homosexuality in almost all of his own creative, anecdotal and theoretical writing, which also contains many discussions of Barthes's personality and writing, and of the place of homosexuality in both. Various aspects of Barthes's later writing are openly developed in Camus's work.

15  'Pierre Loti: *Aziyadé*', in *Le Degré zéro de l'écriture, suivi de nouveaux essais critiques,* Paris, 1972, p. 170.

16  See, for example, Barthes's reading of Charles Clifford's 1854 photograph 'The Alhambra' in *Camera Lucida,* pp. 38–40. It is captioned 'That's where I should like to live . . .' and contains details attributed by Barthes to Loti's thematics of *Déshérence*: grass growing up through the stones of the street, cypress trees and cemeteries ('places of debauchery, of drifting desire', p. 186).

17  See *Incidents,* pp. 21–61 and 71–116.

18  *Empire of Signs,* London, 1983, trans. Richard Howard, p. 79.

19  This photo is not included in the English translation. See *L'Empire des signes,* Paris/Geneva, 1970, p. 40.

20  *Femmes,* Paris, 1983, see especially pp. 150–1.

21  *Chroniques achriennes,* Paris, 1984, pp. 69–70.

**22** 'Preface to Renaud Camus's *Tricks*', in *the Rustle of Language,* p. 295. Barthes gives as an example of a 'generous impulse': 'the one which overcomes the narrator (in the middle of an American *trick*), and makes him rave so amiably on the subject of the author of this preface'. He is referring to his own brief appearance as a character in one of the *Tricks,* where Camus defends Barthes's work energetically in an argument and then fears that he may have spoiled his chances with the currently fancied 'Jeremy': 'If, thanks to them [Barthes and the photographer Daniel Boudinet], I'd messed up this particular trick, I'd make them pay for it!' (*Tricks*, Paris, 1982, p. 441). Barthes returns the compliment in his preface with a coy 'Of course, speaking literally, it must be very pleasant to be "tricked" by Renaud Camus' (p. 295). This particular intertextual chain is continued by Camus's brief cameo appearance in *Soirées de Paris* (p. 93).

**23** *Sade, Fourier, Loyola,* Paris, 1976, trans. Richard Miller, p. 101.

**24** 'Inaugural lecture, Collège de France', in *Barthes: Selected Writings,* p. 478.

**25** 'Radioscopie', in Jacques Chancel, *Radioscopies,* IV, Paris, 1976, p. 265.

**26** 'Réponses', *Tel Quel,* XLVII, 1971, p. 99.

**27** *S/Z,* New York, 1974, trans. Richard Miller, pp. 211–12.

# Autobiography as intertext:
# Barthes, Sarraute, Robbe-Grillet

The conjunction of autobiography and fiction in actual writing practice is still apt to be felt as something of a scandal. When Alain Robbe-Grillet and Nathalie Sarraute published autobiographies within a year of each other in the early 1980s, both clearly felt that the move would be seen as more or less heretical in the context of their previous fiction – whose principles are perhaps even more profoundly inimical than are those of most novels to Philippe Lejeune's canonic definition of autobiography as 'the retrospective account that a real person gives of their own existence, when the emphasis is on their individual life, and in particular on the history of their personality'.[1] The *nouveau roman*'s subversion of character and plot, its erosion of distinctions between real and imaginary, and its subordination of representation to a self-reflexive process of writing all conspired to set it at odds with the basic generic presuppositions of autobiography.

Sarraute's *Childhood* (1983) immediately spells out the reader's anticipated incredulity when the narrator's *alter ego* asks, 'wouldn't it mean that you were retiring? standing aside? abandoning your element?', as if autobiography were an outright defection from fiction.[2] Similarly, Robbe-Grillet's *Le Miroir qui revient* (1984), followed by a sequel *Angélique, ou l'enchantement* (1987), which in turn promises a third – and by implication final – volume, devotes a long prolegomena to a gleeful highlighting of the apostasy implied in his opening autobiographical claim, 'I have never talked about anything other than myself', a claim which reneges on the supposedly anti-humanist and anti-representational principles of the previous fiction.[3] What these autobiographers are recognising in differing ways is that autobiography is bound to be seen as a departure from the kind of fiction that each had been associated with, both in its practice and in its underlying principles. At the very least, they are suggesting that autobiography in these instances is, if not necessarily ultimately unassimilable to the fiction, then at least disturbingly different. It is this difference that I want to examine in this essay, by approaching the relations between the autobiographies and the fiction as intertextual relations.

In invoking the heresy and scandal associated with the *nouveaux romanciers'* recourse to autobiography, I am not, however, attempting to deny the fictional component of autobiography, least of all in the autobiographies in question. Indeed, the peculiar, fascinating character of these autobiographies owes as much to the way in which they elaborate a certain fictional practice as it does to the ways in which they deviate from it. It is this hovering in the intertextual relations between autobiography and fiction that I want to explore. In doing so I shall nevertheless continue to presuppose that there are generic distinctions between novels and autobiographies, even while the fiction is being revealed as autobiographical and the autobiographies as fictional, since in this sphere (if not in all others) generic differences need to be respected as an effect of reading, even if they cannot be defined as intrinsic qualities of the texts in question.[4]

One major reason for the heretical character of the autobiographies of the *nouveaux romanciers* was that the genre implies an authorial figure which the *nouveau roman* had always vigorously denounced. In the introduction to *Towards a New Novel*, Robbe-Grillet specifically rejects what he calls the nineteenth-century myth of the author as 'a sort of irresponsible and fatal monster' whose life was traditionally chock-full with biographically narratable substance: 'alcoholism, unhappiness, drugs, mystic passions, madness'.[5] The authorial myth produced a massive distortion of the literary text which was compounded by the critic whose task was, classically, to interpret the work in terms of the life on the presumption that authors never talk of anything except themselves.[6] For the *nouveaux romanciers*, their novels were to be seen in relation not to their lives but to an evolving and largely autonomous fictional tradition in which the novelist mattered only as a more or less anonymous and entirely insignificant vehicle through which the genre could develop and advance. The novelist constituted such a vehicle in so far as his/her preoccupations were those of language and form, and the content that a traditional critic would have ascribed to the author's alcoholism or unhappiness is now to be evaluated simply as a product of the novelist's preoccupation with form, a secondary substance that is 'as if it were secreted in the very writing' (*Snapshots*, p. 72). As a consequence, authors who had placed themselves in the service of the self-denying artefact that is fiction were liable to find themselves under suspicion of apostasy when they resorted to the self-affirming forms of autobiography.

But, far from recanting, both Sarraute and Robbe-Grillet (albeit very differently) insist on presenting their autobiographies as continuations of their ever-evolving fictional enterprise. The thrust of Sarraute's autobiographical venture seems specifically designed to demonstrate how apt the fictional principles continue to be despite the apparently antagonistic demands of autobiography. And in the case of Robbe-Grillet, although the autobiographical text is announced as a break with certain fictional assumptions, it is also presented as being more in keeping with the underlying values of the *nouveau roman* than would be a simple development of the old fictional vein. For him, the *nouveau roman* had latterly become a victim of its own critical orthodoxy in a way that is antithetical to its essentially revolutionary vocation. Although Robbe-Grillet appears to flirt with the old 'bureaucracy' of the authorial myth through his claim that his writing has always been about himself, his ultimate aim is to kill at least two bureaucracies (the old and the new) with one stone by writing an autobiography which he simultaneously insists on defining as 'still a fictional enterprise' (p. 13).

At the same time, there is a third function that these autobiographies are laying claim to – that of *metatextual* commentary on the fictional works – and this shift from practice to commentary reintroduces a disjunctive relation between autobiography and novel. In this perspective the autobiographies constitute a metatext in relation to the novels that recalls (sometimes obliquely) that of the critical and theoretical essays. A little technical precision might help to clarify the different kinds of intertextual relation that I am seeking to identify. In using the term 'metatext' I am borrowing from Gérard Genette's terminology in *Palimpsestes*; but as far as I know there doesn't exist a term to describe the relations between one text and another within the corpus (and more particularly between those texts which fall within the same generic category) of a given author. These relations are not actively intertextual in that they don't entail explicit or implied comment on one text by another, nor any

metatext / ? ta-text

transformation through rewriting of one text by another, but it is nevertheless an intertextual relationship that is enormously powerful for readers: one of the first moves in any reading is to place a new text in the interextual context of the corpus to which it belongs. Since we are dealing here with texts that are 'from the same stable', I coin the term *sister-text* to describe the relation between novel and novel – and novel and autobiography when the latter is regarded as a continuation of the former.

In addition to this tacit relationship, the autobiographies maintain a more active form of intertextuality which has always existed in Robbe-Grillet's fiction, an element of what Jean Ricardou has called 'a restricted intertextuality' i.e. 'the reduplication of an item from another text' within the same corpus.[7] For example, the *voyeur*'s bicycle appears inexplicably at the Villa Bleue in *The House of Assignation*, just as the mannequins of the latter reappear in *Djinn*.[8] These are instances of a more general intertextual phenomenon which Genette calls *hypertextuality*, a form which (unlike the sister-textual category) does imply some active transformation or rewriting of one text by another. Genette defines it as 'any relation that links a text B [the *hypertext*] to a prior text A [the *hypotext*] to which it is conncected in a manner that is not that of commentary',[9] and he cites Joyce's *Ulysses* (which is hypertextually grafted onto the *Odyssey*) as the classic example. This *hypertextual* relation not only constitutes the 'restricted intertextuality' of Robbe-Grillet's fictional corpus, but is also one of the intertextual relations which in turn graft the autobiography onto that corpus.

The term *metatextuality* is used by Genette to describe the relation of commentary to text. It is, he says, 'the relation which links a text to another text which it discusses', and is, in short, '*par excellence*, the *critical* relation' (p. 10). Thus, for example, Robbe-Grillet's remarks in *Le Miroir* (p. 39) about *The Voyeur* offer a straightforward critical reading of his novel which does not differ in kind (Robbe-Grillet suggests that content might be another matter) from that of a professional critic. So we now have three categories of intertextuality – the sister-textual, the hypertextual and the metatextual – that bind the autobiographies to the novels. The last two terms in particular, however, are mutually incompatible in the sense that the intertextual relations between one text and the other are not of the same order: hypertextual relations are always relations between equals, whereas metatextual relations presuppose a relation of subordination (whether this is conceived of as a subordination of text to commentary or of commentary to text) that is due to the fact that the metatext, unlike its object, is 'by definition non-fictional' (*Palimpsestes*, p. 450). The autobiographies (and especially Robbe-Grillet's) exploit the ambivalence associated with this incompatibility in a variety of ways, but in doing so they are following an influential precedent established by Barthes's *Roland Barthes* in 1975. So I propose now to explore how Barthes sets up an ambivalence between sister-, hyper- and metatextuality, and to see how fundamental his exemplary and supremely subtle handling of these relations are to his whole (bizarre) autobiographical practice.

## Roland Barthes: *Roland Barthes*

The series in which Barthes's *Barthes* appears proclaims it – architextually,[10] – as metatextual. The book is part of a publisher's list which includes some of the finest criticism on the authors treated.[11] The series' former subtitle (*par lui-même* – 'by him-/herself') gives it a latent autobiographical slant which Barthes chooses to exploit on a large if decidedly idiosyncratic scale. But he does so without the series' usual self-quotation, and with the aim, paradoxically, of subverting the metatextual demands of the critical genre.

In fact he dismisses the metatextual as a broadly excremental activity.[12] The autobiography is introduced as a means of undermining all metatextual expectations; rather than provide self-elucidation, the book is offered as 'the book of my *resistances* to my own ideas' (p. 119, my italics). The relationship of this text to its predecessors is one of addition rather than of encapsulation, and the metatextual is rejected in favour of a sister-textual one: 'my texts are disjointed, no one of them caps any other; the latter is just a *further* text, the last of the series, not the ultimate in meaning; texts about texts never illuminate anything' (p. 120).

And yet Barthes does not renounce self-commentary entirely, and it's worth reading what he has to say about his *Michelet*, the *Critical Essays*, *The Pleasure of the Text*, or *S/Z*. Perhaps the most consistent and critically revealing self-commentary concerns Barthes's style, and the remarks he makes on this topic are both metatextual and illuminating. Even so, there is something odd about this self-commentary, for it is designed to obstruct any serious evaluation of his ideas or of his development as a thinker by insisting instead that content should be viewed as style. Thus, having recalled a number of oppositions that have held key positions in his thought (*denotation/ connotation, readerly/writerly*, etc.) he dismisses their intellectual value and claims instead that they are mere 'artefacts' whose function is simply to make it possible 'to say something' (pp. 91–2). So although there is a metatextual function at work here, it has a decidedly subversive character in that it chooses to foreground factors that in traditional critical terms would appear too marginal or too superficial to warrant serious attention.

This subversion is reinforced by the self-reflexive or retroactive character of a great number of these metatextual remarks in which the metatext is implicated as a text in the phenomenon it is describing. Take, for instance, Barthes's comment on what he suggests is a characteristic stylistic tic of his: 'Sometimes he [this is Barthes referring to himself] translates himself, doubles one phrase by another' (p. 58). This sentence performs exactly the self-translation which it identifies and goes on to illustrate it (somewhat redundantly in the circumstances) with a quote from *The Pleasure of the Text*. It is then followed – even more redundantly – by a further sentence that repeats the trick, so that the sentences enact, both in relation to each other, as well as individually, the reflexivity or what Barthes calls the 'autonymy' of this self-implicating kind of commentary. In doing so they ultimately erode the distinction in status (hypertext/hypotext) on which the metatextual commentary initially depended, and the metatext reveals itself in these moments to be a sister-text.

The metatextual dimension of Barthes's text is even more thoroughly disturbed by his recourse – or appeal – to fiction. Alongside Barthes's insistence that his text is operating at a surface level of style and not at the 'deep' level of ideas, there is a repeated claim that his text is a fiction, a claim which serves to invalidate the text's status as metatext. The fictional for Barthes is not synonymous with the invented or the untrue, or even the unserious: it consists in an *undecidability* about a text's seriousness which is the effect of a certain (or more precisely, an uncertain) use of quotation marks. All writing, says Barthes, is a rewriting of the already-said. So his own writing is a rewriting of his intellectual intertexts, of the Imaginary, and even of himself. Barthes's rewriting of these various 'languages' is a fictionalising strategy which works by surrounding them with (usually invisible) quotation marks. Forced (inevitably) to speak the language of the other, Barthes prefers to *stage* it rather than attempt to adopt it as the language of his own sincerity (since sincerity is itself a part of the language of the other that is the Imaginary). As fiction Barthes's writing is a 'staging' of the languages of the other (and principally, he says, of the languages of the Imaginary), which the stage-director achieves by 'arranging the flats one in front of the other, distributing the roles, establishing levels' (p. 105). Discourse must always be attributed to a fictional source, and inevitably this will apply also to the discourse of Barthes himself in *Roland Barthes*. His intermittent use of the third person is designed to mark the text as fictional and supports his injunction that 'All this must be considered as if spoken by a character in a novel' (p. 119).

The key aspect of the fictionality of Barthes's writing, however, lies in the 'bathmology', or play of 'degrees', which characterises the generalised citationality of his staging of discourse. It is the instability of the placing of the quotation marks that decisively constitutes the fictional and renders it unrecuperable. The ideal text would be 'a text with uncertain quotation marks, with floating parentheses' (p. 106), in which each undecidable component would work like a mouthful of good wine where, says Barthes, 'the mouthful swallowed does not have quite the same taste as the next mouthful taken' (p. 96). In fiction the degree of quotedness of each mouthful of discourse is constantly drifting. So that if his text is fictional, it is seeking not the lucidity of the metatext, but the shifting quality of the citational. In making metatextual claims the bathmological principle of the novelistic immediately fictionalises those claims. In the process, the intertextual relations which comprise the text are transformed from the metatextual to the hypertextual, and Barthes turns out to be rewriting his (and others') texts in the same way that *Ulysses* rewrites the *Odyssey*.

However, if we over-privilege the status of the novelistic in *Roland Barthes* and read it only as a fiction, we risk repressing the full ambivalence in Barthes's writing. The fiction/metatext contradiction is unresolvable and should probably remain so, for there is an element of the Cretan liar paradox endemic in the whole operation of the text, whereby to read it as fictional depends on reading the injunction to do so as non-fictional. And this paradox is precisely a product of the complex intertextual relations of *Roland Barthes* with its component languages, relations which are simultaneously, if incompatibly, sister-textual, metatextual and hypertextual. Or, to quote Barthes (to whom – fiction or no fiction – one wants constantly to give the last, authoritative word) 'let the essay avow itself *almost* a novel' (p. 120).

## Nathalie Sarraute: *Childhood*

Like *Roland Barthes, Childhood* is anxious to present itself first and foremost as a continuation of Sarraute's existing *oeuvre* – a sister-text rather than a metatext in relation to the novels. Much of the text's self-commentary takes the form of a dialogue between the narrator and her *alter ego*, and the opening pages exploit this dialogue to spell out the autobiography's relation to its fictional predecessors. The *alter ego*'s fear that the narrator's plan to write her 'childhood memories' would represent an unacceptable departure from her previous 'element' is energetically countered by the narrator. In particular, the *alter ego*'s worry that there will be no new material to be found in the subject of childhood remembered is contradicted by the narrator in terms which are immediately recognisable as having all the hallmarks of her fictional values: 'it's still vacillating, no written word, no word of any sort has yet touched it, I think it *is* still faintly quivering . . . outside words . . . as usual . . . little bits of something still alive' (*Childhood*, p. 3). The 'vacillating' is opposed to the 'fixed', the unwritten to the already-said, the alive to the dead in line with oppositions which have been repeatedly mobilised in the fiction in order to ground a notion of authenticity. These, for example, are exactly the values used by the novelist in *Between Life and Death* when judging his own writing and trying to decide whether what he has written is entirely fixed ('dead' as the novel's title would have it), or whether something living can be salvaged from it.[13]

Just as the values of the writing in the fiction and the autobiography are the same, so too are the forms taken by that writing. Like the novels from *The Golden Fruits* onwards, *Childhood* is a sequence of scenes with no apparent chronological or narrative link. Many of them are focused on a central utterance (the 'conversation') whose *sous-conversation* the scene is designed to explore and unmask. Thus the first scene from Sarraute's memories is launched and sustained by the phrase 'Nein, das tusst du nicht'. The life is resurrected through the narrator's unpacking[14] of these key utterances: 'It isn't your home' (p. 115), 'Tiebia podbrossili' (p. 172), and so on. This kind of structure is used with increasing frequency in

Sarraute's later fiction, and it culminates in *The Use of Speech* where each section is headed by a title which contains the key phrase which it will worry until its every implication has been unravelled: 'Ich sterbe', 'Your father. Your sister', and so on.[15]

The dominant tense of each of the scenes is, as in the novels, the present – the past being resurrected and relived rather than narrated. The characteristic style of the novels is also largely maintained in the autobiography: the tentative sentence structures, the *points de suspension*. And the dialogue between the narrator and her *alter ego*, while undoubtedly an innovation as far as autobiography in general is concerned, is simply an expansion and development of a strategy that was already a feature of the novels, particularly, once again, in *The Use of Speech* which begins with a question and answer session that makes manifest the suspicion which, in Sarraute's view, surrounds all novel writing in the modern era, and which, to judge by its use in *Childhood*, also affects autobiography.[16]

So Sarraute's *Childhood* proclaims its sisterhood with her fiction both in its value-system and in its use of fictional form. But, paradoxically, in repeating the forms and values of the fiction, the autobiography is also being called into service as a means of endorsing their validity through the authority of its implicit basis in lived experience. The generic presupposition that autobiography is the retrospective account that someone gives of their own existence allows *Childhood* to make claims for the fiction – notably for its veracity – through its intertextual association with it. The novels' preoccupation with authenticity requires that their writing be grounded in something real. Indeed Sarraute has always insisted that what she writes about in her novels (her 'tropisms') is *true*. This is precisely the claim she is making in the French preface to *The Era of Suspicion* when, talking about her first published text, *Tropisms*, she writes:

The texts which make up this first work were the spontaneous expression of very vivid impressions, and their form was as spontaneous and natural as the impressions to which they gave life.
    As I wrote, I became aware that these impressions were produced by certain movements, certain internal actions on which my attention had long been fixed. In fact, I believe, since my *childhood*.[17]

The denial of artifice in her writing, and the insistence on the spontaneity and naturalness of the 'impressions' which it seeks to convey are a way of claiming authenticity both for the represented

experience (the 'movements') and for the means of that representation (the 'form'). The claim is clinched by the appeal to their source in
the *childhood* subsequently recalled in the autobiography. If nothing
else, *Childhood* is substantiating the two major assertions being
made in this preface: first, that tropisms, 'have continued to be the
living substance of all my books' (*L'Ere du soupçon*, p. 9); and
second, that they are based on real experience that has its origins in
Sarraute's early childhood. These assertions demonstrate that there
is another chronology – and thus another intertextuality – at work in
the autobiography: for although *Childhood* is written in remarkable
conformity to the principles and forms of the novels, the 'childhood'
which it recalls actually precedes them and provides them with the
guarantee of veracity to which they continually appeal. The sisterhood of texts is accompanied by a rather different kind of intertextual relation in which the autobiography is ascribed a priority and
an authority whose metatextual message is: the novels are true.

This message is also inscribed within *Childhood* itself, and is not
simply the effect of my juxtaposing of the essays alongside the novels
and the autobiography. The message emerges from two recurrent
features of the autobiography: one is the narration of what I shall call
'bad intertextuality'; and the other from the interventions of the *alter
ego* in the text. The 'bad intertextuality' is associated with two
episodes where the young Natasha tries her hand at writing. Its
purpose is to show that writing can only come from experience, and
not from other books. In the first of these episodes Natasha shows
her novel to a writer friend of her mother's who snubs her with his
comment that, 'Before setting out to write a *novel*, you should first
learn to spell' (*Childhood*, p. 173). But the real problem with the
'novel' isn't the spelling, but, in the eyes of the adult narrator, its
thoroughgoing inauthenticity.

Natasha's chief crime was to have used words that weren't part of
her life, and to have put them into the service of characters and
situations that were also quite outside her own experience –
Georgian princes and princesses living in the mountains of the Cau-
casus. The enterprise is doomed and inevitably (in the Sarrautean
scheme) falls victim to the deadly effects of a language that is
borrowed from ready-made examples. Instead of trying to capture
the palpitating 'virtuality' of lived experience, it uses literary cliché to
lasso a fairy-tale scenario which is itself also entirely 'known in
advance'.[18] The other episode recalls an assignment for her French

teacher at school (pp. 194–203); and it makes the same point, providing its young protagonist with the same salutary moral as that of the Caucasian novel episode: borrowed words are not the stuff of proper writing, a moral whose lesson, it can be assumed, the present autobiography has duly taken on board.

The role of the *alter ego* is chiefly to act as a counter-weight to any incipient intertextual lapses on the part of the narrator. Although she begins by playing devil's advocate to the autobiographical project, she is quickly co-opted into ensuring its success through her sceptical and somewhat suspicious line of questioning. Her interventions lend the episodes they comment on the status of what Michael Shering-ham has called an 'autobiographical incident'. Sheringham uses the term to refer to 'minor events [in autobiography] to which discourse attributes a heavy payload of meaning'.[19] In the case of Sarraute, incidents acquire autobiographical significance not so much through a straight attribution of meaning, but rather through being placed in a history which includes and implicates the writing subject of the present.[20]

For instance, in the scene that is launched by the phrase, 'What a tragedy, though, to have no mother', the narrator's efforts are concentrated, as usual, on describing the effect these words had upon her: ' "tragedy", which had never approached me, never touched me, has struck me. [. . .] I am enclosed in it. In tragedy' (p. 106). The scene stands by itself as a fragment suspended in an apparently atemporal kaleidoscope of memories until the *alter ego* intervenes to ask, 'Was that the first time you had been trapped like that, in a word?' (p. 107). The response elicited from the narrator reinscribes the event in a historical sequence which embraces not only the narrator's subsequent experience, but also – implicitly – the countless episodes in Sarraute's novels where characters find themselves trapped by words which pursue them with the predatory insistence described here: 'I don't remember it happening to me before. But *how many times since*, have I not escaped, terrified, out of words which pounce on you and hold you captive' (*ibid.*, my italics). Thus the autobiographical incident as narrated here constitutes an originary instance of this exemplary experience. Its function is not only to give chronological shape to childhood memories, but to validate parallel episodes in the novels by providing them with an origin in real-life experience.

The autobiography here departs from the non-narrative and a-

historical fictional practice in order to establish a historical conti-
nuum; but it does so with the ultimate purpose of bolstering the
truth-claims of that fiction. In the process it also recalls the metatextual commentary of the essays in *The Era of Suspicion* and more
particularly the remarks Sarraute makes in the preface about
*Tropisms* and its aftermath in her work. Seen from this perspective,
*Childhood* has also taken up the metatextual baton dropped by *The
Era of Suspicion* in so far as the essays in it are devoted to defending
new fictional forms in the name of an authentic experiential truth.
Thus, somewhat like Barthes's *Roland Barthes*, *Childhood*
comprises the configuration of the different kinds of intertextual
relation that this essay has been charting in autobiographical texts:
sister-textual in relation to the novels in so far as it is a continuation
of their forms and values; hypertextual in relation to them in so far as
its function is to repeat the message of the metatext that is *The Era of
Suspicion*.

### Alain Robbe-Grillet: *Le Miroir qui revient, Angélique, ou l'enchantement*

Whereas Sarraute's autobiography seeks to repeat the message of her
critical and theoretical essays, Robbe-Grillet's aim in his two
volumes of autobiography is, on the contrary, to free himself from
the conceptual apparatus that he himself helped to establish in
*Towards a New Novel* (see *Le Miroir*, p. 12).

But the autobiographical project is not written only in relation to
the essays, and it constructs an important intertextual link for itself
in relation to the novels. At one level this is a metatextual link: for
instance, the assertion that 'I have never talked about anything other
than myself' is an implied critical directive which demands that the
novels be read (reread) as an autobiographical testament in their
own right. At the same time the autobiography has a sister-textual
relation to the novels to the extent that it claims to be continuing
Robbe-Grillet's fictional practice. It does this partly through simple
affirmation, and also partly through the inclusion of narratives
whose fantastic components mark them as 'fiction', rather than, say,
memoirs (the Corinthe stories and all those concerning Mina, Jean-
Coeur Simon,[21] Manrica, and so on). The complexity and ambivalence of the generic status of these texts is emphasised by the way
that Robbe-Grillet has had his publishers set out the list of 'Books by

the same author' in the front of *Angélique* where the two autobiographical titles appear separately from the rest under the rubric
*'romanesques'*.[22] So that in addition both to the explicit claims to
fictional status made in the autobiographical texts, and to the
fictional 'interpolations' and echoes in them, *Le Miroir* and
*Angélique* invite a reading on the basis of the most general generic
affiliations that treats them as a continuation of the fictional corpus.

Once again we have in autobiography the configuration of the
metatextual and the sister-textual which when taken together produce the third relation of the hypertextual – although the arrange-
ment of the configuration and its function is different from those in
Barthes and Sarraute. Where Barthes seemed anxious above all
about the relation between his own discourse and that of the *doxa*,
and where Sarraute was chiefly concerned to relate her writing to an
experiential 'truth', Robbe-Grillet is perpetually shadow-boxing
with a reader to whose ideologically inspired interpretations he
refuses to submit. The imbrication of fiction in autobiography in the
*'romanesque'* texts seems designed to keep the reader at arm's length
by producing systematic generic confusions: read as fiction, the texts
confound the reader with their claims about autobiographical
origins; and yet read as autobiography, the fictional component of
the texts undermines any inclination the reader might have to tie him
down to his 'truth'. The texts play consistently on these ambiguities,
and in what follows I shall look first at the way in which Robbe-
Grillet undermines a 'dogmatic' reading of the fiction through his use
of autobiography, and then at the way in which the fiction undermines the autobiography, before finally returning to consider more
directly the question of Robbe-Grillet's problems with his readers.

Robbe-Grillet's assertion that his novels were all along a form of
veiled self-disclosure is a jibe at readers who had taken their metatextual cues from the essays. The writer is not, after all, someone
whose head is filled with sentence structures and grammatical patterns, but someone who writes about himself. What is involved in
this shift is not just a theoretical realignment, but a disempowering of
the reader. Robbe-Grillet attacks his readers for having been too
short-sighted to have seen 'the monsters' in his texts.[23] And as he
perversely lays autobiographical claim to a whole variety of elements
in his novels, the critics are routed: Jean Ricardou was, he says,
wrong about the door in *Project for a Revolution in New York* which
he saw as a mechanical generator of the whole text: it was actually a

description of the front door of Robbe-Grillet's grandparents' house at Kerangoff.[24] The supreme example of this kind is the young girl whose name is used as the title for the second autobiographical volume. Angélique proves to be the prototype for Jacqueline/Violette in *The Voyeur*, from her sexual precociousness to her mysterious death on the cliffs of Brittany. The penultimate episode in *Angélique* recounts her manipulative seduction of the young Robbe-Grillet, which leaves him believing that her menstrual blood is the result of some inadvertent but terrible damage that he has done to her and for which she puts a spell of impotence on him. The ropes and chains which appear more and more frequently on the wrists and ankles of the women in his films and novels, the red pubic hair which is the object of so much sadistic violence in them, and the obsessive linking of sex and blood are now all given an autobiographical and highly traumatic origin.

But lest the autobiographical cues become the basis of a new dogma in their own right, Robbe-Grillet succeeds in undermining them through his repeated slides into fiction. In addition to defining the entire project as a fiction, Robbe-Grillet makes the fairly standard point that autobiography inevitably adopts the forms and conventions of the novel. For example, in an interview with Jean-Jacques Brochier he says that, 'in *Le Miroir* my father also becomes a fictitious character. Any person in a book is a character from a novel'.[25] And in *Le Miroir* itself, he undermines what would otherwise seem a fairly seminal scene (the young Robbe-Grillet in bed at night, both terrified by the monsters of his nocturnal fantasies and indulging in 'solitary pleasures which already had a strong sadistic streak' under the intermittent gaze of his mother as she sits reading in the next room) by drawing attention to the fictional quality of the whole description (p. 17).

In addition to these self-fictionalising remarks Robbe-Grillet is keen to map out the fictional intertexts of the autobiographical volumes, and both use their opening pages to establish a new inter-textual repertoire (largely fictional) within which Robbe-Grillet's writing might be placed. The Breton legends of his childhood provide a framework of presuppositions with which both volumes exten-sively associate themselves. There is also some critical discussion of Camus's *The Outsider* and of Sartre's novels (*Le Miroir*, pp. 28–30), and the interweaving of self-portraiture and biography in *Nausea* is recalled both in the Robbe-Grillet/Corinthe parallel which runs through both volumes of the autobiography, and more overtly in Robbe-Grillet's momentary confusion between Sartre's Rollebon and his own Corinthe on account of their similar shadowy involvements with Russian politics. And as part of the same intertextualising strategy, *Angélique* opens with the narrator's deciphering of human faces in the furniture and wallpaper surrounding him, including those of many fictional characters: 'Gauvain, Tristan de Léonnois, Perceval, Lancelot du Lac, Arthur de Bretagne' (pp. 8–9), a list which establishes the chivalric intertexts which the remainder of the text exploits at some length. These are followed in turn, first by Mazeppa and Brunehaut, and then by 'Richard of Gloucester, Macbeth Count of Glamis, Joseph K., Sartoris, Ivan Karamazov and his brother Dmitri, Boris the usurper, Edouard Manneret, Nicolas Stavroguine' (p. 9). Through this very heterogeneous procession of figures Robbe-Grillet can be seen to be establishing a fictional tradition in which he wishes his own work to make sense (a tradition which includes his own earlier work). In this he is doing something very similar to what he was doing in *Towards a New Novel* but at the same time he departs from it by making the new tradition distinctly (and provocatively) less modernist than the one outlined in the essays.

This intertextual repertoire is also part of a general strategy designed to blur the autobiographical and the fictional in the two autobiographical/*romanesque* texts. In *Angélique* Robbe-Grillet insists that he is as deeply marked by the lives of fictional characters as by those of 'real' people, and the implications of this claim are borne out by the text's interweaving of the 'fiction' of the Corinthe story and the 'reality' of Robbe-Grillet's. Corinthe, who has already appeared intermittently in Robbe-Grillet's films and novels, is the central character of a discontinuous 'fictional' narrative which is bound to the discontinous autobiographical narrative through a series of the shifts which are so characteristic of Robbe-Grillet's later fiction. He claims at the beginning of *Le Miroir* that his autobiographical venture is motivated not by desire for self-knowledge, but by a wish to find out more about Corinthe whom he treats as if he had been a 'real' person on the fringes of his family's acquaintance (which he may have been, for all I know).

Within each strand – the 'fictional' Corinthe one, and the 'real' Robbe-Grillet one – there is a further mixing of genres as the 'fictional' Corinthe is pursued and reconstructed from a series of documentary sources: an article in the *Manchester Guardian* based on an interview at the time of the *Anschluss (Angélique*, p. 18); an edition of an autobiography by a cousin of Corinthe's on the German side of the family for which Robbe-Grillet gives precise biblio-graphical references (p. 156), and so on. Conversely, the war memories of Robbe-Grillet's father slide gradually into a series of pseudo-chivalric fictional episodes in which the *ankou* (death-figure) of Brittany legend also figures prominently. So that the two texts (*Angélique* perhaps more radically and markedly so than *Le Miroir*) comprise a sort of patchwork where fiction is juxtaposed with child-hood memory, critical comment with anecdote about events in Robbe-Grillet's recent past, a defence of pornographic fantasy with a eulogy of Barthes, and an indignant and highly detailed narrative account of the prosecution of *Glissements progressifs du plaisir* in the Italian courts with general quasi-philosophical statements about the nature of art. This patchwork effect is reinforced by Robbe-Grill-et's occasional signalling of their different contexts and origins. Moreover, the generally fragmented composition of the text is regularly foregrounded by Robbe-Grillet's intermittent comments about where and when he is writing or revising it: in Brittany, in New York, in 'the peaceful plains of the Middle West' (*sic, Angélique*, p. 40).

The variety of discursive genres used in these texts highlights the broadly intertextual character of Robbe-Grillet's autobiographical practice, and this in itself aligns it to the intertextual nature of his fictional practice. But the *glissements* that link the different intertex-tual fragments also embody what for Robbe-Grillet is ultimately a fictional principle, and so give priority to the fictional status of these apparently autobiographical texts. The 'productive' use of the auto-biographical material means that 'I see very little difference between my work as a novelist and this, my more recent work as an autobiographer' (*Angélique*, p. 68). On the one hand the fiction derives from a quasi-autobiographical impulse and is propelled by a search for answers to the questions 'What am I? and what am I doing here?' (p. 69); and yet on the other hand, the underlying autobiogra-phical quest boils down in both genres to 'problems of structure' (p. 69) – always the key factor of the fiction in the 1950s. But in writing the fiction that comprises this 'autobiographical pseudo-research' (p. 69), Robbe-Grillet is at the same time dramatically changing the direction of his previous fictional enterprise. By associating problems of structure with problems of identity, and giving them an autobiographical dimension, Robbe-Grillet is reneging on the old orthodoxy which held that structure was synonymous with absence of biographical content.

The effect of Robbe-Grillet's defection is primarily designed to wrong-foot his readers in an attempt to reclaim his writing – both the former fiction and the present autobiography – from the critical apparatus which he feels they have institutionalised at his expense. The allusions he makes to his readers in the two texts invariably cast them as gullible victims of a variety of different orthodoxies – marxist, feminist, psycho-analytic, and even that of the *nouveau roman*. His uneasiness about the reception of his texts shows up early in *Le Miroir* in the form of defensive anticipations of Freudian recuperations of his autobiographical narrative (e.g. *Le Miroir*, p. 13). Later on he defines the modern novel as a 'trap' designed to capture every kind of modern critical orthodoxy: the 'machinery' of the novel 'should only "operate" with the transparent strangeness of a trap with multiple springs, a trap for humanist readings, for politico-marxist or Freudian readings, etc., and finally, a trap for devotees of structures devoid of meaning' (p. 41). The reader, regardless of his or her particular critical bias, is portrayed as the necessary victim of the text's manipulations (see p. 41). In turning against his own metatextual commentary in *Towards a New Novel*, Robbe-Grillet seems to be turning against the readers who have armed themselves with its critical keys in order to penetrate his texts and claim mastery of them. The autobiography not only refutes a former critical orthodoxy, but in the process of supplanting one metatext takes care to avoid establishing itself as a new metatext. As fictional hypertext rather than critical metatext, the autobiography is able to generate a new reading of the novels which will liberate them from institutionalised critical readings, while at the same time denying its readers the satisfaction of acquiring a new metatextual apparatus with which to construct any new critical control. In pronouncing itself a fiction the autobiography is defining itself as a trap in which readers cannot expect to find any mastery, and where the experiences which await them will be frustration, deception and finally ejection from a text which only let them in in order to put them in their place. It is not readers, but Robbe-Grillet who rules OK.

The careful intertextual positioning of Robbe-Grillet's autobiography seems, then, to be ultimately connected to his anxieties
about the reception of his texts. However, this concern with reading
is not confined to Robbe-Grillet; it is equally – if less obviously – true
of Barthes and Sarraute, and it may partly explain their recourse to
autobiography. Some critics have suggested that the ambivalent
status of Barthes's autobiography is proof of a general crisis of
commentary, and Barthes himself has defined modernist writing as
'that which rejects commentary'.[26] One could then say that the
autobiographies discussed here all refuse, or at least complicate, the
metatextual function because the modernity of the would-be object-
texts makes it impossible for the would-be metatexts to relate them
except as hypertext: as fiction to fiction rather than as commentary
to fiction.

But what is at stake is less the status of commentary or the question
of modernity as an intrinsic textual feature, than the uneasy awareness evidenced by all three writers that the modernity which they
exemplify has been associated with a very powerful and complex
system of reception. Ironically, it is a system which seems not the
least perturbed by the so-called crisis of commentary, and which,
even in paying lip-service to it, relentlessly pursues the metatextual
aims of the profession which sustains it.[27] In this sense they could all
be seen as writing less against their precursors (amongst whom one
could include their former selves), than against their readers. Theirs
is an 'anxiety of anticipation'[28] rather than one of influence; and the
mapping of the intertextual field, along with their careful positioning
of the autobiographies within that field, are both a symptom of this
anxiety and also a response to it. For this reason, the intertexts need
to be considered as much in relation to the texts' reception as their
origins. The case of Sarraute probably presents the simplest version
of the manoeuvre, but it is one that testifies to a very keen awareness
on her part of the current critical intertexts. *The Era of Suspicion* is
largely concerned with staking out an intertextual field in which her
fiction may be seen by its readers as both intelligible and true. Her
appeal to the examples of Dostoevsky, Proust, Henry Green, Ivy
Compton Burnett and Virginia Woolf, and her denunciation of both
Balzac and the modern behaviourists are an implied request to be
read in a context which will validate both the experience she is
seeking to represent ('psychology', as she calls it) and the formal
techniques by means of which those experiences are represented. The

autobiography has the same broad aims, except that she, like Robbe-Grillet, has now to reckon with the critical orthodoxies that have grown up with the *nouveau roman* and which are profoundly at odds with the assumptions of all her writing. Indeed, she has consistently opposed the view that fiction is just a game played with words. It is this critical credo above all that she is countering by using the autobiography to demonstrate – against the critical orthodoxy of the late 60s and 70s – that the fiction is thoroughly and genuinely grounded in experience.

Barthes has a more complex relation with his anticipated reception. Aware that each move in his own career has seen subversion solidified into system, and *paradoxa* revert to *doxa* in the institutionalising wake of his readers, he cannot fail to see that *Roland Barthes* risks being drawn into the same pattern. The use of fiction constitutes an important means of avoiding the impasse of this pendulum swing; and as a corollary it substantially alters his relations to his over-zealous readers. Through the fictional, Barthes is seeking to co-opt his readers into playing out his bathmological games with him, to seduce them into joining in the writing process, and so prevent his text from becoming the object of the critical discourses of the *doxa*.

Fiction having implicated the reader in the text, Barthes sees the ideal reader not as someone who will receive his text in a particular intertextual context (the Freudianism/marxism/feminism of which Robbe-Grillet is so suspicious), but someone who will participate in Barthes's citational play with these contexts and use the intertext with rather than against him. Barthes's vision of the ideal text, in which the languages of the Imaginary are staggered in various shifting relations to each other through the deployment of quotation and parenthesis, may be utopian, but it is conceived as a utopia that requires the reader's participation in the process which it comprises (see *Roland Barthes*, p. 161). Barthes's response to the anxiety of anticipation is thus to entice his reader across the barrier that lies between text and reception – not, like Robbe-Grillet's, to browbeat him or her into a submissive recognition of their inferior status. But in its own way it too is a mark of the acute consciousness, shared by all three writers, of the enormously powerful role of reception.

More specifically it shows how aware they are of the critical assumptions that currently operate within the institution of reception. The institutionalisation of reception through its growing professionalisation in the academy has been accompanied by the spawning of terms like *intertextuality* itself whose counterpart has been a dismantling of the notion of a 'founding subject'.[29] Autobiography more than any other genre has been linked with this idea of a founding subject – albeit only vestigially and nostalgically now – and it is therefore perhaps not a coincidence to find these three writers turning to autobiography. They may not be seeking to retrieve or reinstate a founding subject, but they are undoubtedly exploiting the genre traditionally associated with such a figure in order to protest against the vulnerability of their texts, be they fictional or autobiographical, to the new-found power of readers. Their protest is directed against readings and receptions that are legitimated not just by the intertextual field of the critic, but also by the reader's recourse to a critical repertoire containing concepts like the intertextual itself which has so drastically stripped authors of the authority once enjoyed by the founding subjects who preceded them.

### Notes

1  *Le Pacte autobiographique*, Paris, 1975, p. 14. My translation.

2  Sarraute, *Enfance*, Paris, 1983. The English translation is taken from *Childhood*, trans. Barbara Wright, London, 1984 (pp. 1–2) from which all further translations will be taken, with occasional minor adjustments.

3  Alain Robbe-Grillet, *Le Miroir qui revient*, Paris, 1984, p. 10. See also *Angélique, ou l'enchantement*, Paris, 1987. All translations from both these volumes are my own.

4  As Paul de Man has it, 'Autobiography . . . is not a genre or a mode, but a figure of reading or of understanding that occurs, to some degree, in all texts', 'Autobiography as de-facement', in *The Rhetoric of Romanticism*, New York, 1984, p. 70.

5  Alain Robbe-Grillet, *Pour un nouveau roman*, Paris, 1970 (first published in 1963). The translation comes from Barbara Wright, *Snapshots and Towards a New Novel*, London, 1965, p. 46 (also with some minor adjustments), from which all further translations will be taken.

6  And this is no doubt the reason why Sarraute always refuses to recognize the relevance of gender to her writing, for example, in her conversations with Simone Benmussa published as *Nathalie Sarraute: Qui êtes-vous?*, Lyon, 1987. See esp. pp. 139 ff.

7  'Terrorisme, théorie', in *Robbe-Grillet: Colloque de Cerisy*, Paris, 1976, Vol. 1, p. 23. My translation.

8  See Christian Rullier, '*Djinn*: vers une théorie de la ré-écriture', *Critique*, CCCCXI–XII, 1981, pp. 857–68. Rullier argues that through this recycling Robbe-Grillet is using one novel to rewrite previous ones. I shall be trying to show that the autobiography is doing the same kind of thing, but in a more extensive and radical way.

9   *Palimpsestes*, Paris, 1982, pp. 11–12. My translations. I follow Genette in my categorisation of intertextual relations.

10   Genette defines the architextual relation as 'a relation . . . which is of a purely taxonomic order', *Palimpsestes*, p. 11.

11   See, for example, Barthes, *Michelet*, Oxford, 1987, trans. Richard Howard (first published in French, 1954).

12   See *Roland Barthes by Roland Barthes*, London, 1977, trans. Richard Howard, p. 73 (first published in French, 1975). I have followed Howard's translation with occasional alterations.

13   *Entre la vie et la mort*, Paris, 1968.

14   The metaphor is Sarraute's: the narrator of *Childhood* describes her mother's remark that 'Vera is stupid' as a *package* like the ones that parents give to children when they are sent away to boarding school.

15   *L'Usage de la parole*, Paris, 1980. For a discussion of the technical and structural similarities between Sarraute's novels and *Childhood*, see Françoise van Roey-Roux, '*Enfance* de Nathalie Sarraute, ou de la fiction à l'autobiographie', *Etudes littéraires*, xvii:2, 1984, pp. 273–82. Roey-Roux also draws attention to the slight ambiguity concerning the gender of the narrator's interlocutor in the text.

16   See Sarraute's *The Era of Suspicion*, whose title alone makes this point.

17   My translation and my italics. *L'Ere du soupçon*, Paris, 1970 (first published 1956), p. 8. The English translation (by Maria Jolas) of these essays in *Tropisms and The Age of Suspicion*, London, 1963 has a different preface, which makes the same general point.

18   Sarraute's mother was a writer of children's fiction of the kind that Natasha is aping here. Valerie Minogue's reading of *Enfance* sees all Sarraute's writing as an unwriting of her mother's kind of literature: see 'Fragments of a childhood: Nathalie Sarraute's *Enfance*', *Romance Studies*, IX, 1986, pp. 71–83.

19   See 'Chateaubriand and the poetics of the autobiographical incident', *Romance Studies*, VIII, 1986, p. 30. I am indebted to Michael Sheringham for advice and discussion concerning a number of points that have arisen in this paper.

20   I owe the inspiration behind this line of thinking to Johnnie Gratton who drew my attention to some of the ways in which narrative increasingly encroaches on the apparently a-chronological structure of *Enfance*.

21   The name, which is discussed at some length in *Angélique*, is itself a clear echo of *Djinn* and its narrator-hero Simon Lecoeur.

22   The term 'romanesque' almost certainly comes from Barthes who uses it in opposition to 'le roman' to define a certain quality of writing which he distinguishes from the specific conventions associated with the genre: plot, proper-names, etc.

23   Only the critic Maurice Blanchot is credited with having seen them, but his article was ignored as the orthodoxy, bolstered by Barthes's pieces on Robbe-Grillet, took hold. See Maurice Blanchot, 'La clarté romanesque', in *Le Livre à venir*, Paris, 1959. However, Robbe-Grillet forgives Barthes for his role in the bureaucratising of his fiction by saying that his comments were

those of a novelist, and that the relations between Barthes and Robbe-Grillet were really 'relations between novelist and novelist, and not any more between novelist and critic' ('Pourquoi j'aime Barthes', *Prétexte: Roland Barthes*, Paris, 1978, p. 259), in other words, hypertextual rather than metatextual.

24  *Le Miroir*, p. 32. Ricardou's (brief) discussion of this door is in *Le nouveau roman*, Paris, 1973, pp. 118–19. My own reading of this door treated it as auto-referential rather than biographical, in so far as I saw it as an emblem of 'the false and the imitated' (and still would, regardless of its autobiographical origins). See Ann Jefferson, *The Nouveau Roman and the Poetics of Fiction*, Cambridge, 1980, pp. 96–7.

25  Jean-Jacques Brochier, *Alain Robbe-Grillet: Qui suis-je?*, Lyon, 1985, p. 147.

26  In Robbe-Grillet, 'Pourquoi j'aime Barthes', p. 266. For a discussion of the problematic nature of commentary see Leyla Perrone-Moisés, 'L'intertextualité critique', *Poétique*, XXVII, 1976, pp. 372–84, which contains an excellent discussion of commentary as critical intertextuality.

27  Obviously, in denouncing this practice I nevertheless have to include myself in it. But this simply confirms the point by showing how easily the system can accommodate this kind of attack.

28  This is the title of a recent number of *Yale French Studies* (LXVI, 1984, ed. Sima Godfrey). Although Robbe-Grillet seems to share the wish he attributes to Corinthe in *Angélique* to be 'the last writer', his anxieties are directed more against the critical readings he anticipates than against the writers who will come after him.

29  As Marc Angenot has shrewdly noted. See 'L'"intertextualité"; enquête sur l'émergence et la diffusion d'un champ notionnel', *Revue des sciences humaines*, CLXXXIX, 1983, pp. 121–35.

# Intertextuality or influence: Kristeva, Bloom and the *Poésies* of Isidore Ducasse

Any text is constructed as a mosaic of quotations; any text is the absorption and transformation of another. The notion of *intertextuality* replaces that of intersubjectivity, and poetic language is read as at least *double*.[1]

Close critical attention is rarely paid to Ducasse's *Poésies,* the seemingly slight, 'other' work by the author of *Maldoror,*[2] and its double importance for Kristeva, as a typically 'intertextual' *and* typically 'avant-garde' work, is a valuable redress of such neglect. That neglect itself had afforded the text a privileged place in a Post-Modern canon of the misread avant-garde, from Sade to Céline, a tradition that Kristeva and her contemporaries on *Tel Quel,*[3] all textual practitioners, boldly continue in their own critical practice, effacing the distinction between literature and criticism: in this 'multiple textual space', all are equal. Such a bold gesture finds a precedent in the double character of *Poésies* itself, as both poetry and criticism, and finds a rationale in the theory of intertextuality, of which *Poésies* is, for Kristeva, an exemplary illustration. But it is exemplary in its most peculiar feature, the seventy-five or so 'corrective' citations that appropriate another's text and by slight modification reverse its sense, and a difficulty arises when 'the absorption of a multiplicity of texts (of meanings) in the poetic message'[4] is illustrated with citations from *Poésies* that actually articulate only two texts: the appropriated pre-text and its correction. Hence the closest Kristeva comes to a close reading of *Poésies* in fact evokes not the 'multiple textual space' of Kristevan intertextuality but a closed arena where two combatants, or their texts, are, as the theorist of a different tradition might say, locked in poetic warfare.[5] The inappropriateness of taking Ducasse's citational practice in *Poésies* as 'a striking example' of intertextuality's 'dialogue between discourses' is the more unfortunate in that *Poésies* is by far the example most frequently used by Kristeva.[6] The same tendency to illustrate generalities with examples too particular for the task characterises her description of historical context. The dialogic process, she claims, 'is observable throughout literary history', a history which is then epitomised in the following observations: Poe was translated by Baudelaire, who influenced Mallarmé, who then translated Poe, who had been influenced by De Quincey, who had also been translated by Baudelaire. Not only is it highly cutaneous to treat influence, translation and citation as instances of the same phenomenon, but in taking for example so historically situated a conjunction in literature – the 'situation de Baudelaire', in Valéry's phrase[7] – Kristeva undoes her own claim to have discovered in the 'complex movement of affirmation and negation' between texts a 'fundamental law' of specifically modern poetic production. 'The network can be multiplied, it would always express the same law', she insists, but on closer inspection the network proves less receptive. To give one example, as 'the simultaneous absorption and destruction of another text from the intertextual space', Alfred de Musset's thoroughly Romantic and un-modern 1828 adaptation of De Quincey should also belong in the network – but then dialogue between discourses would no longer be specifically a phenomenon of modernity. Or, to take another, the network might reach from Baudelaire and Mallarmé towards Valéry, three French poets who, in Eliot's words, 'represent the beginning, the middle and the end of a particular tradition in poetry',[8] but that would be to foreclose intertextual multiplicity and substitute a defunct High Modernism for Kristeva's still-thriving Post-Modernity (a tradition that has thrived in France not least upon the determined wresting of Mallarmé from the misprisions of Valéry). In whichever circumstances, it is not Kristeva's ambition to include Musset, Valéry or Eliot along with Ducasse among the forebears of her own textual practice. That it can be done shows, perhaps, that her critical attention to *Poésies* itself needs our closer attention.

Kristeva's double error is firstly to read *Poésies* as no more than citational, and then to assimilate it to a generalising theory of intertextuality ill-adapted to its particular citational manner. *Poésies* is a text that needs both a continual re-thinking of its place in several literary traditions, poetic and otherwise, and a close attention to its unassimilable particularity. Following Sima Godfrey's 'Anxiety of anticipation: ulterior motives in French poetry',[9] a Bloomian approach might satisfy those needs left unfulfilled by Kristeva, although it is not, despite the many citations in his writing, as a theorist of citational intertextuality that Bloom proves useful. His close reading of the connections between texts is unlikely to elucidate Ducasse's citational practice, since it is Bloom's personal swerve away from convention to read together texts that wilfully deny their explicit relations. The Bloomian agon of strong poet and strong poet can be fought without either reading the other's text, and it is not imitation but antithesis that locks them in battle; for Bloom an unwillingness to cite each other is proof of relations between poets.

In its use of different critical vocabularies, however, Bloom's writing is objectively intertextual, and throws light on *Poésies* by analogy. The greater part of Ducasse's text is not, in fact, in Kristeva's sense 'a mosaic of citations', or a tesselation in Bloom's sense,[10] but like both *Revolution in Poetic Language* and *The Anxiety of Influence*, *Poésies* is a montage of diverse theories. Whereas the mark of such diversity in Kristeva's work is its fourteen pages of bibliography, in Bloom it is the nomenclature of the 'six revisionary ratios': *clinamen, tessera, kenosis, daemonization, askesis, apophrades,* credited respectively to Lucretius (via Alfred Jarry), ancient mystery cults, Saint Paul, Neo-Platonism, Empedocles and Athenian civic ritual. If the vocabulary of *Poésies* is just as diverse, its immediate origins in contemporary philosophy, from Proudhon to Taine, are only hinted at (and Ducasse includes no bibliography). The display of names is saved for the familiarly Bloomian genealogies of imagination that proliferate in *Poésies*: Corneille and Racine; Dante and Milton; Hugo, Lamartine and Musset – the text is littered with the great dead names, entered in lists, grouped into parties and pitted against each other, fathers against sons. In an adaptation of Bloom to the context of French Romanticism, the solitary struggle of the poet with his precursor gives way to a theatre of cultural war, the critical scene where the combatants are schools of thought and polemical judgements, and the prize is institutionalised authority. *Poésies* itself is this 'staged scene', a 'court of judgement' such as Bloom discovers in Browning's *Childe Roland* and a play of authors-as-puppets, 'marionettes with frayed strings',[11] animate only in the critical discourse that puts them to use. The primal scene of this drama was enacted by Victor

Hugo in his *Preface to Cromwell* to criticise just such a critical practice:

Again, the names of the dead are always thrown in the teeth of the living; Corneille stoned with Tasso and Guarini (Guarini!) as later Racine will be stoned with Corneille, Voltaire with Racine, and as every genius who shows his face today is stoned with Corneille, Racine and Voltaire. These tactics, as we see, are played out, but still they must have some merit, for they are still resorted to.[12]

As they are resorted to forty years later when Ducasse turns on Hugo: 'The barbarous vaudevilles of Hugo do not proclaim duty. The melodramas of Racine, of Corneille, the novels of La Calprenède do. Lamartine is incapable of composing Pradon's *Phèdre*; nor Hugo, Rotrou's *Venceslas*; nor Sainte-Beuve, the tragedies of Laharpe or of Marmontel . . .' (*Poésies*, p. 68). Ducasse contests such 'insane prefaces as the preface to *Cromwell*' (*Poésies*, p. 34) by making a pawn of the giant Hugo, kept down as much by the lesser (Rotrou!) as the great. The pre-texts of Ducasse's critique are not those particular plays by Pradon and Rotrou, nor the dramatic works of Laharpe and Marmontel. The Scenes of Instruction are commonplace ones: the schoolroom, where it is taught that Rotrou and Pradon are nothing more than the lesser contemporaries of Corneille and Racine, and the discourse of conventional criticism in which Laharpe and Marmontel are Voltaire's lesser disciples and nothing more. The hundred or so names wielded in *Poésies* are commonly read as the precursors of the poet Ducasse, but they are merely quotations from Literature, agents of institutional precursors (School, Press and Academy) which are collectively invulnerable to the assaults of the individual poet. Ducasse's tactical response is to play off these institutions against their agents, picking them off one by one: 'I isolate the most beautiful poems of Lamartine, Victor Hugo, Alfred de Musset, Byron and Baudelaire, and I correct them in the sense of hope; I show what ought to have been done' (*Poésies*, p. 126). Of these subjects for revision, only Hugo is still alive in 1870. It is Hugo who, in Bloom's overview of influences on Baudelaire, alone among French poets fits the type of the strong poet with whom the lesser must compete: 'Valéry, unlike both Formalist and Post-Structuralist critics, understood that Hugo was to French poetry what Whitman was to American poetry, and Wordsworth was to all British poetry after him: the inescapable precursor.'[13] Baudelaire's failure to escape Hugo's influence is made much of by Bloom, too much, given Godfrey's persuasive demonstration that the truly inescapable authority over modern French poets, even over Baudelaire, is Boileau: 'Charles Baudelaire ou Boileau hystérique' is the formula she cites from a critic of the 1860's.[14] For a modern poet like Baudelaire, or for the author of *Maldoror*, each readily the Satan of a Bloomian scenario, Hugo may be, in Bloom's words for Milton's God, the dead but still embarrassingly potent and present ancestor (*AI*, p. 20). But for both, such Satanism is role-playing, a fact Ducasse underscores by assuming the name and persona of the Comte de Lautréamont, last of the 'poètes maudits' (*Poésies*, p. 124) and only a fiction, a marionette operated by Ducasse for the purpose of exploding the myths of literary Satanism. That done, Ducasse takes up, unhysterically, the properly French concern with poetic theory that starts from Boileau – and his own 'art poétique' is *Poésies*. This is not to say that his *œuvre* cannot accommodate an orthodox Bloomian reading. If ever Bloom comes to preface a volume of Modern Critical Views on Lautréamont, he might well choose to cite this passage, the post-scriptum to a letter from the young Ducasse to Hugo, into which can be read all the tremulous subjection of the ephebe before the ancestral poet: 'You cannot know how happy you might make a human being, if you were to write me a few words. [. . .] Having come to the end of my letter, I contemplate my audacity more calmly, and I tremble at having written to you, I who am still nothing in this century, whereas you, you are All.'[15] So suitable a candidate for the role of ephebe in a Bloomian agon might reasonably be expected to have developed, as theorist, into a theorist of poetic influence, even if, as Bloom might contend, a pathological refusal to be Bloomian is as likely an outcome and as compatible with the theory. Ducasse's critical revision of Literature does make several Bloomian gestures. *Poésies* is criticism of the kind that, as Bloom would have it, tends to become poetry as poetry tends to become criticism. Ducasse, like Bloom, meditates upon misreading and, at least no less than does Bloom, offers instruction in the practical criticism of poetry. But what Ducasse means by practical criticism is the correctional citation of deviant texts, refusing the authority Bloom invests in 'the poet as poet' and, to paraphrase Kristeva, installing intertextuality in the place of intersubjectivity. The overwhelming personal prestige of Victor Hugo, who still awes Bloom today, no longer impresses the ephebe Ducasse: Hugo belongs with Baudelaire, Lamartine and

Sainte-Beuve, among the deceased (though he actually outlived Ducasse by fifteen years). In a Bloomian history, Hugo's longevity is a dark shadow cast over the period's literature, dominating four generations of ˜ontemporaries. In Ducasse's literary history, all poets, from Aeschylus to Zorrilla, are dead poets, 'poètes maudits', and contemporaries in the grave. The mission of *Poésies* is the salvation of their texts.

In *Poésies II*, six stanzas from Hugo's *Tristesse d'Olympio* are revised by Ducasse, but the citation is not of the kind that for Kristeva exemplifies intertextuality (inverting key terms, reversing the sense and retaining the form). If the beginning and end of the passage are recognisably out of Hugo,[16] between them the text has been purged of its own language and opened to a quite extraneous voice: '[Love] is no longer severe towards the object of its wishes, rendering justice unto itself: the expansion is accepted. The senses no longer have their thorn to excite the sexes of the flesh. The love of humanity is beginning.' (*Poésies*, p. 70) At least one allusion here can be traced: 'l'aiguillon de la chair', the thorn in the flesh, is the 'messenger of Satan' that St Paul describes buffeting him (II Corinthians XII:7). The point of this allusion is clear enough since in this chapter and in the epistle as a whole Paul describes the incursion into the human province (the world, the body, the heart) of the extra-human, be it by the grace of God in Christ's Incarnation or by the operation of Satan. In *Poésies* Paul's text repeats the gesture by entering Hugo's poem as an agent of the divine. 'An intermediary being, neither divine or human, enters into the adept to aid him', Bloom might say (*AI*, p. 15). But what Paul describes is not quite Bloom's *daemonization*. Satan, standing here, as in the Book of Job, in God's service as man's 'adversary', is a close but an external threat, the enemy 'before you', as are the inhabitants of the land before the Israelites, in the Old Testament passage to which Paul's text alludes:

And an angel of the Lord came up from Gilgal to Bochim, and said, I made you to go up out of Egypt, and have brought you unto the land which I sware unto your fathers: and I said, I will never break my convenant with you.
And ye shall make no league with the inhabitants of this land; ye shall throw down their altars: but ye have not obeyed my voice: why have ye done this? Wherefore I also said, I will not drive them out from before you; but they shall be as *thorns in your sides*, and their gods shall be a snare unto you.
(Judges II: 1–3, Revised Version, my italics.)

The same God, with the same intent, lays a different landscape before man in Hugo's *Tristesse d'Olympio*: 'Gods lends us a moment the meadows and the fountains to place there our hearts, our dreams, our loves. Then He takes them from us.'[17] This sentimentalised nature, the physical world of externalised passions, is discarded by Ducasse in the textual revision of Hugo's poem. He expands Paul's phrase to include love, the object of Hugo's morbid nostalgia, here purged of its mystery at the source: 'the sexes of the flesh'. The hostile, Old Testament terrain and its ensnaring gods were left behind by Paul in his conversion to Christ. Repeating the gesture, Ducasse repudiates the passions, strange gods of the romantic landscape, as Paul repudiates the merely physical persecutions of Satan. 'And when he tells us There was given to me a thorn in the flesh, the messenger of Satan, what is he saying but that his suffering was confined to the physical domain' (St John Chrysostom, *Sixth homily on Saint Paul*).[18] This is the suffering of which Hugo's poem is purged by Ducasse when he excises reference to the landscape: this textual revision is, literally, a conversion. The poem that remains in *Poésies* is only apparently diminished, converted from verse to prose and emptied of its properly poetical content (an emptying-out – *kenosis* – not in Bloom's sense,[19] though he takes it from St Paul). The communicant text is made open to receive, quite literally, the 'flesh' of another. Citation is a form of grace:

For this thing I besought the Lord thrice, that it might depart from me.
And he said unto me, My grace is sufficient for thee: for my strength is made perfect in weakness. Most gladly therefore will I rather glory in my infirmities, that the power of Christ may rest upon me. (II Corinthians XII: 8–10)

This 'return of the dead', of Christ in His power, is not the dismal or unlucky day of Bloom's *apophrades,* when 'the dead returned to reinhabit the houses in which they had lived' (*AI,* p. 15), but an occasion to glory. If Paul's words describe the Devil's external influence, their citation by Ducasse is an Imitation of Christ, an appropriation of the force of the Christian covenant in its corrective movement: a *clinamen*, or swerve 'so as to make change possible in the universe', (*AI,* p. 14).[20] Bloom's taking of Lucretius' language of physics to describe poetic misreading is, of course, itself a misreading, the critic's gesture an Imitation of the poet's: the swerve from a 'true' sense of the appropriated vocabulary is always intended. My figural use of grace for misprision in *Poésies* does the same, in imitation of Ducasse's secularising appropriation of Christianity's true sense.[21] In *Tristesse d'Olympio* Hugo is a Christian poet: 'The soul, in a dark recess where all seems to expire, senses something throbbing still beneath a veil . . . It is you who sleeps in the shadows, o sacred memory!' In *Poésies* (p. 70) this text is converted to that of the anti-Christian Ducasse: 'The love of humanity is beginning. In these days when man senses that he becomes an altar adorned with his virtues . . . the soul, in a recess of the heart where all seems to be reborn, senses something that no longer throbs. I have named memory.' Ducasse's removal of the 'veil' from Hugo's text imitates the gesture performed by Christ, in the New Testament passage to which Hugo alludes:

for until this day remaineth the same vail untaken away in the reading of the old testament; which vail is done away with in Christ.
But even unto this day, when Moses is read, the vail is upon their heart.
Nevertheless, when it shall turn to the Lord, the vail shall be taken away.
(II Corinthians III: 14–16)

The 'veil' is lifted, and that which was hidden beneath the veil is abolished, 'no longer throbs. I have named memory.' Conversion of the heretic here swerves from the true Christian sense by desecrating, literally, the converted text: Hugo's 'memory' is purged of its epithet ('sacred') so that he might receive a secular grace. By contracting Hugo's poem into prose, Ducasse has made possible the reading of the precursor text: correction is redemption. By redeeming the text Ducasse lifts the burden of the past and becomes the Christ of a secular humanism, whose grace is this death of memory.[22]

Ducasse's projected correction of his forebears Hugo, Lamartine, Musset, Byron and Baudelaire was to feature 'at the same time six of the wickedest passages from my cursed books'. The only trace of this is on p. 68 of *Poésies,* a revision of strophe 5 from the first *Chant de Maldoror*. This pre-text from *Maldoror* acts there as preface to a Sadeian burlesque of Christian redemption. Its last lines are a derisive prayer for the gift of grace: 'God [. . .] it is you I invoke. Show me a man who is good! – But let your grace centuple my natural powers, for I may die of terror beholding the monster; men have died of less.'[23] In using his own text as pre-text Ducasse seems to have avoided 'the immense anxieties of indebtedness' that 'self-appropriation involves' necessarily for Bloom (*AI*, p. 5), but the pre-text itself is indebted to a pre-text, a discussion of grace from Ernest Naville's

1868 *Le Problème du mal*: 'It is sometimes asked, Why did not God make the creature incapable of sin, that is to say, *necessarily* good?'[24] The incredible 'monster' of the *Chants de Maldoror* is clearly a perversion of Naville's Christ:

> Not only do you think that there has never been a man who has always chosen Good; but, in the actual condition of humanity, you do not believe it possible for a perfectly good man to exist. No one believes it; and I could desire no better proof than the controversies which are ever waging around the name of Jesus of Nazareth. Those who pronounce Him perfectly good infer without hesitation from this perfect goodness His Divine nature, and those who deny His divinity do not hesitate to deny the historical reality of this perfectly good man. (*The Problem of Evil*, pp. 119–120)

When in *Poésies* the *Chants de Maldoror* are corrected, the passage is purged of its explicit reference to grace and distanced from this pre-text in Naville. If Ducasse will have a strong precursor, it will be not Hugo but Christ, the strongest of all and not 'simply a figure for any truly strong poet'.[25] And when His strength is dissipated in mediation through texts, there will be no more strong precursors to speak of. The weak remain to remind us of what might have been: in the place of the precursor stands Naville. Not only is his Christian reading of modern poetry the archetype and test of Ducasse's own judgements but, as Ducasse points out to his publisher, he is also a tangible forebear whom the ephebe might, reversing the flow in Bloomian style, influence in turn.[26] But it seems Ducasse has missed an important point: the ephebe must challenge the strong, not the weak (as Coleridge does Milton, now Cowper), if he is to be a strong poet himself; or, if he is to become a critic, challenge a strong critic (as Pater does Ruskin, not Swinburne); or else convert all precursors into critics of some kind and pitch against their collective strength (as Bloom does). Ducasse does 'follow' Bloom in this last respect, except that he challenges the collective weakness of his precursors. The oppositions in *Poésies* between groups of writers result in minor victories (Hugo and Lamartine over Musset, Racine and Corneille over Hugo), but in the lists of his precursors Ducasse is ultimately, in the last of them (*Poésies* p. 76), a leveller: 'Poor Hugo! Poor Racine! Poor Coppée! Poor Corneille! Poor Boileau! Poor Scarron! Tics, tics, tics.'

The ratios may be different from Bloom's, but the point is still that readings are necessarily misreadings, and there is a map to be drawn of the Ducassian landscape. Bloom uses ratios to determine 'the poet's stance – rhetorical, psychological, imagistic – as he writes his poem': 'The figure that a poet makes, not so much in or by his poem, but as the poem relates to other poems, is the figure I seek to isolate, define, and describe by adequate gradations' (*BV*, p. 7). Possession, Conversion, Salvation, Redemption, etc. are all terms available if the ratios in *Poésies* need names. But the anti-messianic figure made in and by that text (the poet as ant*i*- not ant*e*christ) is made not by the poet but by the reader, as s/he relates the poem to other, messianic, poems, and it is as much the stance of the reader that the names adequately describe. 'No reader [. . .] can describe her or his relationship to a prior text without taking up a stance no less tropological than that occupied by the text itself' (*BV*, p. 30). When Sollers writes of 'Lautréamont's science' and Kristeva uses algebraic equations to represent what happens in *Poésies*,[27] not only is their stance 'no less tropological' than Ducasse's, but it is so in what they believe is the same way, troping on both poet and critics as 'scientists of the text' and effacing the distinctions between them. Bloom's different stance may have the advantage of accounting for such wayward tropologies, but in arguing that the language of poetry and the language of criticism are equally tropological he shares with Kristeva and Sollers a desire to assume the same stance as that 'occupied by the text itself', effacing the distinction between critic and poet: their languages 'cannot differ, in more than degree' (*BV*, p. 29).

Bloom has eloquently argued that criticism is as tropological as its object: 'all poetry necessarily becomes verse criticism, just as all criticism becomes prose-poetry' (*AI*, p. 95), and he enjoys the scandal this has spread among those traditional critics who have always behaved as if criticism could avoid contagion from its tropological object. But it may not be literature that corrupts. When Bloom seems so often to make the poems he reads read as if he had written them, and when readings of Bloom – even this one – seem momentarily unable to avoid the same impression, it is he who becomes the carrier: 'Influence is Influenza – an astral disease' (*AI*, p. 95). How he caught this disease and how he passes it on is a story told in his books. His description of poetic influence is a description of how he was influenced by poets, and he is interested only in the theory of influence and of relations between poets insofar as he himself – the Critic as Poet – has relations of his own with other poets, or insofar as relations between other poets serve as figures for those relations of his own. When he supports the theory of misprision with quotations from Shelley, Stevens or Ashbery that describe the same process figuratively, he makes of these poets the types of poetical critic that he has become. Poetry necessarily becomes verse-criticism, certainly, when it is read by a critic bent on writing prose-poetry. In such circumstances he is right to insist that criticism is as tropological as poetry, even if that insistence too is necessarily a trope. But poetry need not be tropological 'in the same way' as criticism, need not assume the same stance as the critic himself, and the assumption that it does is also, just as necessarily, a trope, one that serves Bloom's ambition. *Poésies* is poetry that resists such wholesale appropriation by the critic: my reading of Ducasse through Bloom can use only those parts of *Poésies* (the relation to precursors and the appropriation of 'other', authoritative language) that anticipate the theory of influence, albeit antithetically; Kristeva can use *Poésies* to illustrate intertextuality where the theory of intertextuality is anticipated by its citational practice, albeit partially. The object of the reading is troped, anxiously perhaps,[28] as an anticipation of the reading. The evident partiality of such readings leaves the text's integrity untouched and available to other readings. Shelley, Stevens and Ashbery, if they are strong poets, will survive Bloom's reading of them, as Ducasse has survived Symbolists, Surrealists, Existentialists and Scientists of the Text. The relative appropriateness of Bloom's theory of influence and of Kristeva's intertextuality as approaches to reading Ducasse may be measured, finally, by the distance each keeps: the misappropriations of each remain obvious, and it is the usefulness of such readings that they never come close, since they then may still serve as the ante- (or anti-) models for other, if not closer, readings.

## Notes

1   Julia Kristeva, 'Word, dialogue and novel' in *The Kristeva Reader*, ed. Toril Moi, Oxford, 1986, p. 37.
2   *Lautréamont's Maldoror*, trans. Alexis Lykiard, London, 1970.
3   Cf. *Théorie d'ensemble*, Paris, 1968.
4   Kristeva, *Sémiotiké, recherches pour une sémanalyse*, Paris, 1969 (re-issued 1978), p. 194. All citations from Kristeva are from this and the following page. Her principal discussions of *Poésies* are in this chapter, 'Poésie et négativité', and in the section on 'Le contexte présupposé' from *La Révolution du langage poétique*, Paris, 1974, pp. 337–58. The English translation of this book omits Kristeva's discussions of Ducasse's work.
5   'A poetic "text" [. . .] is a psychic battlefield upon which authentic

forces struggle for the only victory worth winning, the divinating triumph over oblivion.' Harold Bloom, *Poetry and Repression,* New Haven, 1976, p. 2.

6   In what follows I am indebted to Jonathan Culler's discussion of Kristeva and Bloom, in his chapter on 'Presupposition and intertextuality' in *The Pursuit of Signs,* London, 1981, pp. 105–111.

7   Paul Valéry, 'Situation de Baudelaire' in *Variétés II, Œuvres I,* Paris, 1957, pp. 598–613.

8   T. S. Eliot, 'From Poe to Valéry' in *To Criticise the Critic,* London, 1965, p. 28.

9   Sima Godfrey (ed.), *Yale French Studies,* LXVI, 1984, pp. 1–26.

10   'I take the word *(tessera)* not from mosaic-making.' Harold Bloom, *The Anxiety of Influence,* Oxford, 1973, p. 14. Hereinafter *AI* and cited in the text.

11   Ducasse, *Poésies,* trans. Alexis Lykiard, London, 1978, p. 40. Hereinafter *Poésies* and cited in the text. Lykiard's translation is too free to show clearly the relation to certain pre-texts so I have used my own.

12   *Preface to Oliver Cromwell,* in Victor Hugo, *Dramas,* trans. I. G. Burnham, London, 1896, p. 24.

13   Bloom (ed.), *Charles Baudelaire,* New York, 1987, p. 3.

14   Alcide Dusolier, writing in *Le Nain jaune,* April, 1864, cited in Godfrey, op. cit., p. 20.

15   Letter dated 10 November 1868 and recently discovered in a copy of the first *Chant de Maldoror* that had been sent by Ducasse to Hugo. First published in the *Bulletin du bibliophile,* I, 1983, pp. 13–22.

16   Victor Hugo, *Les Rayons et les ombres,* in *Œuvres poétiques complètes,* Montreal, 1944, p. 239–40.

17   Op. cit. My translation.

18   My translation from *Homélies sur Saint Paul,* Paris, 1980, p. 94.

19   For Bloom, *kenosis* 'is a movement towards discontinuity with the precursor' *(AI,* p. 14), whereas the action of grace I am describing is the reverse.

20   To conjoin Lucretian materialism and medieval Christian mysticism as here is not so inappropriate. The publication history of Thomas à Kempis's book could itself be a repertoire of ratios for misprision: issued anonymously under the exhortation to 'Inquire not who said this, but attend to what is said' (I, v); then variously attributed authors until a copyist signed his transcription and gave it his name; then variously rewritten, 'corrected' or truncated, in Protestant translations; then discovered to have been written for the most part not as prose but as poetry; and so on.

21   For a more detailed discussion of Ducasse's anti-Christian stance, see my 'The precursors and pre-texts of *Poésies',* *French Studies Bulletin* XXXIII, 1990.

22   This is akin to Bloom's Death of Love: 'This voiding of the sense of others and otherness, and so of the possibility of any eros save self-love, represents a renewal of the Gnostic "call" of the Alien God, the true estranged Divinity who has been thrust aside by Jehovah the Demiurge, the mere god of nature and the Creation . . .', 'Auras: the sublime crossing and

the death of love', *Oxford Literary Review,* IV, 3, 1984, p. 15.

23    Adapted from John Rodker's translation in *The Lay of Maldoror,* London, 1924, p. 7.

24    *The Problem of Evil. Seven lectures by Ernest Naville, translated from the French by E. W. Shalders,* Edinburgh, 1871, p. 184.

25    Bloom, *The Breaking of the Vessels,* 1982, p. 36. Hereinafter *BV.*

26    For a more detailed discussion of Ducasse's relation to Naville, see my 'The precursors and pre-texts of *Poésies*'.

27    Philippe Sollers, 'La science de Lautréamont' in *Logiques,* Paris, 1968, pp. 250–301, and Kristeva, 'Le contexte présupposé' (op. cit.).

28    This is not the Anxiety of Anticipation of which Godfrey writes (op. cit.).

# Alter ego: intertextuality, irony and the politics of reading

John Frow argues, cogently, that the relation between a literary text and the social discourses its employs (or displays) is not a direct one – say, of 'imitation' – but mediated.[1] It is mediated, Frow proposes, by the literary intertext, that is, by reference to the literary system. Within that system, certain texts have become recognised, that is 'canonised', and so come to stand for the hegemonic social forces, the system of power that gave them their status. In proposing itself as 'not-X' (where 'X' is the intertextual referent), a text claims literary status, but simultaneously distinguishes itself as a negativity with respect to the canon, and in so doing distances itself from the socially marked discourses that, nevertheless, necessarily traverse it. Thus we know that *Madame Bovary* is not a clichéd text but a text 'about' cliché because it sets itself off intertextually from, *inter alia,* the stereotypes of a Romantic literature of sentiment.

Thus two mutually implicating 'alter ego' relationships are set up. The text defines itself by defining an intertext as that which it is not; and the text defines itself as 'text', in similarly negative fashion, against its own 'discourse', with which it should not be identified. In each case, then, no positive term can be identified: we can say only that the text is not its 'alter ego', it is *not not-I,*[2] whether 'not-I' is the intertext against which the text is defining itself, or the discourse that traverses it and from which it is 'distanced'. This is an essentially ironic and modernist understanding of the nature of textuality; and Flaubert is certainly its *locus classicus.* Thus, one might think of the Tweedledum-and-Tweedledee relationship of the two eponymous 'heroes' of *Bouvard et Pécuchet* as figuring the paradoxical relations involved in a text whose cited intertext consists of the encyclopaedia of its own culture and which can only be described, therefore, as a 'text', *against* the encyclopaedic discourse of which it is composed.

*Bouvard et Pécuchet* is certainly an unmentioned intertext of one of Frank Moorhouse's most teasing stories, 'The alter ego interpretation',[3] where the nexus of intertextuality (as text–text relation) and textual irony (as discourse–text distinction) is thematised. It is thematised, interestingly, in terms of the phenomenon of 'camp,' which I take to be a form of irony: the performance of gender-roles ('butch' or *'femme'*) that are so insistently delineated as to constitute the subject of the performance as the negation of those roles. Not the least valuable aspect of the text, then, is its situation of the literary performance of 'alter ego' in terms of a sexual politics. And here again Flaubert, notably the Flaubert of *Salammbô* – one of the campier texts of the European novelistic tradition – is an obvious, if unmentioned intertext.

But 'The alter ego interpretation' is also an *Éducation Sentimentale,* in which the fiasco of an emotional relationship stands for the failures of a social formation, and the characters' blindness to the causes of the fiasco requires an ironic reading that dissociates the text, also, from the society it delineates (but to which it necessarily belongs). What is ironised in 'The alter ego interpretation' is, however, precisely the ironic structure of the 'alter ego' relation as a model of textuality: it is shown to be politically dubious (in terms of sexual politics) and fatally incomplete (as an 'interpretation' of the nature of art). For a text can only produce itself, or be produced, as having the ironic 'alter ego' structure of the 'literary' by virtue of an act that simultaneously locates it, politically, in the social world. The act in question is called reading.

In this sense, the condition of the text's belonging to the *literary* system – that is, its intertextuality and its ironic relation to its 'own' discourse – is the fact of its belonging to the domain of *social* relations and *political* conflict. For 'literarity', as the mode of irony that defines text as the *not not-I* with respect to social discourses – that is, both to the canonised intertext and to its own textual discourse – is itself dependent on the social phenomenon of its being recognised by a readership, and I mean 'recognised' in the sense of 'noticed' and in the sense of 'accepted'. There can be no intertextuality (constitutive of the literary system) except as it is produced by a reader in the act of perceiving the textual discourse as part of the literary system; and it is in thus recognising the text as belonging to a form of discourse historically produced as subject to 'interpretation', that the reader constitutes the text as an 'alter ego' with respect to itself, that is as meaning 'more', or rather *other,* than it says. In other words, the supposed 'alter ego' relations of literary textuality are in fact a triangulated system, since the text does not become 'text' until it is read.

I will argue that two paradoxes result, and that these two paradoxes permit 'The alter ego interpretation' to ironise its own ironic structure. The first is that the literary system only becomes literary – constituted by the 'alter ego' relation – in the presence of a third, and that that third contaminates the specificity, with respect to the social, that the literary claims as an autonomous system. The second paradox is that, if intertextuality functions within the literary system as an oppositional gesture toward (socially) canonised texts of the 'tradition', it constitutes at the same time, by virtue of its own implicit but necessary address to a readership that will so recognise it, an appeal for canonisation on its own behalf, that is for the (social) acceptance of its own (socially and literarily) oppositional gesture. It is not only, then, that the reader is *necessary* to the functioning of the 'alter ego' relation that defines literature; that reader is also the object of an active *seduction.* Of course, one might make a similar analysis of camp, as an ironically rebellious performance that can function only if it is so recognised, and which therefore tends to address an audience and define itself as a seductive 'entertainment'.

## Alter ego

'The alter ego interpretation' is set in the Sydney suburb of Balmain in the seventies, an old, previously working-class, inner-city neighbourhood now increasingly populated by a recently arrived group of trendies: 'The new mildly-rebellious young adults. Living in old suburbs like cockroaches' (p. 11). I want to suggest that such a formulation does not simply capture the class structure of Balmain but also allegorises the situation of the literary text, rebellious but parasitic on the 'old' culture, the society against which it rebels. Thus, the narrator (whom I shall call 'Frank')[4] lives with his friend Milton and Milton's wife, Hestia, in the Big House, also called the Gatsby House for its size and luxury.

Another thing. We are now beginning to belong in the Big House with its tennis courts, swimming pools, bedrooms with bathrooms. The three of us in an eight bedroom house. At first we were the negroes who had ousted southern gentlemen and ladies, and camped in the mansion. Now we are becoming the gentlemen and the ladies. (p. 10)

'Camping' in a mansion entails becoming 'the gentlemen and the ladies', such – according to the allegory – is the fate of the literary. Why? How?

The story consists largely of a series of conversations, mostly set in restaurants and pubs, around the issue of Frank's and Milton's relationship: they are considering the 'homosexual thing' (p. 11), Frank more urgently than the flirtatious but reluctant Milton. These conversations simultaneously constitute brilliantly executed exempla of what might be called Balmain-speak, which the narrator speaks also in his own right. So the 'dialect' of the text is that of seventies Balmain – except that what constitutes it as *text* is the fact that we read its discourse, precisely, as exemplary. The text is produced, through our reading, as an 'alter ego' relation with respect to its 'own' discourse – the discourse it is ironically 'displaying'. My proposal is that the relation of Frank and Milton figures the 'alter ego' relation of text, and that its failure can therefore tell us something about the nature of textuality.

For when – Hestia having left ('Because of emotional neglect?' p. 10) – the pair finally try sex, the result is a fiasco, which Frank attempts to explain by the 'alter ego interpretation' of the relationship. 'It's really an alter ego relationship – that's why it didn't work in bed. At least not the way we tried it' (p. 13). The 'alter ego' relation, as a *dual* system ('the way we tried it'), with its (acknowledged) narcissistic quality and (unmentioned) Platonic overtones (the intertext is the myth of Aristophanes in the *Symposium*), is insufficiently 'explanatory or predictive' (p. 14). So what relationship *would* work in bed? What interpretation *would* be sufficiently explanatory or predictive?

I have noted some of the intertextual *references* (Flaubert, Plato) and specific *allusions* (*The Great Gatsby*, to which can be added *Vanity Fair*, mentioned as the name of a pub). But at the point where Hestia departs there is a passage that an experienced reader will recognise as making an intertextual *gesture* – one, however, that I think is rather odd. 'Milton sits in the chair opposite my bed. [. . .] I lie under the army blankets. Tranquillisers beside my bed. A glass of red wine spilled in the corner. A loaded shotgun beside the bed. The *Portrait of a Lady* beside the bed. Me hardly the portrait of a lady.

My hands behind my head.' (p. 10) It is odd because the reference to James is hardly illuminating. Obviously there is general thematic resemblance between the story of Isabel Archer's mismatch and that of the botched affair between Frank and Milton, so that *The Portrait of a Lady* can be seen as one of the 'alter egos' of 'The alter ego interpretation'. But the resemblance lacks specificity, and at this purely thematic level almost any other account of a troubled relationship would have served as well. What is happening here?

I propose that this intertextual 'reference' in fact functions as a *figure of intertextuality itself,* and thus that it is the title that is important. Intertextuality produces text as the 'portrait of itself', and in campy fashion, as the portrait of itself 'as a lady'. I am reading the sentence: 'Me hardly the portrait of a lady' as being a classic instance of Freudian 'denial', then, and suggesting that it requires us to reflect precisely on the 'portraitness' and on the 'ladyness' of the textual subject, figured by the narrator Frank.

For Frank is clearly *posed* here (hands behind head) as if for a portrait, among some symbolic icons that indicate Balmain 'life-style' (army blankets, tranquillisers, red wine – I'm not sure I understand the shotgun, however). The issue is not whether he is posing but whether he is posing *as a lady* or – as the comment 'Me hardly the portrait of a lady' would have it – *as himself.* For is it not contradictory to *pose* as 'oneself'? Does not such a pose produce one rather as 'alter ego' than as 'ego'? But what 'ego' would then correspond to the 'alter ego' of the pose? It is notable that Frank defines his identity *only* in terms of what it is not: 'Me hardly the portrait of a lady' leaves us with little that is positive to go on, and that little is itself equivocal. For it is not clear exactly *what* is being denied. Is Frank not the *portrait* of a lady (but a lady)? Is he not the portrait of a *lady* (but of some other kind of woman, say a slut or a whore)? Is he not the portrait of a *woman* at all (but of a man)? The phrase leaves all these conjectures open, plus their permutations and combinations, while admitting also the possibility that Frank *is* the 'portrait of a lady', but *only just* (cf. 'hardly'). Equivalent questions can be asked about the text itself: if it is 'hardly' the *Portrait of a Lady,* what is it? Is it claiming or denying adherence to the class of texts called literary, those that are 'portraits of themselves'? Is it claiming it by denying it?

If 'The alter ego interpretation' belongs to the class of texts that are 'portraits of themselves', then its discourse functions as the 'not-I' of its subject, the narrator Frank, or of its object (the life of Balmain).

But one thing on which the text does seem to be reasonably clear is that if the 'not-I' is a portrait, then so too is the 'not not-I' of identity a representation, for it *is* evident that, since Frank is posing, his denial: 'Me hardly the portrait of a lady' does not really deny his 'portraitness'. The subject or object of representation is itself, then, a representation – so that the whole system is potentially one of infinite regress. And interestingly, questions of representation and portraiture are linked with the question of conversation – i.e. with the major mode of 'portraiture' used in 'The alter ego interpretation' – in 'The ritual of the still photograph'.[5]

There an instructive conversation about conversation occurs. Milton accuses Frank of mimicking 'experience' without living it: 'Your conversations, for instance, are not real – they are imitations of conversations.' 'but fairly perfect imitations,' I say in defence.' ('The ritual of the still photograph', p. 122). Milton concedes that most people can't tell the difference, but insists that Frank's performance (the topic is now his performance of love) 'is like an undetectable forgery . . . the forger alone knows that the money he has is unreal'. To which Frank responds that 'the real currency is unknown to the forger', silently asking himself an unanswered question: 'From what, then are the resemblances copied?' (p. 123). Maurice Blanchot asks somewhere, of literature: what is this resemblance that has nothing to resemble?

Jean Baudrillard would answer Blanchot's question by saying of Frank's conversations and of his performance of love that they are *simulacra*, i.e. copies without an original. They have the uncanniness – or the campiness? – of the hyperreal, i.e. of a reality *produced by signs* that resembles 'real reality' without having its substance.[6] But Frank cannily leaves open the issue of whether there *is* perhaps an original while forcing us to define that 'original' as negativity (and while strongly suggesting, in 'The alter ego interpretation', that it is itself a 'portrait').

Two comments are necessary. One is a reminder: when push comes to shove, i.e. in bed, the 'alter ego interpretation' of identity does not work, and perhaps now we can glimpse why. In producing identity as 'not not-I', it produces it as an unknowable negativity. Frank wants to believe in the 'alter ego' theory, and clings to it, worrying that 'we should perhaps have gently, slowly masturbated ourselves, simply lain there together, touching, and masturbated. Maybe that was the way' (p. 14). But masturbation, separate (as here) or mutual (as suggested earlier), only emphasises the narcissism and the passivity (the limpness?) that inheres in the 'alter ego inter-pretation'. In this 'interpretation', Frank can only ever be the 'alter' of his own 'alter ego', Milton: ' "I'm your downtown self," I say, "and you're my academic self" ' (p. 13). A chiasmus is sketched, but the failure of the terms to *meet* – as in shared masturbation – is symptomatic: the formulation is calculated not *quite* to legitimate any inference to the effect that therefore Milton is 'uptown' or Frank 'unacademic' ('bohemian'?). Frank is only *other* than academic, Milton is only *other* than downtown: no positive term is admitted.

In terms of the story, the problem of the 'alter ego interpretation' is that, whereas it accounts for the *failure* of desire, it does not fit the brutal fact of Frank's desire for Milton. When he looks 'down inside to see if this fits the way it is, really is, I mean' (p. 14), Frank sees that the theory 'explains to me why I sometimes doubted that I could physically overcome the Sapoderm' – that is, the antidandruff soap associated with Hestia and her alleged attempt to have Milton sell out on Balmain values. It explains the turn-off, then, but it does not explain 'why I buried my face in his underwear' (p. 13). 'I really ache to touch his penis, to hold it, tight and erect. Taste the first oozing juice and then to have it throb into me, mouth or anus. It doesn't appear that the alter ego interpretation is sufficiently explanatory or predictive' (p. 14).

What, then, does account for desire (as well as its failure)? René Girard has shown that, where 'love', considered as a dual relation, is a 'Romantic lie', desire is necessarily mediated by a third party and is therefore the product of a triangulated system in which one desires what one knows to be desirable to others.[7] A desiring relationship, in short, is not simply interpersonal, but is necessarily mediated by the social (i.e. by the discursive production of 'desirability'). In this light, it is its exclusion of the third, mediating party that accounts for the failure of the 'alter ego interpretation' to account for the pheno-menon of Frank's desire. That is my second comment.

In terms of the allegorisation of textuality, it helps us to see why, both in the case of Frank's posing as himself (or herself) and in that of the non-coincidence of his conversation (and his performance of love) with its 'original', a third party is cast in the role of audience to the performance of Frank's identity, or of reader of the undetectable split that constitutes Frank's conversation as text. I am referring to Milton, who 'sits on the chair opposite the bed' where Frank reclines, hands behind head, and who claims the privilege of perceiving the special quality of Frank's conversation. 'Most people can't tell the difference between real conversation and your conversation. But I can' (p. 122). The third party generates desire as the hope of a *meeting*, in identity, of 'not I' and 'not not-I'.

I want to show, then, that in each case – the sexual and the textual – the deficiency of the alter ego interpretation lies in its exclusion of the third party as the mediating social element. However, in the case of the 'homosexual thing' between Frank and Milton, Frank's desire is shown to be mediated by the *women* in Milton's life that the dual relation does not acknowledge. Whereas, in the case of literature – figured by Frank's posing for Milton – it is in the reader as third party that desire is supposed to be generated. The 'alter ego' performance consists of producing a 'portrait' of oneself as the desirable 'not I' – the portrait of oneself as a lady – that can stimulate the reader's desire for the 'not not-I' that is the original, a subject both distinguishable and indistinguishable from the 'alter ego'. It is, in short, the perform-ance of a seduction, mediated by producing a simulacrum of oneself.

So the text is ironic. Clinging to his 'alter ego' theory although aware of its deficiency, Frank shows himself unwilling to acknow-ledge the triangulated systems that are nevertheless readable in the story. The differences between the *discourse* of which Frank is the subject and what the *text* 'knows' that is unavailable to Frank, depends on an act of reading. But in constructing the text as ironic in this sense, I am simultaneously conforming to the (triangulated version of the) 'alter ego' model of its identity, and responding to the act of textual seduction by which I am led to *desire* a textual 'identity' beyond the words of its discourse. The text produces 'me' as the object of its desire in the same movement and by virtue of the same act whereby I produce 'it' as having the duplicitous identity of a seducer.

### Triangulation

All Frank's flirtatious conversations with Milton take place in the presence of third parties who are always women, either Hestia or one of Milton's mistresses. They also occur in carefully delineated social circumstances, especially restaurants and hotels, but also the 'Big House' in which 'the three of us' – i.e. Frank, Milton and Hestia – are 'camped' (p. 10). So these conversations have an *erotic context,* constituted by the presence of a woman, which itself has a *social context*, of which Frank in particular, noting indicators of class and race (a waitress with 'the bevelled vowels of an aborigine', p. 2; a barmaid 'who speaks disciplined Australian' and dresses in middle-class style, p. 6), is conscious.

He is no less conscious of Milton's women, whom we can see as reader figures, not in the sense that they are (like Milton) objects of seduction, but to the extent that they are cast in the role of outsiders who must nevertheless be 'included' in the conversation. Milton and Hestia return from the States, and Frank is self-consciously pleased with the spontaneity with which he is able to welcome them 'both' back (p. 2). Sharing a private joke with Milton in the presence of Lydia, he feels 'guilty now that she is not fully *in* the conversation', and also, 'because of upbringing, obliged to bring her in' (p. 5); she, meanwhile, has withdrawn into the 'safe, alert feminine posture – taking an interest in the life and work of the men – [. . .] but way down, critical, supercilious' (p. 4). Frank offers Hestia a 'pedestal' (how better to isolate her?), and on the pedestal himself, a 'pederast', to Milton: Milton 'laughs, blushes. Hestia doesn't' (pp. 7–8). At the end, the 'alter ego interpretation' is discussed in the presence of Milton's new mistress, the puzzled Cleo 'who is trying to comprehend' (p. 13).

Two episodes do not take place in the presence of women: the portrait scene (the scene of seduction) and the episode of sexual fiasco. On these two occasions, Frank and Milton are – symbolically – 'alone at last' in the Big House. With Hestia's departure, the social has been excluded from their relationship: not coincidentally, the previous scene has been a hair-cutting episode (Biblical intertext!) in which Hestia's shortening of Milton's hair so that he can participate in an official inquiry is interpreted by Frank as her taking him 'back to normality, away from me' (p. 10). But now the two are *so* alone and the Big House *so* big that 'sometimes we can't find each other and there is a frantic shouting and opening of doors, turning on of lights' (p. 10). Thus the sexual fiasco is foreshadowed, as a failure to *find* each other, implying a deficiency of identity. But meanwhile it is Frank's turn to associate himself with women, dreaming of his ex-wife and feeling like a 'haunted house' (p. 11); and being thrown out by Milton for having brought a girl home. 'The girl I brought home had once slept with him' (p. 12).

Thus it becomes clear that, like the 'under-the-table intellectual hand-holding' (p. 5) the pair indulge in with Lydia, their 'alter ego' relationship 'works' only to the extent that it is mediated by a third party, whose absence accounts for the fiasco in bed. And since the third party is consistently female, we are forced to see in the 'alter ego' relation a figure of what Eve Kosofsky Sedgwick calls the homosociality of patriarchal society, in which relations 'between men' are mediated by women – who are included in the system by virtue of this exclusion – but in which homosexual desire is frowned upon (cf. Milton's 'frantic heterosexuality', p. 6, and the failure in bed).[8] By the same token, the excluded women come to represent, in Frank's eyes, the enforced heterosexuality of 'normal' society – the society in which Milton desires acceptance. The point is made in a scene set in the Vanity Fair Hotel, a refuge for marginalised Balmain types, 'city middle-class rejects, fringe whites' (p. 5) who huddle for companionship in the bar.

Here it is the pub-keeper's daughter, she who is 'dressed more for a middle-class social occasion than for work in a bar' (p. 6), who excites Milton's lust and triangulates the relationship. 'We're accepted here', he announces, meaning – as Frank understands – that 'inside the acceptance of "the group" by the publican (and his daughter) is acceptance of, by reduction, him, and acceptance is "love" '. In short, the erotic context in this case is identical with the social context and the 'alter ego' relation is clearly situated in terms of the paradox of homosociality, which both excludes women and enforces heterosexuality. 'I need the warmth of public love', Milton adds, and Frank recognises this as a moment of 'raging self-exposure – look at me, this is the true me'.

He simultaneously experiences a surge of desire. 'I should take his hand, put him to bed, pull down his pyjama pants, gently suck him off, pull them back up, so that he can sleep the deep sleep, satiated sleep' (p. 6). And Milton, for his part, seems ready to 'relax his frantic heterosexuality', thanks to the alcohol. We can take this as evidence that desire appears in the homosocial relation only as a result of its being triangulated by women. And, in terms of the text's self-figuration as literature, we can see that this triangularisation figures the excluded/included reader as both a necessary component of the system and the site of social 'acceptance'.

## Seduction

But this is obviously too simple, for *two* triangles are active in this episode: that of Frank-Milton-and-the-barmaid but also the triangle of Milton-Milton's performance-and-Frank: 'He's moving to raging self-exposure – look at me, this is the true me. Somewhere under the adult voice, husks of provincial pronunciation, is a cry from this exposure, and it whimpers up from a child's bed' (p. 6). It is to this performance ('look at me') of self-exposure, with its *dual* aspect (adult voice, child's whimper), that Frank responds in his own sexual fantasy of putting to bed and giving maternal comfort. The two triangles are articulated by Milton's ambivalence: he seems willing to sleep either with the barmaid or with Frank 'as long as he's sure of a fuck somewhere in the night' (pp. 6–7), and his desire for the barmaid and her acceptance takes the form of a performance that is nevertheless addressed to Frank: 'He knows I'm watching him. He performs' (p. 6). So there is symmetry between Milton's performance of self-exposure, addressed here to Frank, and Frank's performance of identity in the 'portrait of a lady' scene, which has Milton as its object of seduction.

In these two cases, however, the 'readers' are men, and the symmetry of the scenes of seduction enacts the 'alter ego' relation as one of mutual desire – albeit of a desire that 'works' only when the other appears as a socially identified figure. For Milton's 'self-exposure' takes the form of his desire for the barmaid's love and for social acceptance: *that* is what stimulates Frank's desire for him. But Frank, in his role as 'portrait of a lady', can be said to be presenting to Milton a socially identified image of himself that corresponds, for Milton, to another pole of attraction: the pole of 'Balmain' and of 'campiness'. As 'portrait of a lady', he makes a campy appeal within homosexuality to Milton's 'frantic heterosexuality'; while as 'me hardly the portrait of a lady', with the army blankets, tranquillisers, spilled wine and shotgun, he identifies himself with another social group, in which it is less of a 'crazy illusion' (p. 6) that Milton might be accepted.

We can see, then, that literature is being figured in the story as requiring, in homosocial society, *two kinds of reader*, whom I will call the 'excluded' and the 'complicitous'. The excluded reader, figured as a woman, perhaps suspects that there is an in-joke that she cannot quite fathom, and is forced, like Lydia, into the 'safe, alert feminine posture' of withdrawn 'interest'. Where the mediation of women is necessary for the 'alter ego' relation constitutive of litera- ture to *work*, this identity performance is, however, posited on the *exclusion* of women and is addressed, by men, to the figures of power that are men, whom it seeks to seduce into a relationship of love. There is no hint that the male reader does not *understand* the duplicitous identity-performance, as is the case with the mediating women ('Lydia is oblivious', p. 4), or needs to adopt the attitude of detached 'interest' described as typically feminine. On the contrary, Milton, as the only person who can detect Frank's conversations as forgeries, knows how to *read* him (as dual); and it is a similar act of reading that Frank performs when he sees Milton moving to a (dual) 'self-exposure'. In short, their mutual readability – as a figure of homosociality – seems to be the secret of the bond between them: their reading of each other is not detached but complicitous. It is a reading infused with (homosexual) desire – a desire that must go unsatisfied, however, to the extent that it is mediated by the exclu- sion of the female. Complicitous reading stimulates desire and excludes the female; its consummation, however, does not 'work' because it coincides with the complete absence of the female, whose 'interest' is indispensable to the economy of the homosocial.

So we should not be surprised to see that 'between men' seduction is mediated by images of what the relation excludes. The 'alter ego' that Frank and Milton produce, each for the other, is of a kind calculated to be attractive to the other man. Milton becomes a helpless child, whimpering from 'somewhere under the adult voice' (p. 6); Frank presents the 'portrait of a lady', i.e. of the figure most likely to inspire desire in the frantically heterosexual Milton. 'I'm too conventionally feminine with him at times', he confirms in another place (p. 9); and it is, of course, a conventional version of motherly femininity that responds in him to Milton-the-child in the fantasy of putting him to bed and sucking him off. 'The many times, when my own physical solitude and from occasional gladness of my own femaleness, which straggles about my personality, from my own need to rest in submission, I unobservably twitch with unfulfilled, blocked impulses, to touch him, to say put my head against him, touch his hair' (p. 7). Thus the excluded third party is smuggled back in to the relation of mutual seduction, triangulating it through the production of simulacra of identity that reintroduce helplessness and femininity into a 'between men' situation that cannot 'work' without them.

## Prostitution

In literary terms, these models of seduction suggest that the 'alter
ego' structure of textuality – the 'pose' or 'performance' it produces
for a reader conscious, however, of the split that constitutes the 'true'
textual identity as 'not not-I' – is designed to be seductive to figures
of social power. In the homosocial world, literature must pose, in
order to gain acceptance, as a figure of powerlessness, helpless or
charming: a child or a woman (we can relate this to Frank's submis-
siveness and passivity in bed). Literature, in short, must camp it up;
and however true it may be that 'me hardly the portrait of a lady', it is
the portrait of a lady that the desire to be loved produces, stimulating
in turn the readerly desire to realise the text's (problematic) identity.
These models of seductiveness are consequently figures of literary
success, the signs of literature's appeal for acceptance and cano-
nicity.

The politics of reading derive from the fact that the reader must be
either complicitous with the text (and so, with the homosocial structure of the social formation) or else excluded from the in-joke, like
women in homosocial society, but playing the part of detached
'interest' without which there could not *be* an in-joke (without which
it could not 'work'). Or perhaps empirical readers tend to combine
these roles? For there *is* a reader figure in 'The alter-ego interpretation' who is in a situation both of complicity and of exclusion, a
woman seduced as if she were a man. Early in the story, Frank recalls
the episode of his having gone with an aboriginal prostitute, an
episode that seems to produce prostitution on one hand as a figure
for literary camping and on the other for a mode of reading that
*might* be seen as existing outside the structures of power, the world
of 'the gentlemen and the ladies'.

For prostitution has the same 'alter ego' structure as Frank's
posing as himself or his conversational 'forgery': 'It puzzles me that
the behaviour of a person who does something for payment, tip or
bribe is often as congenial, and as cooperative, undetectably so, as
that of a person doing it for good will' (p. 3). The unprofessional
performance of the young prostitute, a beginner at her trade, further
underlines the resemblance with Frank's own amateurism in his
campy performance for Milton as a sexual whore ('Me hardly the
portrait of a lady'). But it is clearly implied that in this encounter too
it is Frank's sexual performance that has proved deficient; so that the

prostitute's attempted seduction of him – which is not without its own political and social point ('She was determined . . . to give me a demonstration fuck – an advertisement for the primitive sexuality of her race', p. 3)[9] – turns in the end into a purely discursive perform-ance, of dubious efficacy. 'She talked too much, lying there in that room . . . talked too much, that is, for a prostitute' (p. 3). So she ends up being a figure of literary performance as a rather incompetent act of seductive prostitution.

But she becomes a reader figure when Frank in his turn produces a discursive performance, designed simultaneously to cover for and to redeem his deficient sexual performance. 'I told her I was camp to explain my careless performance; to get her to arouse me; will you love me though I fail as a man; the search for lost passive moments of infant sexuality' (p. 3). 'Camp' in Australian English is a synonym for 'gay'; but here the avowal of camp-ness is simultaneously a demonstration of campiness, of which it has the characteristic 'alter ego' structure. We cannot be sure whether telling the prostitute he is 'camp' is a genuine *explanation* on Frank's part of his 'careless performance,' or whether it is only a way of accounting *to her,* in a way she will *accept,* for something more complex – an underlying identity – that he does not himself have access to (as his meditation on the episode suggests). In short, he is camping in telling her he is camp, in an act of 'self-exposure' that is both true and not-the-whole-truth, a 'portrait' of himself produced for, and determined by, the audience.[10]

She, in any case, is cast here in the role of 'female' reader (like Hestia, Lydia, Cleo . . .), that of the women mediators of the 'alter ego' relation who are not expected to *understand* – yet at the same time cast as the object of Frank's seductive effort, like the 'male' audience that is Milton, who *does* know how to read. For the aim is 'to get her to arouse me' – that is, to arouse *her* desire so that she will arouse *mine*. Frank can hope in this way to achieve acceptance – 'will you love me though I fail as a man' – and thus to produce the ideal sexual relation (*his* ideal sexual relation): one that contrasts both with the flop with the prostitute and with the fiasco with Milton. The 'alter ego' relation fails because it excludes the necessary mediation of women; the relation to women fails because they are not in a position to read the 'alter ego' relation. The prostitute, fantasised as a *women who reads,* embodies the solution to this dilemma. She solves it because female prostitution is the mirror image of Frank's own campy performance as whorish 'portrait of a lady,' and so permits the prostitute to occupy the position in the 'alter ego' relation that is 'normally' Milton's.

The difficulty, however, is obvious. All this, on Frank's part, is a 'crazy illusion' of acceptance that corresponds to Milton's similar delusion in the pub. It simply writes out the sexual, class, and in this case, racial politics of prostitution, as if they did not exist – whereas the text, of course, alerts us to them. The prostitute, paid or not ('She would've fucked without payment. I made her take it', says Frank), is a proletarian of desire, whose social function, as an exploited woman, is to produce the seductive *images* of desirability that are demanded, for the satisfaction of men, in male-dominated culture. Frank's desire for acceptance by the working class simply reverses Milton's desire for acceptance by the middle class, and it is no less illusory. Indeed, it is narcissistic in its flight from the political, and regressive in its erotic character, simply 'the search for lost passive moments of infant sexuality'.

Consequently, the figuration of literature as a campy form of whoring and of reading as a corresponding practice of prostitution does not remove the literary from its social context, but ironically demonstrates the illusoriness of the belief that it can function as a self-enclosed, asocial system. Frank's experience with the prostitute is embedded in the story as the in-joke he shares with Milton and keeps from Lydia. And nothing tells us that his seductive ploy with her *works* any better than, at the other end of the story, his sexual episode with Milton, in Hestia's absence. The two flops correspond. With respect to the social, literature is inescapably in the *nec tecum nec sine te* position: as an 'alter ego' relation that, by irony, produces its identity as separate from the 'world', it can only work by being *read* in that world, and so in the context of the world's politics.

I seem to have come some distance from intertextuality. But my proposition has been that intertextuality necessarily produces textuality in terms of an ironic 'alter ego' structure of identity, and so, equally necessarily, involves it in the politics of reading. There is, to summarise, the politics of the textual *need to be read,* which I hope to have shown produces the would-be autonomous text as a necessarily social form of discourse, and the would-be rebellious work as appealing for acceptance, and canonisation. But there is also, for the reader, the political problem that takes the form of a question: *who is*

*the reader to be?* For complicity with the textual desire to be read is a
social complicity as well; but the alternative is an exclusion that itself
reproduces the patterns of exclusion on which the social formation
rests (and which it consequently *includes*). Most of us, I fear, are
prostitutes, willing to be complicitous – to adopt the persona corresponding to the text's seductive structure – while very largely ignoring
the in-jokes – literary and social – in which we play our role by being
excluded from them.

## Notes

1   See *Marxism and Literary History,* Cambridge, 1986.
2   Thanks to Paul Erb for teaching me to use this formulation.
3   In *Tales of Mystery and Romance,* London, 1977.
4   These are scare quotes, and they register Moorhouse's prefatory
disclaimer: 'Following speculation surrounding some of the stories when
they first appeared, the author states that no identification is intended with
living people.' Such disclaimers, of course, can always be read as cases of
Freudian denial; but 'Frank' is *not* the author. He is, if one will, in an 'alter
ego' relation with the author-figure, who can only be constructed by a reader
as the *not not-I* corresponding to the narrator as 'not-I.' 'Frank', finally, is a
nicely ironic name for the duplex if not duplicitous narrator; it goes with a
pattern of ironic naming in the story – Milton, named after the poet of
'paradise lost', is coupled with Hestia, the Greek goddess of hearth, home
and domesticity.
5   It is worth pointing out that all the stories in the collection form part of
a linked series.
6   See, for instance, *De la séduction,* Paris, 1979, the essay by Baudrillard
most pertinent to my concerns here.
7   See in the first instance *Deceit, Desire and the Novel,* Baltimore, 1966.
8   *Between Men: English Literature and Male Homosocial Desire,* New
York, 1985.
9   The prostitute episode figures as the inside story of Frank's
'experiences with aborigines', known to Frank and Milton but not to Lydia,
who is told the phrase refers to political activism (an adult-education class).
It thus stands for the would-be asociality of the literary, here ironically
undermined and demonstrated to be, as I will point out below, an illusion.
10   Needless to say, this constitutes a *mise en abyme* of the story itself, as
a campy 'explanation' of a sexual fiasco. The narrator's affirmation: 'I am
camp' corresponds to the textual avowal of involvement in the economy of
homosocial desire.

# Fiction, fact and madness: intertextual relations among Gide's female characters

Gide's writing is characterised not only by a high level of literary self-consciousness involving allusions to other authors, but also by the extent to which these references go beyond a solely literary intertextuality. The ideological confrontations that take place within his novels are simultaneously confrontations between different discourses: Protestant, hedonistic, romantic, medical, legal, etc. Moreover, the intertextuality operates on two different levels. Firstly there is the massive use made by characters of other discourses – particularly biblical, but also literary – as a means of rationalising and disguising their own feelings (Alissa in *La Porte étroite,* the pasteur in *La Symphonie pastorale*),[1] and the correlative search for a way out of this kind of cultural and psychological bad faith – in other words, the quest for an individual *authentic* discourse, perhaps most obviously embodied in Michel, the narrator of *L'Immoraliste,* whose attempt at personal liberation is based on the idea that 'What separated me – distinguished me – from other people was crucial; what no one said, what no-one could say but myself, *that* it was my task to say' (p. 90).

Secondly, however, there is a less overt type of intertextuality that by-passes the character's consciousness. It is this that I intend to concentrate on, and in particular on one example – typical in that it starts off within the area of fictional references, but ultimately leads out of literature and into other discourses – which concerns in the first place the figure of Lucile in *La Porte étroite.*

This is a character who is not developed to any great extent in the novel, and seems at first to serve merely as a foil to her daughter Alissa's virtue. The descriptions of her are extremely stereotyped; they do little more than evoke a woman who is immoral and sensual (versus Alissa's purity), hysterical (versus Alissa's spiritual serenity) and black (versus Alissa's reiterated 'pallor'). Nevertheless, her importance is greater than this rather crude portrayal might suggest; that is, it goes beyond the psychological, and both relies on and reactivates a network of symbolic intertextual allusions. Indeed, it might be argued that the only credibility that this otherwise caricatural figure of the dusky temptress possesses derives from the invisible support provided by its occurrences elsewhere in literature. One thinks first, perhaps, of Baudelaire's Creole mistress; and it is noticeable that other quotations from Baudelaire in the text seem implicitly connected to this image, alluding to the contrast between northern and tropical climates – 'soon we will plunge into cold darkness / Farewell vivid brightness of our too brief summers' (p. 31) – or to the idea of travel, as in the meditation on the phrase 'weighing anchor' (p. 34) which recalls Baudelaire's 'Invitation au voyage'.

However, it is not with Jeanne Duval that the most detailed and elaborate series of echoes is set in play, but with another far less glamorous figure: the first Mrs Rochester from *Jane Eyre*.[2] (The presence of Miss Ashburton, the English governess, in *La Porte étroite* already serves to link the two novels.) Both Bertha Rochester and Lucile are Creole women who have been brought, more or less forcibly, from the West Indies to Europe, by a European man who then assumes control over them: Mr Rochester as husband, Vautier as adoptive father. They also share psychological features, and narrative and symbolic functions – although in Lucile's case these are always less emphatic, as though Gide's text is able to present its character through a kind of intertextual shorthand, producing a swift and economical evocation of a certain stereotype which relies for its effect on recalling a model more fully developed elsewhere. Thus both are – or were, in Bertha's case – beautiful and alluring: to the somewhat rapid 'Lucile Bucolin was very beautiful' (p. 5) corresponds Mr Rochester's account of Bertha as 'the boast of Spanish Town for her beauty . . . tall, dark and majestic . . . she . . . lavishly displayed for my pleasure her charms and accomplishments . . . I was dazzled, stimulated: my senses were excited' (p. 332).

But, equally, both are lacking in any moral sense, lascivious, foul-mouthed and sexually demanding. In the case of Lucile, this seme of promiscuity is conveyed above all through the symbolism of the 'porte large' and its variant, the 'porte ouverte', which is throughout associated with her, and contrasted with the 'porte étroite' of the title, which stands for virtue and chastity.[3] The open door comes to act as a signal for a set of characteristics – promiscuity, immorality, sensuality – attached in the first instance to Lucile. Here again, Gide's relatively restrained and elliptical description contrasts with the lengthy condemnation of Bertha as having 'neither modesty nor benevolence, nor candour nor refinement . . . a turn at once coarse and trite, perverse and imbecile' (p. 333), 'no professed harlot ever had a fouler vocabulary than she' (p. 335); and 'What a pigmy intellect she had, and what giant propensities! . . . Bertha Mason . . . dragged me through all the hideous and degrading agonies which must attend a man bound to a wife at once intemperate and unchaste' (p. 334). A further similarity lies in the two women's screaming fits. Bertha is definitely mad and howls like a wild animal, whereas Lucile merely has hysterical attacks which may or may not be genuine: 'There were certain days on which Lucile Bucolin had one of her "attacks" . . . it was impossible to stifle . . . the dreadful screams' (p. 9).

The likeness extends to specific incidents in the two narratives: both Bertha and Lucile physically attack a helpless man. Lucile's attempted 'rape' of Jérôme (p. 8) is paralleled, again in a more extreme form, by Bertha's attack on her brother; and in both cases the man has to be *washed* (Mason by Jane, p. 239), or to wash himself: Jérôme's immediate reaction is to scrub 'every part of me the woman had touched' (p. 9). And, in a more symbolic form of violence, Lucile's tearing of Jérôme's jacket (p. 8) is paralleled by the incident in *Jane Eyre* in which Bertha comes into Jane's bedroom while she is asleep and tears her wedding veil in half. In terms of the plot of both narratives, both women are instrumental in preventing marriages: Mr Rochester and Jane are unable to marry until Bertha dies, because she is his wife; whereas there is the suggestion that Lucile's immorality is indirectly responsible for Alissa's sense of sexual guilt and her consequent refusal to marry Jérôme. Bertha, interestingly, has the same effect on Jane, albeit only temporarily: after seeing Bertha, 'Jane Eyre who had been an ardent expectant woman – almost a bride – was a cold solitary girl again' (p. 323).

Underlying all these parallels, however, is a deeper and more structural relation between the two women, and one which encompasses both similarity and difference. It has to do with the way they are associated with concealment, repression and absence, and the interplay between these three concepts. Bertha is kept hidden in the attic for the first part of *Jane Eyre,* and this literal concealment also functions as a metaphor for the psychic repression of sexuality and madness; her death is the necessary precondition for the happy ending, i.e., the marriage of Jane and Mr Rochester. But one could also argue that from Jane's point of view, Bertha's concealment produces an *absence* of knowledge in the first part of the narrative – an absence which the text returns to again and again, constructing it as a mystery that is built up even as it is gradually unravelled.

Lucile's position, once again, is by contrast extremely understated; but she too has her 'attacks' which have to be *concealed* from the outside world; she too serves as an image for the dangerous and destructive consequences of unrepressed sexual desires: and she too forms an absence in the narrative because she runs away and is never heard of again. But, whereas Bertha's principal effect on the structure of the novel as a whole results from her concealment – her existence as a mystery – Lucile, paradoxically, is effective above all as an absence: in other words, *after,* and because of, her disappearance. Bertha's trajectory through the narrative takes the form of a kind of volcanic eruption. The pressure generated by her confinement – 'What crime was this, that lived incarnate in this sequestered mansion, and could neither be expelled nor subdued by the owner?' (p. 239) – and by the momentum of the mystery, builds up until she bursts forth into the open – 'What mystery, that broke out, now in fire and now in blood, at the deadest hours of night?' (ibid.) – after which her force is quickly dissipated.

But with Lucile there is no climax; her presence in the early part of the novel remains strangely diffuse – a vague source of menace and repulsion, but which never comes to a head. Also, her absence is simply that – there is no mystery, nothing is concealed or revealed: she just goes away. We are not even told definitely whether she is with her presumed lover, the young lieutenant, or not. In fact, the strangest aspect of this event is the lack of curiosity which surrounds it; none of the characters makes any attempt to find her, and the text barely comments on it. Nevertheless, it does have a decisive effect on the subsequent development of the narrative: not, as with Bertha's death, as a means of clearing the air and removing the obstacles which separate the couple of lovers, but rather the opposite. It is as though Lucile's presence provided a concentrated focus of sensuality, which was perceived as a dangerous source of possible infection, but which in fact also served to localise and contain the seme of sensuality – and so, in a sense, to enable all the other characters to remain pure and uncontaminated. Consequently, her disappearance sets in motion a curious process of dissemination whereby traces of her particular features suddenly begin to appear in other characters: it is, paradoxically, in her absence that she becomes contagious. This prompts a possible double interpretation of the 'open door', as standing both for her sensuality and for her *exit* from the text: the open space through which she vanishes but, equally, the open space *of sensuality* which she leaves behind her, to be filled in by other characters.

The 'contagion' undermines the individuality of the female characters; the boundaries that separate them become more fluid and they begin to overlap, firstly with Lucile, but also to some extent with each other. This muddying of the waters, so to speak, has already been prefigured in the name of the place where the Bucolin family lives: Fongueusemare, with its equation of passion ('fougue') with filth and stagnation ('fangeuse mare', i.e., 'slimy pool') exerts an increasing influence on its inhabitants.

For instance, Juliette's passionate love for Jérôme constitutes yet another obstacle to union between him and Alissa, and so repeats, in an explosive fashion more characteristic of Mrs Rochester, one of the narrative and symbolic functions of Lucile. Moreover, it erupts into the text like one of Lucile's attacks: 'Her face was flaming . . . her eyes shone as if she were feverish . . . A sort of fury inspired her; notwithstanding my anxiety I was astonished – embarrassed almost – by her beauty' (p. 57) – and is framed by yet another sequence of opening and closing doors: saying she must speak to him, she opens the door to the garden and disappears; then, when he fails to realise what she is suggesting, ' "Now I know what there remains for me to do" she added indistinctly, as she opened the door of the garden which she slammed violently behind her' (ibid.). Rejected by Jérôme, Juliette decides to accept her 'not cultivated – very ugly – very vulgar – rather ridiculous' (p. 41) suitor, Edouard Teissières. There would seem to be little to link this local businessman with the exotic langorous Creole, but even he, with his vulgar desire for Juliette, is presented in terms which evoke Lucile: not only is the engagement formalised in 'the entrance hall, the doors of which had been left open' (p. 61), but he seems to have acquired her racial characteristics as well: 'Taller, stronger, more highly *coloured* ['plus coloré'] than any of us, almost bald, of a different class, a different world, a different *race,* he seems to realise that he was a stranger ['se sentir *étranger*', i.e. foreign] among us' (p. 61, my italics).

The engagement provokes a nervous crisis in Juliette (pp. 61–2) which, in its similarity to Lucile's hysteria, can be read as yet another trace of her contaminating influence. In fact, the feature of the 'attack' has already spread as far as Jérôme's mother. There is something very strange about the way in which her gentle decline towards death nevertheless results in a sentence which is almost identical to an earlier one describing Lucile's screaming fits – which are scornfully dismissed, moreover, by Jérôme's mother as 'play-acting'. On p. 21 of the French text we read: 'Un soir que *la crise avait été particulièrement forte* et que j'étais resté avec ma mère . . .', and on p. 38, with reference to Jérôme's mother: 'Au cours d'*une crise particulièrement forte,* elle me fit approcher d'elle' (my italics).[4] It is as though, beneath the overt and over-stated *contrasts* between Lucile and the 'good' women in the novel, the text is constantly working to recall the absent Lucile through these small subterranean connections woven between her and the remaining characters.

However, the extent to which Jérôme's mother and Juliette are drawn into Lucile's semantic field is relatively marginal compared to the implication of Alissa herself. The way in which the initial *opposition* between her and Lucile is gradually eroded in the course of the narrative is central to its whole structure. Its works not only through direct comparisons between them, but also indirectly, in construct-ing links between all four women. Thus as early as p. 10 (i.e., before Lucile disappears), Jérôme simultaneously expresses and denies Alissa's similarity to her mother: 'No doubt she was very like her mother; but the expression of her eyes was so different that it was not till later that I became aware of this likeness'. It is in fact *Jérôme*'s mother whom Alissa most obviously resembles, as Miss Ashburton points out (p. 29); and yet the scene in which he proposes to her contains clear traces of Lucile. His unauthorised entry into her bedroom (' "Why", said she, "wasn't the door shut?" ' (p. 36)) reveals her getting ready for dinner: 'She was putting on a coral necklace, and . . . with her back turned to the door, looking at herself over her shoulder, in a mirror between two lighted candles' (ibid.). The mention of the 'tropical' necklace recalls Lucile's exoticism, and the two candles echo Jérôme's earlier horrified glimpse of Lucile with the young lieutenant in her bedroom 'illuminated by the cheerful light of two candelabra full of candles' (p. 12). In fact a further transformation of the scene occurs after Juliette's rejection by Jérôme: she takes refuge in *Alissa*'s bedroom, where she is discovered by Abel, who has similarly entered without permission – 'I pushed open the door of the room' (p. 60) – to find her in exactly the same position, with her back to the door, looking at herself in the mirror (ibid.). Again, Alissa effects a superimposition of her mother and Jérôme's mother when she wears the crucifix that he has given her 'in memory of my mother' (p. 55), 'in the opening of her bodice' (ibid.); the English version omits a significant adjective here – the original is: 'dans l'échancrure de son corsage *clair*' (p. 78, my italics), making a link with Lucile's 'corsages légers' and the pale bright colours she wears when she should be in mourning. In fact there is a more specific echo as well: Lucile also wears a medallion 'in the opening of her bodice' (p. 5) ('dans l'échancrure du corsage' (p. 16)). Conversely, Alissa's final rejection of Jérôme (i.e., by implication, of her own sexual identity) is accompanied by her wearing what the English version gives as 'an unbecoming dress, dull in colour' (p. 98), but which in the French is a clearer contrast with the earlier 'corsage clair': 'un malséant *corsage*, de couleur morne' (p. 134, my italics).

Alissa's journal shows that she finally becomes conscious of her affinity with her mother, and also that it is this which makes it psychologically impossible for her to marry Jérôme (pp. 124–5); but this awareness has already been pre-empted by a more purely textual construction of meanings; even the phonetic interplay of their names, while it suggests an inversion – '-cile'/'-liss-', also *reverses* the symbolism of the doors: the only sounds which occur in one name but not the other are /a/ and /u/ – but it is Lucile who is given the *closed* vowel, and whose name ends phonetically with a consonant, while the initial and final *open* vowel /a/ present Alissa as, precisely, open-ended. The representation of Alissa, in other words, traces the movement whereby, in Barbara Johnson's words, a difference *between* entities is revealed to be based on the repression of a difference *within* an entity – 'an attempt to follow the subtle, powerful effects of differences already at work within the illusion of a binary opposition'.[5]

There are, however, two features prominently associated with Bertha which are *not* shared by Lucile: she is imprisoned, and is like an animal. Jane's first sight of her is described as follows:

In the deep shade, at the far end of the room, a figure ran backwards and forwards. What it was, whether beast or human being, one could not, at first sight tell: it grovelled, seemingly, on all fours; it snatched and growled like some strange wild animal: but it was covered with clothing, and a quantity of dark, grizzled hair, wild as a mane, hid its face. (p. 321)

At this point the intertextual activity moves beyond *La Porte étroite*; because while the above description has nothing in common with Lucile, it is extremely reminiscent of the minister's first sight of Gertrude in *La Symphonie pastorale*: 'I could make out, crouching in the fireplace, apparently asleep, a nondescript-looking creature ['un être incertain'], whose face was entirely hidden by a thick mass of hair' (p. 11). Gertrude cannot speak, but emits 'odd moans' (p. 13), and 'there was nothing human in the sounds she made; they were more like the plaintive whines of a puppy' (p. 14); when approached, 'she began to groan and grunt like an animal' (p. 19); and later on the minister realises that before he found her she had never been out of doors, and that 'Her little universe of darkness was bounded by the walls of the single room she never left' (p. 25). These are the only ways in which the two figures are similar – indeed, the spiritual and restrained character into which Gertrude develops is, psychologically and morally, the exact opposite of Bertha – but the imprisonment, the animality, the matted hair and inability to speak nevertheless set up an intertextual link which is all the more significant for being disavowed in the subsequent narrative development – although it could be argued that the image of Gertrude as the 'lost sheep', fundamental to the whole structure of *La Symphonie pastorale,* shifts its meaning from the biblical return to the fold, in the direction of a more sensual animality through being reinscribed in the intertext of female madness and animality, the matted 'woolly' Creole hair of Bertha Mason and Lucile's 'masse de . . . cheveux crépelés' (p. 16) ('the masses of her curly hair', p. 5 – but 'crépelés' is better translated as 'frizzy').

The figure of the mad woman locked up in the attic, who is like an animal because of her lustfulness and/or her inability to use language, is an extremely powerful one;[6] and some indication of the hold it exerts on Gide's writing in general is given by its reappearance yet again in a much later text – a non-fictional one: the ultimate and quintessential version is the 'Séquestrée de Poitiers'. Here it is a real woman, Mélanie Bastian, who was discovered in 1901 to have been imprisoned by her mother and brother for twenty-four years in an upstairs room, to be living in filth and degradation and to have apparently gone insane. Gide wrote an account of the case twenty-eight years later,[7] in which he quotes at length from the report of the police commissioners:

> We also observed that [Mlle Bastian], who cannot be seen, is lying on a thin mattress and covered with a blanket – the whole bed being of a repulsive dirtiness; that insects and vermin are crawling over this same mattress and feeding on the excrement on this unfortunate woman's bed. We tried to uncover her face, but she clung to the blanket in which she was completely wrapped, uttering shrill cries like a savage. (p. 208)

This is followed by extracts from the subsequent report of the *juge d'instruction* which repeat certain features of the discovery almost word for word:

> The unfortunate woman lies completely naked on a piece of rotten matting . . . The latter is covered with vermin. We speak to her: she cries out and clings to her bed, at the same time trying to cover up her face even more. Mlle Bastian is frighteningly thin; her hair is in a thick braid which has not been combed or untangled for a long time' (pp. 208–9).

In both these quoted passages the similarities between Mélanie and Gertrude are striking. The extreme filth and squalor, the darkness, the animal cries, the covering of the face, the matted hair, the vermin, all occur also in the fictional portrayal of Gertrude. Gertrude, of course, was not so much literally imprisoned as too frightened to leave the house – although even this becomes more applicable to Mélanie as the investigation into her insanity is pursued and the 'fact' of her being kept in the room against her will becomes less certain. But Mélanie's main initial characteristics – imprisonment and madness – are also fully shared by Bertha Mason. Equally, there is a rumour, although it is never proved, that Mélanie was incarcerated for her sexual misdemeanours (p. 203); and her 'very lewd expressions' (p. 219) correspond to Bertha's 'foul vocabulary' (*Jane Eyre*, p. 335).

One might conclude, therefore, that the figure of Gertrude in her initial state is derived from a double source: the fictional character of Bertha Mason and the real-life case of Mélanie Bastian. Even the names involved seem to act as clues that this is the case: not only are the initials of Gide's title – *La Symphonie pastorale* – the same as those of the 'Séquestrée de Poitiers'; but we even learn that Mélanie's brother's nickname for her was, precisely, *Gertrude* (p. 252). But the most interesting aspect of the relation between the two figures works on a more concretely textual level – i.e., it concerns the intertextual

links between *La Symphonie pastorale* and, not the actual event of
the Bastian trial, but the *text* which Gide wrote about it. On this
level, it becomes more difficult to argue that Gide's construction of
the character of Gertrude was 'influenced' in any straightforward
way by his familiarity with the true story of the 'Séquestrée de
Poitiers', simply because he wrote his own account of the case ten
years *after La Symphonie pastorale.*

In other words, the chronological position of 'La Séquestrée de
Poitiers' means that it cannot be seen as a documentary source for a
subsequent fictional creation in *La Symphonie pastorale*; rather, it is
*itself* 'influenced' by the preceding *fictional* figures of Bertha,
Gertrude, and to a lesser extent Lucile. That is, the usual hierarchical
relation between fact and fiction is inverted, insofar as here a factual
account is to some extent determined by a fictional discourse. The
literary figure of the imprisoned mad woman *infiltrates* the factual
discourse of 'La Séquestrée de Poitiers'. Gide, for instance, chooses
to include in his very selective account the not particularly relevant
information that Mélanie's brother was 'married to a Spanish
woman, whose temperament was less calm than his own', and 'had
returned alone to Poitiers' (p. 202): a fleeting reappearance of the
tempestuous southern wife whose husband cannot live with her
(Bertha/Mr Rochester, Lucile/Bucolin).

Thus the trail of associations leading from Lucile in *La Porte étroite*,
to Bertha Mason in *Jane Eyre*, to Gertrude in *La Symphonie
pastorale,* has ultimately taken us out of fiction and brought us into
factual writing: but this is not so much a *return* to some solid ground
of reality, as an excursion into a text which is in some ways similar to
fiction, and in some ways actually more complex and less secure than
fiction. The figure of Mélanie Bastian is central to it – even more than
Gertrude, for instance, is central to *La Symphonie pastorale* – but
nevertheless as soon as one moves back from an exclusive focus on
her and looks at the text in more general terms, it becomes clear that
it is extremely heterogeneous and dispersed. Mélanie acts simply as a
passive point of intersection of a number of different discourses:
journalistic, medical, legal, and so on. In an obvious sense, these do
not 'belong' to Gide. He quotes them verbatim, and often at length;
indeed he opens his account with the following disclaimer: 'I have
some misgivings about putting my name to the account of this
strange affair. In the wholly impersonal exposition that I shall give of
it, I have been concerned solely to put together the documents that I

have been able to collect, and to let them speak for themselves' (de m'effacer devant eux', p. 202). Although one might argue that the extent of his 'effacement' diminishes considerably as the account proceeds, it is nevertheless indisputable that this text presents a far more overtly and completely intertextual character than any of his fiction. In this context, it can almost be seen as a caricature of fiction's capacity to contain and juxtapose different, and indeed conflicting, discourses.

It is precisely this capacity of prose fiction that Bakhtin singles out as its fundamental defining feature.[8] He argues that the novel differs radically from other genres in that it is never a single discourse, but a representation or 'image' of *other discourses*: 'all essentially novelistic images share this quality: they are internally dialogised images – of the languages, styles, world views of another (all of which are inseparable from their concrete linguistic and stylistic embodiment)' (*Dialogic Imagination*, p. 46). Each of these discourses thus does not 'represent' so much as it is 'represented': it functions not as a *means*, but as an *object* of representation (ibid, p. 44). In Bakhtin's terms, it is 'objectified'; we read it not for what it has to say so much as for what the text is 'saying' about it.

In Gide's writing the objectification of other discourses most typically takes the form of a sliding confrontation between fictional and non-fictional discourses, whereby these are held in balance one against the other. Thus, for instance, *La Symphonie pastorale* is a fairly straightforward case of a 'Bakhtinian' objectification of *medical discourse*. Martins, the minister's doctor friend, describes Gertrude's condition in an odd mixture of biblical and scientific vocabulary: 'Songe que tout est chaos dans cette âme et que même les premiers linéaments n'en sont pas encore arrêtées. Il s'agit, pour commencer, de lier en faisceau quelques sensations tactiles et gustatives . . .' (p. 34),[9] and explains the method which the minister must adopt in order to teach Gertrude to speak – a method which he has taken from the comparable case of 'the poor girl . . . discovered somewhere in England towards the middle of the last century by a doctor who devoted himself to educating her. Her name was Laura Bridgeman' (p. 21). This reference to a factual event situates Gide's narrative very directly in relation to an extra-textual reality, but the realistic impact which such an injection of documentary truth might have had on the narrative is simultaneously weakened by the doctor's inability to remember where he read about it and his vagueness about its details (pp. 21–2). The situation is further complicated by being placed in relation to *another* fictional text which it supposedly inspired: 'Then he told me of one of Dickens's stories – which he thinks was directly inspired by Laura Bridgeman's case . . . *The Cricket on the Hearth,* which I read with the greatest pleasure' (p. 22), and which is itself objectified through the minister's criticism of it: 'It is a rather lengthy but at times very touching tale of a little blind girl, maintained by her father, a poor toy-maker, in an illusory world of comfort, wealth and happiness. Dickens exerts all his art in representing this deception as an act of piety, but, thank Heaven, I shall not have to make use of any such falsehood with Gertrude' (ibid). Thus the true story of Laura Bridgeman's cure both acts as a reference point for the fictional Gertrude's cure, while at the same time the terms in which it is presented slightly undermine its authority. That is, *La Symphonie pastorale* is fiction which incorporates and simultaneously distances a non-fictional medical discourse. In 'La Séquestrée de Poitiers' this relation is inverted, because here a non-fictional text draws on certain fictional figures and conventions, while at the same time distancing them.

The situation with this text is more complicated, because the 'fictional' elements are not nearly as explicit as is the medical discourse in *La Symphonie pastorale.* Gide starts his account by reprinting, in his preface, the report of the case that was published in *La Vie illustrée*: in other words, a 'factual' journalistic narrative. It reads, however, very much more like the opening pages of a novel – and, specifically, a novel by Balzac. It is entitled, in what could almost be a deliberate reference to the beginning of *Le Père Goriot*: 'Les *drames cachés*. La Séquestrée de Poitiers [my italics]' ('Hidden dramas. The Imprisoned Woman of Poitiers'); and it starts as follows: 'In Poitiers, in a quiet peaceful street with a monastic name, 'la rue de la Visitation', lived a family of the haute bourgeoisie, respected by everyone throughout the region. Mme Bastian, widow, née de Chartreux, descendant of a most aristocratic local family, lived there with her son . . .' (p. 201). The setting, the antecedents of the family, the ironic comment on the street name, the imperfect tense, are all in perfect conformity with the conventions of Balzacian realism. Equally, the final summing up of the situation runs through almost all Balzac's favourite adjectives:

It is an *appalling drama,* a *drama of prejudice,* of respectability, of *exacerbated virtue* – virtue based on *hideous* convention – but what is even more *abominable* is the cowardice of the witnesses who come forward en masse today and who, for a quarter of a century, for as long as it appeared less safe to speak out, remained *fiercely* silent. (p. 203, my italics)

By placing this piece in the 'Avant-propos', and thus setting it apart from the rest of his text, Gide seems in some way to be also setting it up as target for attack. On one level, this is simply an instance of the main theme of the whole collection, summed up in its title: *Ne jugez pas* ('Do not pass judgement') – in other words, the theme that guilt is often more apparent than real and that neither the public nor the courts should make hasty judgements. Thus the concern of this section on the 'Séquestrée' is to *justify* the apparently shocking acquittal of Mme Bastian and her son, in the face of the public outcry which greeted it and which is vehemently expressed in the piece in *La Vie illustrée*. As the blurb on the back cover puts it: 'How was it that this affair, in which the guilt of Mme Bastian and her son seemed obvious, could result in the acquittal of the accused? André Gide's account *enables us to understand* that decision and clarifies this now legendary affair in a *masterly* fashion' (my italics). Gide, in other words, is engaged in explaining and proving the facts of the case, and thus countering the emotional reaction of the public.

At the same time, however, he is also working against the particular *discourse* exemplified in *La Vie illustrée*. This is based in the first place on emotion; as he says, 'One can discern in the very tone of this article a reflection of the indignation which immediately aroused public opinion at the time' (pp. 203–4). It is in fact more than a mere 'reflection' of public indignation: it contributes actively to the creation of such a feeling. Moreover, the style which achieves this is, as I have discussed above, essentially drawn from and nourished by *fiction* – the Balzacian novel. So Gide's 'own' text (although it is in some ways equally 'other' to him), in unravelling the sober reality behind the sensational half-truths of journalism, also undermines the *discourse of the novel*; and it does so not by any explicit comment but through a typically Bakhtinian distancing and relativising of the discourse.

At this point, however, another feature of Bakhtin's poetics of the novel becomes relevant. Bakhtin is at pains to point out that there is no absolute dichotomy between the author's 'own' discourse and the others, but rather a question of relative weighting: the *more* a discourse is represented, the *less* it represents. Moreover, the author in objectifying a certain discourse at the same time need not, and sometimes cannot, separate himself from it completely: there are degrees of desolidarisation. In the case of 'La Séquestrée de Poitiers', there are several traces in the body of the text of the fictional conventions that Gide is elsewhere opposing. For instance, his presentation of the witnesses in the case is done in a way that evokes the 'live' situation of a court-room drama. He introduces 'living witnesses whom we shall soon hear' (p. 213); both witnesses and accused are consistently presented as *voices* to be 'listened' to: 'But first we will listen to the accused' (p. 213), 'Let us first listen to Pierre Bastian' (p. 214), etc.

In any case the conjuction of factual and pseudo-fictional disccurses here is not in fact a simple binary opposition, because the fictional stereotype is opposed by not one but two non-fictional discourses, and these are in turn opposed to each other: on the one hand that of the legal and medical authorities (and hence of *authority*), and on the other the speech of Mélanie Bastian herself. Thus a very Foucauldian[10] conjunction of knowledge, rationality and power is set up against a discourse of *madness,* abundantly illustrated in the text (when interrogated, Mélanie 'quickly becomes angry, and her usual immobility gives way to a state of violent agitation . . . she hides her face in her pillow and merely mumbles unintelligible words and sentences with no discernible meaning, interspersed with numerous swear words' (p. 224)) and defined as such by three 'forensic doctors' who 'expressed their judgement that Mlle Bastian would never regain her sanity' (p. 259). Within this triangular structure of *fiction* versus *authoritative knowledge* versus *madness,* Gide's unquestioning reliance on fact assumes a less enlightening role than when it is simply used to undermine journalistic melodrama; here it is identified with the discourse of authority and becomes the point of view from which the mad discourse of the 'séquestrée' is objectified. In this way a hierarchy is set up which ironically reinstates the fictional relation of authorial voice to character: Gide's appropriation of the legal-medical discourse enables him to act like the author of a novel dominating and containing his 'character's' discourse. In fact Mélanie's words are a particularly extreme case of objectification: their meaning is not so much relativised as nullified. The Bakhtinian balance between 'representing' and 'being represented' is here completely swept aside; Mélanie's speech cannot itself represent anything at all, precisely because it is represented as meaningless in Gide's text. He refers to it as 'the screams, cries and extraordinary illogicalities ['extra-ordinaires inconséquences'] of an unbalanced personality' (p. 258), and concludes a transcript of an interview with her with the dismissive comment: 'Followed by many other replies as nonsensical ['déraisonnables'] as the above' (p. 262).

There is thus a parallel between Alissa's biblical discourse in *La Portre étroite*, for instance, and this mad discourse in 'La Séquestrée'. Textually, both are objectified through a confrontation with other opposing discourses; psychologically, both are signs of a distorted view of reality. With the biblical discourse this can be seen as a form of emotional alienation; and the mad discourse is also alienated in a very literal and precise sense. As legal–medical subject, Mélanie is of course officially defined in French as 'aliénée', but what is more significant is the way in which she defines herself as *other*: in response to questioning she at first says she has no name, then, when asked if she is not called Mélanie Bastian, says, 'There's more than one with that name' (p. 260). Later, asked whether anyone washed her or combed her hair when she was living in rue de la Visitation, she replies (having had her head shaved): 'It wasn't me who had so much hair, it was another woman; there are other people who have the same name as me' (p. 262).

The 'illogicality' of her remarks stems above all from this refusal to assume a consistent singular identity. Paradoxically, even the subject's alienation from her discourse is here internalised and reproduced in the discourse itself in an 'illogical', and hence private, form.

In fact while Mélanie's discourse, to judge from the transcript of the interview with her, is by no means totally unintelligible, it is to large extent *private* – for instance in the name it gives to her room: 'mon cher grand fond Malampia' – very roughly translateable as 'my dear big Malampia at the bottom' – and in its refusal to name its referents identifiably: 'Wasn't there a nice garden?' 'Yes, yes, when they take me back there I'll jump on someone else's spine' (p. 261). Her retreat into madness, as well as and even more than her physical isolation, has cut her off from the influence of the surrounding ideology. The cultural ties which Michel the 'immoralist' struggles so hard to cut himself loose from have here fallen away without any deliberate effort on the part of the individual: Mélanie finds herself more radically *outside* the cultural intertext than Michel could ever aspire to be.

In this rather ironic sense Mélanie's mad discourse is actually the closest that any of Gide's 'characters' gets to the ideal of authentic discourse, as this is positively formulated by Michel and negatively implied by Alissa, Jérôme and the minister. That is, it is entirely individual, unique, spontaneous, untouched by pre-existing literary or biblical or medical discourses, and free from any rhetorical concern with its effect on a listener. Therefore one might have expected Gide to treat it more sympathetically than he does; there is something strange about his refusal to 'hear' Mélanie's voice in the same way as he 'hears' those of the witnesses, and about his repeated dismissals of it as crazy gibberish. For instance, he cites but takes no account of the conflicting testimony produced in an article written by the hospital chaplain who claims Mélanie has been declared insane merely in order to exculpate her mother and brother, and that 'the victim is gentle, quiet and well-behaved . . . she has never given the slightest indication of malicious or dangerous madness' (p. 233). Instead, he assumes her madness to be self-evident, saying: 'There is no need for me to stress the extraordinary illogicality of Mélanie Bastian's replies. The reader will certainly notice them for himself' (p. 227). The only way in which he can read Mélanie's discourse is by the extremely reductive operation of trying to impose on it a single consistent meaning which will stand up in court – which not surprisingly fails: 'Our efforts, unconscious or otherwise, in the course of an interrogation, to reduce these incoherences in order to render the defendant's remarks consistent, are doomed to total failure, and particularly in the case of Mélanie Bastian' (ibid.) – one wonders also why he refers to the *victim* here as a 'defendant'.

The reasons behind his resistance to a possibly authentic mad discourse may lie in its relationship to free will. One of the defining characteristics of Gide's authentic discourse is that it is freely chosen, as the result of an individual *prise de conscience* on the part of the subject. However, the *séquestrée*'s mad discourse cannot in any definable sense be seen as the result of a free and conscious choice. If, therefore, it were to be counted as a valid type of authentic discourse, the equation between authenticity and freedom would no longer hold. Mélanie speaks in the way that she does because she cannot speak in any other way, or possibly is not even aware that there is any other way of speaking. She thus illustrates with exemplary force the *inseparability* of psyche and language: this is not a mind selecting a way of speaking which most truly expresses its originality, but rather a discourse which constitutes a particular subjectivity and provides the only possibility of access to it – a possibility which Gide seems unable to take up. The final irony of this very consciously ironic body of texts, but one that escapes its author, perhaps lies in the idea that the most heavily objectified discourse is also the most authentic.

## Notes

1   References are to the Dorothy Bussy translations of these two texts, and of *L'Immoraliste* – i.e., *Strait is the Gate*, Harmondsworth, 1924; *The Immoralist*, Harmondsworth, 1930; and *La Symphonie pastorale*, Harmondsworth, 1963. Occasionally I have felt it necessary to give the original French version as well, and here I have referred to the Folio editions. The original dates of publication are: *L'Immoraliste*, 1902; *La Porte étroite*, 1909; *La Symphonie pastorale*, 1919.

2   Charlotte Bronte, *Jane Eyre*, Harmondsworth, 1966.

3   'La porte étroite' and 'la porte large' are taken from the French version of the bible, Luke 13: 24: 'Enter ye in at the strait gate: for wide is the gate and broad is the way that leadeth to destruction, and many there be that go in thereat. Because strait is the gate, and narrow is the way, which leadeth unto life, and few there be that find it.' The English distinction between 'door' and 'gate' does not exist in French, and most of the textual echoes of the biblical quotation in fact refer to doors rather than gates: the English translation therefore inevitably loses many of the intertextual resonances of the original.

4   'One evening when the [Lucile's] attack had been particularly acute and I was being kept in my mother's room' (p. 9); 'In the course of a particularly severe attack she sent for me' (p. 23).

5   *The Critical Difference*, Baltimore, 1980, p. xi.

6   It has of course been treated at length in Sandra Gilbert and Susan Gubar, *The Madwoman in the Attic*, New Haven, 1979.

7   'La Séquestrée de Poitiers', in *Ne jugez pas*, Paris, 1930, pp. 200–66. Translations from this text are my own, and page references to the original.

8   See, for instance, *The Dialogic Imagination*, ed. Michael Holquist, Austin, 1981.

9   The stylistic peculiarity of this is considerably toned down in the English translation, which has: 'You must reflect that her whole mind ['âme', i.e., soul] is in a state of chaos and that even its first lineaments are as yet unformed. The first thing to be done is to make her connect together one or two sensations of touch and taste [literally, 'tactile and gustatory sensations'] (p. 20).

10   See, for instance, '*I, Pierre Riviere, Having Slaughtered My Mother, My Sister and My Brother . . .*' *A Case of Parricide in the Nineteenth Century*, trans. F. Jellinek, New York, 1975; *Discipline and Punish: The Birth of the Prison*, trans. Alan Sheridan, London, 1977; *The Birth of the Clinic: An Archaeology of Medical Perception*, trans. A. M. Sheridan, London, 1973.

# Literature/cinema/television: intertextuality in Jean Renoir's *Le Testament du docteur Cordelier*

If anything is axiomatic about intertextuality, it is that any and every textual medium is, in principle at least, at home in a book on it. (I propose to deal with the vexed question of what a 'text' is by ignoring it.) Why, then, here cinema? – or (perhaps better) *how* cinema? What is specific about filmic intertextuality?

For Hollywood cinema at least, stardom provides a good starting-point. The very concept of a film *star* is an intertextual one, relying as it does on correspondences of similarity and difference from one film to the next, and sometimes too on supposed resemblances between on- and off-screen personae. Thus, Sergio Leone's *Once upon a Time in the West* ironically inverts Henry Fonda's normal heroic role to make of him a particularly sadistic villain; Mike Nichols's *Who's Afraid of Virginia Woolf?* exploits parallels between the stormy domestic life of George and Martha on screen and that of Richard Burton and Elizabeth Taylor off it.[1]

To invoke the names of directors is to suggest a further important element, paradoxically most influential in Hollywood. This influence is surprising because the director's role as *auteur* in 'art' cinema, like the author's for a literary text, has long been taken for granted (*8½* is more often categorised as a 'Fellini' film than as a psychological drama or a film about film-making). Hollywood movies, on the other hand, were predominantly thought of as instances of particular genres (the Western, the horror film, the melodrama), until in the 1950s the French critics of *Cahiers du cinéma* began to write of Hollywood directors too as *auteurs*. This approach, despite almost unrecognisably different vocabulary, had much in common with early literary structuralism, for both sought 'to uncover behind the superficial contrasts of subject and treatment a hard core of basic and often recondite motifs'.[2] Thus, a film such as *To Have and Have Not*, directed by Howard Hawks, came to be read in conjunction with its director's other works in widely differing genres (ranging from the screwball comedy *Bringing Up Baby* to the musical *Gentlemen Prefer Blondes*), with which it has in common such themes as the importance of male camaraderie and an uneasily stoical cynicism.

The strengths and weaknesses of this approach are less important here than its interaction with other ways of viewing films. For *To Have and Have Not*, the most important of these would be based upon genre (an amalgam of *film noir* and spy thriller) and upon stars (Lauren Bacall and Humphrey Bogart who fell in love on and off screen), though there are also important subtexts relating to character actors (Walter Brennan's grizzled veteran transposable from one genre to the next) and Hollywood's relationship with the 'high art' of literature (the script co-authored by William Faulkner from a novel by Ernest Hemingway). For Henri Langlois, founder of the Paris Cinémathèque, Hawks's is a 'constructivist, almost abstract art';[3] for audiences who have never heard of Langlois or the *auteur* theory, *To Have and Have Not* is one of the greatest Bogart vehicles. The intertextuality of Hollywood, like its appeal, crosses established lines of cultural division. Robin Wood's study of Hawks (which compares him to Yeats) was first published in 1968 and written from an explicitly 'Leavisite' perspective; yet its remarks on *El Dorado* could pass for a working definition of (one kind of) intertextuality:

The difficulty for the critic arises not only from the fact that the superficial resemblances to *Rio Bravo*, though so close, are misleading; there is also the fact that, although everything in *El Dorado* is new, it is in many ways dependent on the earlier film for its significance. It is precisely our *awareness* of its differences from *Rio Bravo* that matters.[4]

It would be reasonable to ask at this point why I have not chosen a film by Hawks (or one of the other pantheon *auteurs*, such as John Ford or Samuel Fuller) to discuss here. Inconsistency in a series of essays otherwise devoted to unambiguously 'high' culture is hardly a problem; Hollywood is the most seasoned cultural parvenu in town. It is rather that the *auteur* theory seems largely to have fulfilled its function. It provided what had hitherto been widely dismissed as an undifferentiated commercial mass with a basis for classification and a cultural and artistic legitimacy. Once that had been secured, weaknesses in auteurism came to the fore which actually militate against an intertextual approach – most notably its stress on the director as virtual demiurge. The 'art' cinema, where the director's importance has always been unquestioned and thus never needed to be polemically stressed in the same way, seemed in many ways a more promising place to start. Why, then, Renoir's comparatively little-known (and in Britain long since unviewable) *Le Testament du Docteur Cordelier*?

One major reason is that *Cordelier* is a dramatised adaptation of R. L. Stevenson's *Dr Jekyll and Mr Hyde,* originally intended to be shown on television, and shot in the studios using up to eight cameras and twelve microphones variously disposed. It thus provides an excellent opportunity to interrogate the relationship between cinema and the three artistic media with which it is most commonly related: narrative fiction (from which it in a sense borrowed its first attempts at self-legitimation, as the very term *auteur* suggests), the theatre (a meeting on the terrain of acting and performance), and television (its upstart, and conceivably even parricidal, rival). Renoir himself said, in an interview with *Cahiers du cinéma*: 'By making this experiment possible for me, television has made a splendid present to the cinema'.[5] Such presents were certainly not the norm, in those days before co-production became widespread. Hollywood films in the early days of television often featured television sets exploding or being violently assaulted, which serves to show the resentment that has often dominated the relationship between the two media. French cinema managers called for a boycott of *Cordelier* abroad, objecting to their taxes helping to finance a rival industry.

This already draws attention to what will be the main thread of my reading of the film – that it is an example of what Harold Bloom would call an *agonistic* text, whose relationship with other texts is one of competition and rivalry. Bloom has developed a complex theory of revisionism, understood not as deviation from the highway of Marxism–Leninism but as the processes by which a text wrestles with its 'anxiety of influence' from previous texts. To quote from his *Agon: Towards a Theory of Revisionism*: 'Revisionism, as Nietzsche said of every spirit, unfolds itself *only in fighting.* The spirit portrays itself as agonistic, as contesting for supremacy, with other spirits, with anteriority, and finally with every earlier version of itself.'[6]

By converting a literary classic into a televisual adaptation, by in turn converting that adaptation into a cinematic film, and by incorporating within that film a number of references to other films (most notably Renoir's own), *Cordelier* can be seen as cinema's attempt to avenge itself on the three media mentioned earlier. Notions of vengeance and rivalry are fundamental to the Jekyll and Hyde story, and figured within Renoir's film by the contrast between Doctor Cordelier (the Jekyll equivalent) and Opale (his Hydean other). This evokes a frame of reference stretching from the Christian split between the worthy soul and the unworthy senses to its Freudian equivalent between superego and id, by way of the dialectic of good and evil in Faust and Mephistopheles. The soul/senses rivalry is much more marked in the film than in the novel, for Cordelier is driven to turn himself into Opale by guilt at taking sexual advantage of his female patients. The fact that Cordelier and Opale are played by the same actor, Jean-Louis Barrault, visually reinforces the idea that the splits referred to are in an important sense illusory, that superego or soul is always-already inhabited by id and senses.[7]

Such an idea is profoundly destructive of Western bourgeois morality, and suggests the subversive import of Renoir's text – memorably articulated by the director himself in voice-over, at the very end of the film: 'As for Cordelier, who had paid with his life for the fearsome intoxication of spiritual research, did he not in the end come off best?'[8]

I emphasise this because not the least of the agonistic relationships within the film is that between Renoir himself and the perception of him as jovially unthreatening humanist. It almost beggars belief that the director of *Le Crime de Monsieur Lange*, a Popular Front film about a workers' co-operative saved from disaster by the killing of its scoundrelly former employer, or of *La Règle du jeu*, whose social satire is so vicious that its first screening in Paris provoked a riot, should be perceived in this way. The comparative mellowness of much of his post-war work and the increasingly rotund benignity of his silhouette doubtless help to account for this, but it is a difficult myth to maintain when considering *Cordelier*, for as Daniel Serceau points out: '*Cordelier*, of all his films, is the soberest. It is also the most surprising. Renoir may well appear unrecognisable. The admirers and eulogists of a humanistic, *bon vivant* Renoir will be disappointed. Nonetheless this cinema of cruelty is an essential link in his work.'[9]

Such 'admirers and eulogists' may well be lulled into a false sense *self-proclamation in prologue.* [handwritten annotation]

of security by the film's opening, which shows Renoir arriving at the studios and shaking hands with his collaborators before installing himself genially in the control booth, 'where there are four little screens each reflecting the image of Jean Renoir' (*Cordelier,* p. 9). This enforced homage from small screen to big does not last long, for three of the four images are replaced by what Renoir tells us in voice-over is 'one of those western Paris suburbs that are residential rather than working' (loc. cit.). The first two buildings identified are Doctor Cordelier's house and the chambers of the lawyer Maître Joly. A great many intertextual relationships seem to me to be at work here, which I shall try to summarise with an eye to their availability to different kinds of audience.

First and most obviously, there are the agonistic relationships between textual media: cinema and television, cinema/television and literary pre-text. Following on from these, there is the agonistic relationship between Renoir as benign 'Father Christmas' figure and Renoir the caustic anatomist of bourgeois 'morality' – one which goes back to *La Règle du jeu* of 1939. In this film, Renoir plays the part of Octave, the bohemian whose attempts at engineering his friends' happiness in the face of social hypocrisy end in disaster. At a fancy-dress party, Octave dons a bearskin in which he later finds himself stuck. The bearskin could signify cuddly innocuousness, to be sure, but more than that if we remember that the French phrase *c'est un vrai ours* ('he's a real bear') denotes an ill-tempered person and that a bear-hug can prove deadly . . . The class referents of the two films are different (*Cordelier*'s main characters are doctors and lawyers, *La Règle du jeu* is a *mise-en-scène* of the terminal decline of the landed aristocracy), but for Daniel Serceau they have in common the fact of being 'the statements of a class that derives its legitimacy only from the image of its natural superiority'.[10] It is this image of superiority that Renoir will undercut.

The rotund *raconteur* promising, with every appearance of benignity, to strip bourgeois pretension bare also evokes Alfred Hitchcock (who, two years before *Cordelier,* had formed a company to produce short spine-chillers for television, which he himself was to introduce). A further cinematic intertext likely to be evoked for audiences at the time of *Cordelier*'s release is Henri-Georges Clouzot's *Les Diaboliques*, made in 1954. This is set in a seedy but superficially respectable boarding-school in the very kind of Parisian suburb Renoir's voice-over describes, beneath whose façade a

† *intertextuality depends (for its realisation) on an audience* [handwritten annotation at bottom]

sadistic domestic murder is plotted and carried out. (It is also worth noting that Adrian Lyne's *Fatal Attraction* borrowed its final bathtub scene from *Les Diaboliques,* which had been re-released two years before.)

Now, revelling in being calculatedly *vieux jeu* and setting a shocking example of *ur*-structuralist reductionism for the younger generation, I propose to reduce this heterodox array of references and relationships to so many instances of a single master-theme, the better subsequently to cash it out through my diachronic reading of the film. This is the untrustworthiness of the bourgeoisie as suggested through a multiplication of apparent signs of its respectability. From Flaubert's M. Homais, through the 'bastards' Antoine Roquentin apostrophises in the art-gallery in *Nausea,* and thence to the Barthesian dismantling of bourgeois myth in *Mythologies* and *Writing Degree Zero,* this is a dominant, and recurrent, theme in modern French writing. This prompts gloomy post-Sartrean musings on the infinite resilience of the class we must all love to hate, but also slightly less gloomy post-post-structuralist ones on how, if intertextuality is even to be thinkable, common sources and stores of meaning have to be thought, whether or not their (non-) existence is felt to be an interesting question.

Few bourgeois are as menacingly untrustworthy as the mad scientist, beloved of nineteenth-century Gothic writing (Frankenstein, many of Poe's protagonists) well before Stevenson and taken up with relish by the cinema. *Cordelier* was in fact the fourth cinematic adaptation of *Dr Jekyll and Mr Hyde,* the others all Hollywood films: a 1920 silent directed by John S. Robertson and starring John Barrymore, a 1932 version by Rouben Mamoulian starring Fredric March, and a Victor Fleming version of 1941 with Spencer Tracy and Ingrid Bergman (there is also, more intriguingly, Roy Baker's 1971 *Dr Jekyll and Sister Hyde*). The reasons for this fascination are not far to seek, in the opportunities the theme provides for camp visual floridity (as in Roger Corman's adaptations of Poe), but also in the sempiternal *frisson* evoked by the idea that knowledge (especially the kind acquired in mysterious darkened rooms, such as the laboratory or the cinema) is dangerous. Renoir austerely eschews the first – with the important exception of Jean-Louis Barrault's performance – but exploits the second for all it is worth. This is particularly marked in the feud between Cordelier and his former admirer Séverin, both psychiatrists, which is conducted with a ferocity that puts the École Freudienne de Paris in the shade. For Sévérin, dictating notes to his adoring secretary: '. . . if we agreed to discuss the statements of a man like Cordelier, it would be the denial not merely of medicine, but of scientific knowledge and progress. Please send a copy of this to that imbecile Cordelier. I take back the word "imbecile". Cordelier is a paranoiac' (*Cordelier*, p. 12).

In Stevenson's novella, Jekyll's former friend Henry Lanyon speaks much less savagely of him:

'But it is more than ten years since Henry Jekyll became too fanciful for me. He began to go wrong, wrong in mind; and though of course I continue to take an interest in him for old sake's sake as they say, I see and I have seen devilishly little of the man. Such unscientific balderdash,' added the doctor, flushing suddenly purple, 'would have estranged Damon and Pythias.'
This little spirt of temper was somewhat of a relief to Mr Utterson. 'They have only differed on some point of science', he thought.[11]

Both doctors will die of their knowledge of Jekyll/Cordelier, which makes their preliminary repudiation of it understandable. But the greater venom of Sévérin's words combines with the erotic power he clearly exercises over his secretary – itself later echoed by Opale's sexual assaults and Cordelier's confession of his sexual misdeeds – to make the film in certain ways a more sinister text than the novella. Renoir's benignity appears more than ever a delusion.

This is reinforced by Opale's first appearance, immediately after Renoir's voice-over. All Stevenson's descriptions of Hyde are significantly vague: thus, at the start of the novella his look is described by Mr Enfield, the witness to his first crime, as 'so ugly that it brought out the sweat on me like running', and Enfield goes on to speak of having 'taken a loathing to my gentleman at first sight' (*JH*, p. 9). Absolute evil, like absolute good, must exist in a realm at once of absolute selfhood and absolute difference – thus, outside any space of textual representability. The Jewish prohibition of likenesses of Yahveh, or even of the pronouncing of certain of His names, instances this. Stevenson's shuddering vagueness works on the edge of this realm, as well as evoking the invisibility of threat – the Freudian 'uncanny' – in nightmares.

Renoir's use of Jean-Louis Barrault for his lead role(s) audaciously does the exact opposite. Barrault remains best known in the cinema for his role as the mime Baptiste in Marcel Carné's *Les Enfants du paradis* – a performance of surpassing agility and androgynous tenderness. As Opale, he flounces along 'with an agile and highly catlike suppleness' (*Cordelier*, p. 9), before picking up a young girl met on his path and flinging her violently to the ground. This, besides recalling Peter Lorre's murder of a little girl in Fritz Lang's *M*, brutally turns the grace of Barrault's performance in *Les Enfants du paradis* against itself.

Opale's gait also evokes, as several commentators have noticed, a Renoir film of twenty-seven years before – *Boudu sauvé des eaux,* starring Michel Simon. Boudu is a tramp, who impulsively jumps into the Seine after losing his pet dog and is rescued by the philan-thropic bookseller Lestingois. Lestingois's attempts at integrating Boudu into bourgeois society lead to a string of 'anti-social' incidents and Boudu's seduction of his benefactor's wife, before Boudu is married off to the servant-girl Anne-Marie (previously Lestingois's mistress), only to fall out of a boat on the way back from his wedding and drift away to resume his vagabond life. Like *Cordelier,* the film derides bourgeois cultural values, but in a very different way, via a species of black comedy that in the river scene at the end takes an incongruously benign turn into the pastoral. Simon's faun-like per-formance contrasts strongly with Barrault's, for all that both are seen as instinctual forces; if Boudu is a noble savage (thus, 'natural'), Opale is an ignoble artefact (thus, 'cultural'). One is the product of (by most standards) an insufficiency of knowledge, the other of an excess, as François Truffaut's description of Barrault/Opale suggests:

> . . . unprecedented right down to his incredible gait, which borrows from Michel Simon in *Boudu* and from Burgess Meredith in *The Diary of a Chambermaid*. To animate a human being one has invented, to have him glide along rather than walking, to dream up a set of gestures for him, to get him beating up passers-by at random, in the middle of the street – there is an artist's, a film-maker's dream.[12]

Renoir – like Jekyll, like Stevenson himself – is thus deliberately constructing a malevolent homunculus. Jacques Siclier's hostile remarks about the film thus miss the point, especially when he says that Opale ought to have been 'the ultimate incarnation of Boudu or of Octave in *La Règle du jeu*',[13] for Opale's leering viciousness is surely an agonistic attack on his less malign predecessors. This is reinforced by the evident constructedness of the studio sets (also criticised by Siclier), from which all the 'naturalness' beloved of humanistic Renoir-worshippers has been expelled. Claude Beylie, in the same article, pronounces himself surprised by how visually unspectacular the film is, and tells us that 'this goes against what I expected of him, what I shall call the "Renoir myth" ', before going on to draw a comparison with Charlie Chaplin's *Monsieur Verdoux,* its director's least humorous and most bleakly acerbic work. Opale's implicit attacks on Boudu and Octave (the latter, be it noted, a parricide) thus also stand, synecdochically, for Renoir's attack on his own myth.

Let us look more closely at the attacks Opale carries out. Some time after his onslaught on the little girl, he tries to snatch a baby from its mother's arms, leers furtively at a courting couple, and, 'with destructive rage' (*Cordelier,* p. 18), batters the old man Demarny to death with his stick. We hear that he has viciously beaten the prostitute Suzy not long before we see him kick away a crippled man's crutches 'like a footballer' (loc. cit.) – both episodes with no equivalents in the novel, as if Renoir needed to go even further in Iago-like motiveless malignity than Stevenson ... The taboo on assaults on handicapped people had been flouted with gusto in the cinema, most memorably by Luis Buñuel in whose *L'Age d'or* Gaston Modot kicks a blind beggar to the ground. Opale's attack is more realistic than Modot's, carried out with venomous determination rather than parodic verve; but *Cordelier* is nonetheless likely to put us in mind of the earlier film, if only because Modot appears in both (for Renoir playing the servant Blaise). A further link in the intertextual chain is provided, once again, by *La Règle du jeu,* in which Modot also plays a servant, the gamekeeper Schumacher. Schumacher's jealousy of the former poacher Marceau's attentions to his wife erupts in armed pursuit at the height of the costume ball which concludes the film. It is difficult not to see in Blaise's pusillanimity an ironic counterpart to – even an undoing of – the antisocial frenzy of Modot's two earlier performances:

Through the door that opens onto the gardens, Blaise enters in a panic. His face is wracked by terror.
BLAISE, stuttering with fear: I can't, no, really, I can't . . . it scares me, me who's never frightened, I can't take it any more. (*Cordelier,* p. 22)

The allusion to *La Règle du jeu* comes reinforced by the parallel between Cordelier's worldly *soirée* and the costume ball in the earlier film, commented on by Daniel Serceau for whom Cordelier's gathering 'conceals, at best, only vanity or a naïvety close to stupidity, at

worst, forms of licence and excess that are in the end analogues to
Cordelier's own'.[14] There is, in other words, no clear dividing line
between social drama and psychodrama – which is to say also
between society and the individual, or even between warring parts of
the same (?) individual (?). The theatricality of Renoir's *œuvre* –
classically in *La Règle du jeu*, but perhaps even more so in *Cordelier*
– thus works against any view of it as a unified whole, however
much the auteurist approach implicit in the very phrase 'Renoir's
*œuvre*' may presuppose such a view.

The film's conclusion may be thought to bring the novel 'up to
date' somewhat fatuously by replacing Jekyll/Hyde's final letter with
Opale/Cordelier's oral confession via the tape-recorder. This,
however, would be to disregard the importance for the film of rival
media technologies, already remarked in the introductory sequence
but also prefigured in the agonistic relationship between Boudu and
Lestingois. Lestingois's austere espousal of the high culture on
which, as a bookseller, he is also economically dependent can be
seen as representing the 'legitimate' world of theatre, anxiously
defending itself against the upstart and anarchistic incursion of the
cinema (Boudu).[15] This reading provides at once a pre-text for
*Cordelier*'s already-discussed *mise-en-scène* of the rivalry between
cinema and television, and a context for the highly charged prosopopoeia of Opale/Cordelier's voice on tape. Jekyll's written confession
may seem as tame by comparison as Lestingois's bellettrism beside
the verve of Boudu.

My use of the term 'prosopopoeia' here may well be challenged.
The term is defined by my Collins English dictionary as 'a figure of
speech that represents an imaginary, absent, or dead person
speaking or acting' – a definition that seems to anchor it in the
worlds of rhetoric and literary representation. The use of the term in
this particular context, where we know that the speaker(s) is/are in
the laboratory, potentially visible, as Maître Joly hears his/their
recorded voice, runs into an aporia that calls the very antithesis of
presence and absence into question. Opale/Cordelier is there or not
there, depending on whether or not we regard the (changing) bodily
presence in the laboratory as that of the speaker. The undecidability
of rhetorical terms – itself a key trope for Paul de Man – clearly
applies to cinema as well as to the written word.

Opale/Cordelier's recorded voice evokes another prosopopoeial
presence – that of Edgar Allan Poe's Monsieur Valdemar,

hypnotised on the point of death by the tale's narrator. Derrida quotes the following extract as one of the epigraphs to *Speech and Phenomena*:

I have spoken both of 'sound' and of 'voice'. I mean to say that the sound was one of distinct – of even wonderfully, thrillingly distinct – syllabification. M. Valdemar *spoke* – obviously in reply to the question I had propounded to him a few minutes before. I had asked him, it will be remembered, if he still slept. He now said:-
'Yes; – no; I *have been* sleeping – and now – now – *I am dead*.'[16]

For Derrida, this ultimately aporetic speech-act is in a sense the precondition of any language: 'The statement "I am alive" is accompanied by my being dead, and its possibility requires the possibility that I be dead; and conversely. This is not an extraordinary tale by Poe, but the ordinary story of language.'[17]

Quotations from Derrida such as this generally act as a cue to plead for the reinscription of the primacy of writing over that of speech. This will not be so here, for reasons suggested by my earlier remarks about the film's technological 'updating' of its pre-text. Jekyll tells us in his confession that even when Hyde has all but taken him over, '. . . of my original character, one part remained to me: I could write my own hand' (*JH*, p. 72) – that, in other words, writing for him is the last remaining ground of identity-through-difference. The tape-recorder replays Cordelier's confession in his own voice, almost as though to reinscribe speech (back) against writing. Opale stops the tape, with a cry of: 'I am not Cordelier, I am Opale. Cordelier has disappeared from me – that is the drama!' (*Cordelier*, p. 35) which might be expected to call a final halt to the play of shifting identities. It does quite the reverse, for Opale shortly afterwards begins to speak 'in Cordelier's voice': 'I'm not asking you to forgive me, Joly. I'm asking you to help me . . . to tolerate me . . . What of Cordelier is left in me can only find refuge with you, if it is not to sink [. . .] Help me to become Cordelier once more' (*Cordelier*, p. 36).

This he does, like Jekyll, by taking a lethal dose of the transformatory potion – ironically recovering the identity he desires in death. Where this identity is grounded seems to me an unanswerable question, for a simple reversal of the novella's prioritising of writing over speech runs into the obvious objection that Opale and Cordelier speak with different voices. Speech recorded on tape – erasable, reversible, thus closer to writing – always-already tells us that 'I am dead' (what else was the *frisson* I and my school-friends got from listening to ourselves and each other on our first tape-recorders?). A 'live' voice conventionally tells us 'I am alive and/because I am here'. For that which we are told by the now-recorded, now-live voice of one who is sometimes one, sometimes two, and who will (both) shortly be dead, no simple predication of presence or absence is even possible. *Cordelier*'s tape-recorder is a technological flourish, to be sure, but it is also much more than that.

I shall not offer any 'conclusion', but rather return to the reasons I have given for my choice of *Cordelier*. I first saw the film in Paris in the summer of 1986 – a one-off screening of a rare Renoir which I was obviously anxious not to miss. I knew that it was an adaptation of *Dr Jekyll and Mr Hyde*, a book I had not read since the age of twelve and had almost entirely forgotten. The film on first viewing made such an impact on me that I determined then and there to write a piece on it at the earliest possible opportunity – only one year afterwards provided by the news of this collection of essays. Inevitably, I reread the Stevenson text while preparing this piece, and (re)discovered within it the description of Sir Danvers Carew, Hyde's murder victim:

. . . the older man bowed and accosted the other with a very pretty manner of politeness. It did not seem as if the subject of his address were of great importance; indeed, from his pointing, it sometimes appeared as if he were only inquiring his way; but the moon shone on his face as he spoke, and the girl was pleased to watch it, it seemed to breathe such innocent and old-world kindness of disposition, yet with something high too, as of a well-founded self-content. (*JH*, p. 25)

This is followed by Hyde's reviling of his gentle inquirer, who responds 'with the air of one very much surprised and a trifle hurt' (*JH*, p. 26). Nor was he the only one; for my rereading returned me to my first encounter with the text, as a troubled schoolboy in whose life at the time there seemed to be a dearth of 'kindness of disposition', and no 'well-founded self-content' at all. That I remembered the desk in the school library where I read the book, and even what the edition looked like, and that my return to those childhood tears was cathartic much as an analytic session can be, is I think not solely a self-indulgent detail, for it shows how our immediacy as persons is constructed by the detours of the intertextual. To think this of a Renoir agonistically constructing himself as *auteur* with and against his earlier work is not especially difficult; to think it of ourselves, however steeped in Proust and Freud we may be, is likely to pose more of a problem. Yet some such attempt, in an era when the discourse industries – political, religious and psychoanalytic – more than ever bombard us with exhortations to wholeness while at the same time setting before us the reasons for its impossibility, seems to me desperately necessary. This is one way in which intertextuality can, and should, address itself to civilisation and its discontents. *[handwritten: ← author's own intertextual play on Freud's Unbehagen in der Kultur & a 'pun' which again relies on what he says on pg 180+ — 'Civilisation and Its Discontents' in the title of the English Translation)]*

**Notes**

Some of the research for this essay was done in Paris with the aid of a grant from the Kingston Polytechnic Research Fund.

1   For this kind of approach see Edgar Morin, *Les Stars*, Paris, 1972, and Richard Dyer, *Stars*, London, 1979.
2   G. Nowell-Smith, in P. Wollen, *Signs and Meaning in the Cinema*, London, 1969, p. 80.
3   In J. McBride, *Focus on Howard Hawks*, Englewood Cliffs, New Jersey, 1972, p. 69.
4   R. Wood, *Howard Hawks*, London, 1981, p. 152.
5   J.-P. Spiéro, 'Jean Renoir tourne *Le Testament du Docteur Cordelier*', *Cahiers du cinéma*, XCV, May 1959, p. 30.
6   H. Bloom, *Agon: Towards a Theory of Revisionism*, New York, 1982, p. viii.
7   The critiques of Lacanian psychoanalysis mounted by Derrida and Lyotard likewise suggest this; see Derrida's 'Le facteur de la vérité'/'The purveyor of truth', in *La Carte postale*, Paris, 1980, pp. 441–524 (English translation in *Yale French Studies*, LII, 1975, pp. 31–113), and Lyotard's *Discours, Figure*, Paris, 1971, pp. 239–70 (English translation 'The Dream-Work does not think' in *Oxford Literary Review*, VI, 1, 1983, pp. 3–34).
8   *Le Testament du Docteur Cordelier*, Paris, 1961, p. 38, hereinafter *Cordelier*. (This and all other translations from the French are my own unless otherwise stated.)
9   D. Serceau, *Jean Renoir*, Paris, 1985, p. 101.
10   D. Serceau, *Jean Renoir: la sagesse du plaisir*, Paris, 1985, p. 78.
11   R. L. Stevenson, *Dr Jekyll and Mr Hyde*, Oxford/New York, 1987, p. 15 (hereinafter *JH*).
12   *Cahiers du cinéma*, 178, May 1966. (*The Diary of a Chambermaid* is one of the films Renoir made in Hollywood during the war.)
13   *Téléciné*, 11 November 1961.
14   *Jean Renoir: la sagesse du plaisir*, p. 79.
15   I am indebted for this suggestion to Dr Michael Sadler of the British Institute in Paris (in conversation).

16 E. A. Poe, *The Facts in the Case of M. Valdemar,* in *Selected Writings,* Harmondsworth, 1967, p. 357.

17 J. Derrida, *Speech and Phenomena,* trans. David B. Allison, Evanston, 1973, pp. 96–7.

# Index

Page references followed by n refer to notes, followed by b refer to the bibliography to the Introduction.